T0294864

Dimensions of Curation

AMERICAN ALLIANCE OF MUSEUMS

The American Alliance of Museums (AAM) has been bringing museums together since 1906, helping to develop standards and best practices, gathering and sharing knowledge, and providing advocacy on issues of concern to the entire museum community. Representing more than 35,000 individual museum professionals and volunteers, institutions, and corporate partners serving the museum field, the Alliance stands for the broad scope of the museum community.

The mission of AAM is to champion museums and nurture excellence in partnership with its members and allies.

Books published by AAM further the Alliance's mission to make standards and best practices for the broad museum community widely available.

Dimensions of Curation

Considering Competing Values
for Intentional Exhibition
Practices

Edited by
Ann Rowson Love and Pat Villeneuve

ROWMAN & LITTLEFIELD
Lanham • Boulder • New York • London

Published by Rowman & Littlefield
An imprint of The Rowman & Littlefield Publishing Group, Inc.
4501 Forbes Boulevard, Suite 200, Lanham, Maryland 20706
www.rowman.com

86-90 Paul Street, London EC2A 4NE

British Library Cataloguing in Publication Information Available

Library of Congress Cataloging-in-Publication Data

Names: Love, Ann Rowson, 1967– editor. | Villeneuve, Pat, 1955– editor.
Title: Dimensions of curation : considering competing values for intentional exhibition
    practices / edited by Ann Rowson Love and Pat Villeneuve.
Description: Lanham : Rowman & Littlefield, [2023] | Series: American alliance of
    museums | Includes bibliographical references and index.
Identifiers: LCCN 2023011084 (print) | LCCN 2023011085 (ebook) | ISBN
    9781538167342 (cloth) | ISBN 9781538167366 (paperback) | ISBN 9781538167359
    (ebook)
Subjects: LCSH: Art museums—Curatorship. | Art museums—Exhibitions.
Classification: LCC N408 .D56 2023 (print) | LCC N408 (ebook) | DDC 708—dc23/
    eng/20230523
LC record available at https://lccn.loc.gov/2023011084
LC ebook record available at https://lccn.loc.gov/2023011085

♾™ The paper used in this publication meets the minimum requirements of American National Standard for Information Sciences—Permanence of Paper for Printed Library Materials, ANSI/NISO Z39.48-1992.

Contents

Acknowledgments   ix
Preface   xv

Part I. Introduction to the Dimensions
of Curation Competing Values Model

Chapter 1: The Dimensions of Curation Competing Values Model   3
Pat Villeneuve and Ann Rowson Love

Part II. Two Dimensions: Traditional, Exclusive,
Sympathetic, and Inclusive Quadrants

Traditional: Object (*x*) + Lone Creative (*y*) = **Traditional**   16

Chapter 2: Queering the Museum: From a Traditional Model Toward
a More Inclusive Practice   17
Kara Fedje

Chapter 3: Using Traditional Practice to Review the Chinese National
Art Exhibition   21
Zida Wang

Exclusive: Object (*x*) + Collaborative (*y*) = **Exclusive**   27

Chapter 4: Iterations of Curating with Matthew Ritchie:
Working Collaboratively During the COVID-19 Pandemic   28
Stefanie Dlugosz-Acton

Chapter 5: The Artist Is No Longer Present: Reconsidering Cross-
Border Exhibition Curating in the Post-Pandemic Era   33
Ting Zhang

Sympathetic: Audience (*x*) + Lone Creative (*y*) = **Sympathetic**   39

Chapter 6: *A Shared Body*: Reenvisioning Curatorial Collaboration
in an Academic Art Museum   40
Annie Booth and Meredith Lynn

Chapter 7: *Ally is a Verb*: Adopting a Sympathetic Curatorial Practice to Build Advocacy and Community within a Teaching Museum   46
Alexia Lobaina

Inclusive: Audience (*x*) + Collaborative (*y*) = **Inclusive**   51

Chapter 8: Art Connects   52
Jennifer Jankauskas and Laura Ashley N. Bocquin

Chapter 9: Responsive, Relational, and Disruptive: A Case Study in Community-Based Curation   58
Marianna Pegno, Christine Brindza, Patricia Lannes, and Cecilia Garibay

Part III. Three Dimensions: Exhibitions That ___

Disseminate: Object (*x*) + Lone Creative (*y*) + Democratization of Culture (*z*) = **Disseminate**   66

Chapter 10: Traditional Practice That Disseminates: *Native Brazil/ Alien Brazil* Anna Bella Geiger   67
Peter Aerts and Aline Van Nereaux

Chapter 11: *Something's Off*: Reconsidering Traditional Practice   73
Michelle Sunset

Discern: Object (*x*) + Lone Creative (*y*) + Cultural Democracy (*z*) = **Discern**   78

Chapter 12: Discerning the Cryosphere: Humans and Climate in Art from the Frances Lehman Loeb Art Center, Vassar College   79
Elizabeth Nogrady

Chapter 13: Discerning with a Good Voice: *Hówaste* at The Heritage Center   85
Ashley Pourier and Audrey Jacobs

Enrich: Object (*x*) + Collaborative (*y*) + Democratization of Culture (*z*) = **Enrich**   90

Chapter 14: Not Just Dissemination, an Enriched Experience: *Ming Dynasty Costume* Exhibition   91
Xiaonan Jiang and Xuejing Dai

Chapter 15: *SKIN*, a Multisensory Art Exhibition for Children Aged Eight and Older and Their Families   96
Stefanie Metsemakers and Gerd Dierckx

Amplify: Object (x) + Collaborative (y) =
Cultural Democracy (z) = **Amplify**   102

Chapter 16: Challenging Romaphobia: The Case of a Romanian Carnival
Mask at Mucem   103
Julia Ferloni and Emilie Sitzia

Chapter 17: *Lock & Key Creative Expression Lab*: A Curated Space During
the Pandemic   109
Ashley Hartman, Melanie Rosato, and Nancy Azria

Mediate: Audience (x) + Lone Creative (y) +
Democratization of Culture = **Mediate**   115

Chapter 18: *The Same Four Walls*: Inspiration and Reflection During
a Global Pandemic   116
Lesley Marchessault

Chapter 19: SCREEN IT: A Mediation-Driven Approach to Art,
Technology, and Audiences   120
Pieter Jan Valgaeren

Inspire: Audience (x) + Lone Creative (y) +
Cultural Democracy (z) = **Inspire**   126

Chapter 20: *The Boneyard*: Inspiring Through In-Gallery Artist
Demonstrations   127
Courtney Taylor, Andy Shaw, and Grant Benoit

Chapter 21: *There Is No Planet B!* An Audience Participation Project
Meant to Inspire   133
Aline Van Nereaux

Empower: Audience (x) + Collaborative (y) +
Democratization of Culture (z) = **Empower**   139

Chapter 22: EmPOWER: Learning from Our Youngest Community
Members at the Clyfford Still Museum   140
Nicole Cromartie and Bailey H. Placzek

Chapter 23: *Anybody Home?*   147
Roselyne Francken and Tammy Wille

Act: Audience (x) + Collaborative (y) +
Cultural Democracy (z) = **Act**   153

Chapter 24: Collaborative Reach of a Site-Specific Exhibition That
Addresses School Segregation   154
Katie Fuller and Patricia O'Rourke

Chapter 25: *Boundless Hospitality*: M from a Different Perspective   158
Sofie Vermeiren

Part IV. Curatorial Change and Tools

Chapter 26: One Museum, Three Dimensions of Curation: A Script   165
Jay Boda, Charlie Farrell, Madison Grigsby, and
Anneliese Hardman

Chapter 27: You Say You Want a Revolution: Empowering the Edu-Curator   177
Emily Dellheim

Chapter 28: M Leuven: A Holistic Approach to Exhibition Making   185
Peter Carpreau and Sofie Vermieren

Chapter 29: Inclusive Curatorial Practice   193
Lynette A. Zimmerman

Chapter 30: Toward an Interactive Model of Competing Values:
From Visualization to Tool Kit   202
Morgan Joseph Hamilton

Chapter 31: Dimensions of Education: Adapting the Curatorial Model
for Museum Education   211
Audrey Jacobs and Ashley Williams

Index   221
About the Contributors   227

Acknowledgments

This book came about through collaborative effort at every step from developing the *Dimensions of Curation Competing Values Model* to field testing to chapter writing. We are so appreciative of all who helped make this book possible.

FROM THE EDITORS

In its earliest stages, then graduate assistant Elise Kieffer, now program director and assistant professor of Nonprofit Leadership Studies at Murray State University, identified possible conceptual frameworks for the model. Amanda Martin Hamon, executive director of the Grove Museum in Tallahassee, Florida, and former associate director of K-12 Education at the University of Kansas' Spencer Museum of Art, provided initial feedback and modeling. She currently pursues her doctoral studies in our Museum Education and Visitor-Centered Curation program at Florida State University.

Our methods for field testing included presenting widely to gain feedback from museum professionals across disciplines and roles. Presenting at national and international conferences such as American Alliance of Museums (AAM), Association of Academic Museums and Galleries, Southeastern Museums Conference, and the International Conference of the Inclusive Museum, among others, was integral, along with museum and university presentations that encouraged us. Ultimately, we have presented this work in the United States, Argentina, Belgium, Germany, the Netherlands, Portugal, Spain, South Korea, and the United Kingdom. In addition to presentations, we published in journals including AAM's *Museum* as well as *Curator: The Museum Journal*, the *International Journal of the Inclusive Museum*, and *Stedelijk Studies*. We would like to acknowledge our co-authors and co-presenters; we could not have done this work without their collaboration. Collaborators include the following: Peter Aerts, head of education and communication, S.M.A.K./ Stedelijk Museum voor Actuele Kunst (Municipal Museum of Contemporary Art), Ghent, Belgium; James Burns, executive director, Western Spirit: Scottsdale's Museum of the West, Arizona, and former president and chief executive officer Arizona Historical Society; Rosario Martinez Garcia, director of public programs, Fundación Proa, Buenos Aires, Argentina; Juliana Forero, chief curator of the Frank Art Gallery and Studio 18 Art Complex in Pembroke Pines, Florida; Xiaonan Jiang, doctoral candidate in Museum Education & Visitor-Centered Curation at Florida State University and associate professor in Shandong College of Arts, China; Hyein Kim, Arts and Policy Research Division, Culture and Tourism Institute, Seoul, Korea; Steven Matijicio, director, Blaffer Art Museum, University of Houston, Texas; Laura Minton, curator of exhibitions, Fralin Art Museum, University of Virginia,

Charlottesville, Virginia; Keidra Daniels Navaroli, McKnight Doctoral Fellow, Texts and Technology, University of Central Florida, Orlando, Florida, and former assistant director and curator, Ruth Funk Center for Textile Arts at Florida Institute of Technology, Melbourne, Florida; Daniel Pfalzgraf, gallery owner, Wheelhouse Art, Louisville, Kentucky, and former curator, Carnegie Center for Art & History, New Albany, Indiana; Deborah Randolph, Co-Founder, International Scholars Group, Raleigh, North Carolina; Adam Scher, vice president for collections, Virginia Museum of History and Culture, Richmond, Virginia; Brooke Wessel, school and teacher programs coordinator, The Ringling, Sarasota, Florida, and doctoral candidate, Museum Education & Visitor-Centered Curation; and Zida Wang, doctoral candidate in Museum Education & Visitor-Centered Curation and museum education assistant, Museum of Fine Arts, Florida State University, Florida.

We are so fortunate to work with amazing master's and doctoral students in our graduate program and thank all who gave feedback and critical reflection in our courses. A number of our students (and former students) are also authors or co-authors of chapters in this volume including Jay Boda, Emily Dellheim, Kara Fedje, Morgan Hamilton, Ashley Hartman, Audrey Jacobs, Xiaonan Jiang, Alexia Lobaina, Michelle Sunset, Ashley Williams, and Zida Wang (see part IV for biographies and affiliations). We are especially indebted to doctoral student Audrey Jacobs, who as a part of her Legacy Fellowship at Florida State University was our editorial assistant; we could not have completed this work without her!

Ann Rowson Love would like to thank the CurCom leadership team and membership of AAM's Curators Committee (CurCom) for continued critical reflection upon and support of the Dimensions of Curation Model. In particular, many thanks to CurCom Chair Stacey Swigert, director, Atwater Kent Collection—Lenfest Center for Cultural Partnerships, Drexel University, Philadelphia, Pennsylvania, and former Chair James Burns, executive director, Western Spirit: Scottsdale's Museum of the West, Arizona. Their support has been instrumental to the development of this book.

Ann is honored to be a member of the CurCom leadership team and the national conversation around the many roles of curators in museums. She would like to thank her mom, Sandy Rowson, and sister, Elizabeth Zahorjan, for support and understanding during this book's development. Thank goodness for Sunday lunch check ins! Ann thanks Deborah Randolph, longtime colleague and co-author on another book, for understanding and persevering during simultaneous writing projects. Ann gratefully acknowledges the love and support of her husband, Eric Love, who endured his wife's even busier schedule, along with the regular demands of teaching and administering a graduate program. Eric especially nurtured and supported Ann, who was still undergoing treatment for breast cancer during a good portion of this book's development. She so appreciates his care and culinary magic!

This book benefited from Pat Villeneuve's ongoing work in Belgium. She would like to thank the Fulbright Commission Belgium and her hosts FARO (Flemish Institution for Cultural Heritage) and KUL/Katholieke Universiteit Leuven (Catholic University of Leuven). She gratefully acknowledges the assistance and support of members of her Flemish work collaborative and their colleagues: Peter Aerts, head of education and communication, S.M.A.K./Stedelijk Museum voor Actuele Kunst (Municipal Museum of Contemporary Art), Ghent; Cathy Pelgrims, head of public and education, MAS/Museum aan de Stroom, Antwerp; Hildegarde Van Genechten, advisor, Education and Participation, FARO, Brussels; and Sofie Vermeiren, head of public mediation, M Leuven. She also wishes to thank Lode Vermeersch, research manager at HIVA (Research Institute for Work and Society), KUL, who always found time for coffee or to help with matters at the university and Isabel Lowyck, director, Gaasbeek Castle, who opened so many doors in Belgium after meeting at the International Conference of the Inclusive Museum in Manchester, United Kingdom, in 2017. Finally, she remembers her Fulbright neighbors at the Groot Begijnhof, Professors David Defries and Wendy Matlock from Kansas State University.

Audrey Jacobs sincerely enjoyed helping usher this book through publication and thanks Ann and Pat for the opportunity. She owes a great debt of gratitude to everyone in her program's learning community who do so much to feed her interests. It was a dream working with her two co-authors in this volume, Ashley Pourier and Ashley Williams—a hearty thanks to them both. She warmly thanks her family who have always encouraged her academic aspirations.

We thank all of our contributing authors (see artist biographies and affiliations in part IV); this book only makes more sense with the practice-based examples provided in their chapters. We also thank the many authors who proposed chapters during the call for proposals—widely distributed across museum networks—for sharing their work. It was an extremely challenging review process, and we hope everyone continues to pursue and publish their work. The museum field benefits from continued reflection and research on practice and theory across many publication venues.

FROM THE CHAPTER AUTHORS

JAY BODA, CHARLIE FARRELL, MADISON GRIGSBY, AND ANNALIESE HARDMAN

Jay thanks his colleagues, professors, classmates, and family for their guidance and support. **Charlie:** I would like to acknowledge all my Sarasota collaborators for trusting me with their work and vision. **Madison:** I would like to acknowledge the guidance and support provided by both my undergraduate and graduate professors at Florida State University, as well as from the staff at the John and Mable Ringling Museum of Art. **Annaliese:** I would like to thank Marie Selby Botanical Garden's hardworking volunteers who inspired my research, as well as staff members Dr. David Berry and Kelsie Childs, who tirelessly supported my internship at Selby and research endeavors of curating in a nontraditional museum setting.

ANNIE BOOTH AND MEREDITH LYNN

The authors would like to thank their colleagues and friends Kelly Hendrickson, Jean Young, Preston McLane, Ivan Peñafiel, and Yawei Xiao for their integral contributions to *A Shared Body.*

NICOLE CROMARTIE AND BAILEY PLACZEK

We'd like to thank all of our *Clyfford Still, Art, and the Young Mind* co-curators, partner schools, thought partners, and teachers for their essential roles in this exhibition project, with a special shout out to Lydia and her mother, Sarah Kruger, for contributing to this chapter. We would also like to recognize Ellen Roth, Manager of community research & collaboration at the Denver Museum of Nature and Science, for introducing us to the spectrum of collaboration.

KARA FEDJE

Thank you to my immediate family—Monae, Viv, Bev, Rachel, Tom, Ann, Sanna, Keir, and the zoo crew. Additionally, thank you to my DMAC family—Jared, Jill, Alison, Tracy, Fej, Mia, Amenda, Maggie, Alex, Kristen, Connie, Haley, Janet, Jessica, Keyana, Laura, Lavonne, Madelyn, Deb, Martha, Megan, Rhonda, Stacey, and Tiffany. Lastly, thank you to my FSU family—Ann, Pat, Audrey, Minki, Dianna, Eliza, Ashley, Maclain, Hsin, Kim, Turbado, Yifeng, Zoe, Jung Shan, Amanda, Emily, Morgan, Amber, Rachel, Sara, Babarba, Charles, Jeff, MLe, Shatha, Yawei, and Zida. Thank you for the community of love and support.

JULIA FERLONI AND EMILIE SITZIA

We would like to thank Françoise Dallemagne, Emilie Girard, and Cristian Padure for their review and their advice.

ROSELYNE FRANCKEN AND TAMMY WILLE

For their essential contributions to the *Anybody Home?* exhibition, the MAS (Museum aan de Stroom, Antwerp) would like to thank all collaborators and the members of the family panel and others who shared their advice, thoughts, and ideas. Our gratitude also goes out to everyone who responded to our calls by sharing their stories, sending photographs, or singing a lullaby on camera.

KATIE FULLER AND PATRICIA O'ROURKE

Katie: The exhibition at the Hartford location would not have been possible without these folks: Larry Ossei-Mensah, Glenn Mitoma, Patricia O'Rourke, The Dodd Center for Research, and the artists: Damien Davis, Marvin Touré, Shervone Neckles, jc lenochan, Uraline Septembre Hager, Nicole Soto-Rodriguez, L. Kasimu Harris, and Carina D. Maye, and Charter Oak Cultural Center. **Patricia:** I would like to thank Kathryn Fuller for the opportunity to contribute to this beautiful project.

AUDREY JACOBS AND ASHLEY WILLIAMS

The authors gratefully acknowledge Ann Rowson Love and Pat Villeneuve, whose coursework influenced our model extension's development. We thank our colleagues from our Visitor-Centered Exhibitions course and the artist Cassia Kite for the opportunity to curate and educate with the models in mind.

JENNIFER JANKAUSKAS AND LAURA BOCQUIN

The authors wish to thank their colleagues at the Montgomery Museum of Fine Arts along with all the participants who contributed to *Art Connects*. We sincerely appreciate their professionalism and enthusiasm in bringing this project to fruition.

XIAONAN JIANG AND XUEJING DAI

Xiaonan Jiang and Xuejing Dai would like to thank Shandong Museum, support from which made this chapter possible.

ALEXIA LOBAINA

Alexia Lobaina extends her thanks to the staff of dedicated museum professionals and students at the Rollins Museum of Art, who tirelessly seek ways to activate and reimagine the interaction between art and community, with special appreciation to museum curator Dr. Gisela Carbonell, Bradley-Otis Fellow, and Nikki Barnes, for their collaboration on the exhibition *Art Encounters: Ally is a Verb*, featured in this book.

ELIZABETH NOGRADY

Cryosphere: Humans and Climate in Art from the Loeb would not have been possible without the partnership of professor Jill Schneiderman, Vassar College, and the team at the Frances Lehman Art Center. Special thanks go as well to Dr. Caroline Culp and Oliver Mendel, Vassar College Class of 2022.

MARIANNA PEGNO, CHRISTINE BRINDZA, PATRICIA LANNES, AND CECILIA GARIBAY

The authors of the chapter would like to thank the support, trust, and dialogue of artists Papay Solomon and Anh-Thuy Nguyen in realizing *People of the West*.

ASHLEY POURIER AND AUDREY JACOBS

The authors wish to thank all the artists and mentors whose invaluable contributions made this project possible: Destiny Big Crow, Randilynn Boucher-Giago, Aloysius Dreaming Bear, Michael He Crow, Emil Her Many Horses, Kristina Iron Cloud, Avery Red Cloud, and James Star Comes Out. Mary Maxon, Director of The Heritage Center, initiated and assisted this project. Our team also included Marques BraveHeart who recorded the audio and video of the residency process. Special thanks to Lily Mendoza, the Red Ribbon Skirt Society, and the Fur Trade Museum in Chadron, Nebraska, for consulting with us. Our generous funders supported this project: the National Endowment for the Arts, the South Dakota Community Foundation, the Walter E. Heller Foundation, and Red Cloud Indian School Inc. Wóphila tȟáŋka!

MICHELLE SUNSET

I greatly appreciate the collaborative spirit of my education department colleagues Katie Christensen, Raechel Cook, Sarita Keller, and Jenn Smith, and the support of Director and Chief Curator Nicole Crawford. Also, my immense gratitude to artists Ron Kroutel and Harold Garde for their trust and generosity.

PIETER JAN VALGAEREN

I would like to thank Hanne, Jean Pierre, Thomas, Jan, Christophe, Leen, Christiaan, Raf, Veerle, team Team, and most of all participating artists for all the amazing times, discussions, and results we had building SCREEN IT!

ZIDA WANG

I would like to express my gratitude to Ann Rowson Love and Pat Villeneuve for making this chapter happen! Their guidance, encouragement, and support have been instrumental in shaping my edu-curation career. I also want to thank the Silk Arts Center's curatorial director, Chen Che, for introducing me to the national exhibition position.

TING ZHANG

I would like to thank Ann Rowson Love and Pat Villeneuve, to be super patient and leave me enough time to write this chapter during the Shanghai lockdown period in 2022. I thank Department of Culture and Education of the German Consulate General Shanghai and Shanghai Liu Haisu Art Museum, who jointly supported me on international curating practice under the hardship of pandemic time. Also, I hope to thank Panpan Wang who introduced this publication open call to me and opened a chance for me to communicate with peers worldwide.

Preface

This book came from years of development and collaboration across the museum field, both nationally and internationally. We are thrilled that the book joins the American Alliance of Museums collection with publisher Rowman & Littlefield. We worked with our editor, Charles Harmon, on our last book endeavor and were excited by his enthusiasm and support for this project. Briefly, the *Dimensions of Curation Competing Values Model* contains three axes of competing values encountered during exhibition development from interpretive focus (*x* axis) to curatorial power (*y* axis) to exhibition intention or purpose (*z* axis). We think that the intersections of the three axes inform intentional planning of museum exhibitions. The development of this model reflects ongoing discussions in the museum field that we have experienced as museum professionals for more that thirty years (and yes, we have worked together much of that time) of continued discourse regarding whether interpretation should be object-centered or visitor-centered, whether curators should retain autonomy or collaborate, and whether exhibitions should be inviting for all audiences or driven by community-specific interests. Rather than picking one or the other, we understand there are a range of options. Theoretically, we adopted Quinn and Rohrbaugh's (1981) organizational behavior competing values model and applied it to exhibition curation. During the development of this model, we presented widely to gain feedback and come to general agreement on terms. We refined the model accordingly. The American Alliance of Museums Annual Meeting was an important national convening crucial for refining this work, along with international presentations.

The *Dimensions of Curation Competing Values Model* is made up of three axes—interpretive focus, curatorial power, and intent. While it may be tempting for readers to assume that competing values present binaries, the axes offer continua to think more deeply about curatorial processes. Chapter authors reflect on the model and where their work fits across the axes, sometimes leaning more toward a polar end and sometimes seeking balance somewhere closer to the middle of the competing values continua. Authors used one of two approaches when applying the model to their exhibition work by either using it as a reflective tool to examine past exhibitions or as a planning tool for upcoming projects. Both approaches, we contend, impact exhibition development moving forward.

We sought to develop a model that assisted art museum curators and their collaborators with reflecting on their past exhibition development practices and intentionally planning for their future exhibitions, realigning their practices and processes to best suit the purpose of a given exhibition. Initially, we thought we were developing a model that complemented the practices and values of our own master's and doctorate program focused on museum education and visitor-centered curation. Our program emphasizes an *edu-curation* approach (our word) for a hybrid form of curation blended with education (Villeneuve and Love, 2017). Yet, as we started to articulate a model for practice, it seemed to us that there were many possibilities across a number of continua and we wanted to not only recognize that, but to reinforce a nonjudgmental approach that acknowledges the range. For instance, we recognized there are curatorial voices that have been disenfranchised or missing in museums. This understanding acknowledges the continued need for more traditional curating that prioritizes the autonomy of marginalized curators (y = lone creative). Likewise, we heard from many in the field about the importance of socially engaged exhibitions that prioritize the power of objects and audiences (x = objects and audiences). The model offers a reflective and proactive tool to approach conversations and to guide goals and outcomes during exhibition curation.

The book is organized into four parts that sequentially introduce the model with case study examples from art museums and similar institutions—nationally and internationally—representing smaller to larger institutions. A good number of contributors represent midsize to smaller museums; we contend that smaller museums have more nimble organizational structures that offer opportunities to use this model for reflection and planning. Part I of the book includes chapter 1, where we introduce the *Dimensions of Curation Competing Values Model* from two dimensions (x and y axes) to three dimensions (adding the z axis).

In part II, authors present practice-based case studies of each of the four quadrants of two-dimensional model practices: Traditional (x = object; y = lone creative), Exclusive (x = object; y = collaborative), Sympathetic (x = audience; y = lone creative), and Inclusive (x = audience; y = collaboration). Each of the four quadrant title pages will feature the model visualization. Representing the Traditional quadrant in chapter 2, Kara Fedje shares the story of the making of the *Queering Abstraction* exhibition at the Des Moines Art Center. In chapter 3, Zida Wang presents the approach used for the Chinese National Exposition featuring contemporary artists. Demonstrating the Exclusive quadrant, in chapter 4 Stefanie Dlugosz-Acton discusses the interdisciplinary approach to curating with contemporary artist Matthew Ritchie at the University of North Texas College of Visual Art and Design Galleries. Chapter 5 examines the curatorial processes Ting Zhang used to co-curate a transnational exhibition series based on-site and online during the pandemic in Berlin and Shanghai. Characterizing the Sympathetic quadrant in chapter 6, Annie Booth and Meredith Lynn frame their approach to presenting contemporary Indigenous artists' work in *A Shared Body*, which examined historic and ongoing effects of colonialism in the United States at the Museum of Fine Arts at Florida State University. In chapter 7, Alexia Lobaina describes how a Sympathetic approach to curation influenced a campus-wide literature program and art exhibition at Rollins College Museum of Art titled *Ally is a Verb*. Representing the Inclusive quadrant, chapter 8 authors Jennifer Jankauskas and Laura Ashley Bocquin share the community-wide co-curation of a permanent collection exhibition, *Art Connects*, at the Montgomery Museum of Fine Arts. Likewise, in chapter 9, Marianna Pegno, Christine Brindza, Patricia

Lannes, and Cecilia Garibay present findings from evaluative work on community co-curation at the Tucson Museum of Art.

Part III of the book moves from the two-dimensional quadrants of the model (x and y axes) to the three-dimensional (x, y, and z axes), presenting eight combinations of the axes resulting in "exhibitions that ___." A tree of the eight combinations will be presented on the section title page. The three-dimensional visualization of the model will introduce each approach followed by two case studies from museums. In exhibitions that disseminate, chapter 10 authors Peter Aerts and Aline Van Nereaux discuss Native *Brazil/Alien Brazil* featuring the work of Anna Bella Geiger at S.M.A.K., Ghent (Municipal Museum of Contemporary Art), and in chapter 11, Michelle Sunset reconsiders dissemination in the curation of a contemporary art exhibition at the University of Wyoming Museum of Art. In exhibitions that Discern, chapter 12 author Elizabeth Nogrady explores her approach to curating an exhibition about climate change from the permanent collection of the Loeb Art Center at Vassar College, and chapter 13 authors Ashley Pourier and Audrey Jacobs discuss *Hówašte*, an exhibition at The Heritage Center at Red Cloud. In exhibitions that Enrich, chapter 14 authors Xiaonan Jiang and Xuejing Dai describe the approach to curating Ming Dynasty costumes at the Shandong Museum, while chapter 15 authors Stefanie Metsemackers and Gerd Diercks discuss the exhibition *SKIN* curated for young children at Bonnefanten Museum. In exhibitions that Amplify, chapter 16's Julia Ferloni and Emilie Sitzia challenge Romaphobia in European culture at Mucem; chapter 17's Ashley Hartman and Melanie Rosato examine their approach to *Lock and Key Creative Expression Lab*, an exhibition that took place during the pandemic at Everhart Museum. The exhibitions that Mediate chapters include chapter 18, where Lesley Marchessault also examines an exhibition strategy during the pandemic for *The Same Four Walls* at the Provincetown Art Association and Museum, and chapter 19, where author Pieter Jan Valgaeren discusses the multimedia exhibition *SCREEN IT* at Stadstriënnale Hasselt-Genk. The exhibitions that Inspire chapters feature chapter 20, where Courtney Taylor, Andy Shaw, and Grant Benoit discuss the curatorial approach to *The Boneyard*, a ceramics exhibition and studio at Louisiana State Museum of Art, and chapter 21 authors Aline Van Nereaux describes the approach to *There Is No Planet B!* at S.M.A.K. The chapters representing exhibitions that Empower include chapter 22, where Nicole Cromartie and Bailey Placzek share their community co-curation with young children and families at the Clyfford Still Museum, and chapter 23, where Roselyne Francken and Tammy Wille discuss the exhibition *Anybody Home?* to explore the many meanings of the concept of *home* at MAS (Museum aan de Stroom). In the chapters representing exhibitions that Act, chapter 24 authors Katie Fuller and Patricia O'Rourke share their approach to community action addressing school segregation, and chapter 25 authors Sofie Vermeiren and Peter Carpreau examine their process of co-curating with immigrant community members in *Boundless Hospitality* at M Leuven.

The last segment of the book, part IV, offers strategies from the field for activating curatorial change and tools to assist implementation using the Dimensions of Curation Competing Values Model. In chapter 26, Jay Boda, Charlie Farrell, Madison Grigsby, and Anneliese Hardman use readers theatre methodology to share their approach to realigning competing values during the curatorial processes of master's capstone exhibition projects at The Ringling. In chapter 27, Emily Dellheim reintroduces edu-curation as a hybrid approach for intentionally changing exhibition development practices. In chapter 28, Sofie Vermeiren reflects on changing curation practices holistically with examples from M Leuven. Chapter 29 author Lynette Zimmerman characterizes the role of directors to support the work of radical curatorial change toward social action and environmental justice. In chapter 30, Morgan Hamilton presents Dimensions of Curation digital tools for implementing the model. Chapter 31 authors Audrey Jacobs and Ashley Williams adapt the Dimensions of Curation Model to offer a complementary model for museum education.

When planning the book, we wanted to include as many voices as possible. Readers will find that there is no single template for the structure of the chapters. As co-editors, we wanted each chapter to reflect authentic voice, character, and preferences of chapter authors and their institutions. To help save word count, we asked authors not to include references to our *Dimensions of Curation* publications in their chapters. You will find them all in our first chapter. Please begin reading there. We hope the book's sequential introduction of the model with examples of practice in museums will help curators and their collaborators to meaningfully reflect on their practices and find utility in the model to further intentional exhibition planning. This model is a collective effort across the field to grapple with and find structure for understanding the competing values we, as curators and educators, face during each new exhibition endeavor. We are pleased to share this volume along with all of the authors, their exhibitions, and their institutions from around the world.

Ann Rowson Love, editor
with Pat Villeneuve, co-editor

REFERENCES

Quinn, R. E., and Rohrbaugh, J. (1981). A competing values approach to organizational effectiveness. *Public Product Review* 5, 122–40.

Villeneuve, P., and Love, A. R. (2017). *Visitor-centered exhibitions and edu-curation in art museums*. Lanham, MD: Rowman & Littlefield.

Part I

Introduction to the Dimensions of Curation Competing Values Model

1

The Dimensions of Curation
Competing Values Model

Pat Villeneuve and Ann Rowson Love

Throughout more than thirty years of professional collaboration in museums and academe, we have followed discourses that have the potential to profoundly influence curatorial practices and in turn museum audiences: Should we focus on objects or visitors? Is curation a singular or shared activity? What are our intentions when curating? Just as Korn (2018) advocated for intentional practices in museums to heighten their impact, we argue for intentional curation. Exhibitions strongly convey what a museum is about and whom it is for. Every curatorial decision, whether implicit or explicit, impacts the final exhibition and influences who will come and who may feel disenfranchised from the exhibition or museum.

For these reasons, we think it is important to have ways to think and speak explicitly about curation in shared ways. We offer the *Dimensions of Curation Competing Values Model* as a tool that can be used to reflect critically on past curatorial practices as well as intentionally plan future exhibitions in art museums and similar institutions. We begin this chapter with examples from the literature that set the stage for the development of the model. We then introduce competing values, the theoretical framework for our work, and discuss our adapted Dimensions of Curation Model using hypothetical examples. Finally, we discuss how to use the model and address curatorial change.

OVERVIEW: KEY TRENDS LEADING TO MODEL DEVELOPMENT

Historically, art museum curatorial functions included collecting, preserving, researching, exhibiting, interpreting, and potentially thinking about the museum as a site for social engagement (Alexander, 1979). Curators had advanced degrees in their content areas and focused on preserving and researching collections and interpreting artworks for exhibitions, relying on education staff for programming

(Love and Villeneuve, 2017). In his pivotal essay from the early 1970s, "The Museum, Temple or Forum," Cameron (1971) raised the question whether a museum's function in society was as a place for quiet reflection or a place for assembly—and potentially social action and engagement. This essay contributed to a renewed interest in debating the role of art museums in society.

During the 1990s, new museology—an interrogation on the traditional functions of museums—began to emerge, rethinking the function of art museums and roles of curators. Van Mensch's (1990) methodological museology conflated traditional exhibition and education roles into one function called *communication*. In the United States, a number of reports addressing diversity and inclusion appeared, including the influential and policy-changing report from the American Alliance of Museums, *Excellence and Equity* (Hirzy, 1992). The report incorporated directives for museum leadership to involve community participation at all levels of decision-making including exhibition development.

Meanwhile, museum theorists including Hooper-Greenfield (1994) and Hein (1998) advocated changing the educational paradigm in museums from a traditional, didactic one to a constructivist approach. Constructivism recognizes that visitors bring their own knowledge and backgrounds to their exhibition experiences and that they may have different preferences for how they would like to engage with artworks and content. This approach promoted multiple interpretive offerings to match different visitor preferences. Similarly, Falk and Dierking (1992) focused on understanding visitor experience in exhibitions through three contexts—*personal*, *social*, and *physical*. By the end of the 1990s, museum theorist Stephen Weil (1999) asserted that museums should be *for* someone rather than being *about* something. His instrumental statement led to continued efforts in the new millennium to further effect visitor-centered approaches.

By the early 2000s, museum theorists and researchers continued to advocate for social inclusion and rethinking of curatorial roles and training (Sandell, 2003; Bennett, 2006), calling for the reduction of oppression caused by systemic sexism, racism, and classism. These systems led to marginalized curatorial voices and limited access for many visitors and audiences. Continued emphasis on visitor-centered practices also led to works like Nina Simon's influential book *The Participatory Museum* (2010), where she offered specific approaches for *co-creating*, *co-producing*, and *co-curating* exhibitions for or with visitors. Research and theory development regarding key characteristics of visitor-centered museums in general (Samis and Michaelson, 2017) and more specifically visitor-centered exhibitions and the advancement of the *edu-curator* (Villeneuve and Love, 2017) also emerged.

New museology has turned toward post-critical museology and the recognition that for museums to maintain relevance in society, and the curating of exhibitions in particular, curators must recognize and address social issues including globalization and climate change (Janes, 2009; Chinnery, 2012). Post-critical museology also emerged from groundbreaking visitor research at the Tate Museums in the United Kingdom (Dewdney, Dibosa, and Walsh, 2013). In their book, *Post-Critical Museology and Practice in the Art Museum*, the researchers asserted that post-critical practice should not only incorporate institutional critique of museums, but also that of traditional academic research and disciplines. They argued that a post-critical understanding of visitor experiences, including in exhibitions, should include collaborative teams offering multi-disciplinary perspectives engaged in reflexive discourse and address associated subjectivities related to political and social issues. Kletchka (2018), curious about a practice-based approach of this theory in the United States, examined practices at her local art museum, the Columbus Museum of Art. Related to exhibition development, she asserted the museum's practices aligned with a post-critical approach through their interdepartmental collaborative methods to de-center institutional hierarchies and authority, to value diversity among visitors and interpretive preferences, and to challenge art historical precedents in favor of championing creativity.

The civic role and value of more visitor-centered approaches in museums continued during and post-pandemic in works including to advance museums as social changemakers working in collaboration with their communities (Murawski, 2021). Efforts to decolonize museums also continue to promote disruption of dominant White narratives through community-specific collaboration (Murawski, 2021; Wheadon, 2022). Decolonizing museums necessitates collaboration between museums and specific communities sharing authority (Lonetree, 2012).

In *The Postcolonial Museum*, museum researchers asked, "How can museums cease being a 'curated' place, a space rendered anesthetized, immune, and impermeable, a story of traumas and wounds?" (De Angelis, Ianniciello, Orabona, and Quadrano, 2013, p. 11). Yet there is continued understanding of the power of museum visitors' encounters with objects as demonstrated in Lonetree's (2012) following statement regarding decolonization and Indigenous objects:

> Objects in museums are living entities. They embody layers of meaning, and they are deeply connected to the past, present, and future of Indigenous communities. Every engagement with objects in museum cases or in collection rooms should begin with this core recognition. We are not just looking at interesting pieces. In the presence of objects from the past, we are privileged to stand as witnesses to living entities that remain intimately and inextricably tied to their descendant communities. (p. xv)

This power of encounters with objects can also be noted in Latham's (2013) research on *numinous objects*, deeply meaningful experiences with museum objects. She found four common threads across this type of engagement: the *unity of the moment*, the *object link* triggering a connection with the viewer, the sensation of *being transported*, and the feeling of *connections bigger than self*. Price et al. (2021) studied visitor experiences of memories and awe during object encounters in science and art museums. They found objects sparked awe through memories of emotional associations or a sense of surprise. Prior knowledge indicated more positive awe-filled experiences. They related awe to learning. Other researchers have studied and promoted object-based learning (Chatterjee and Hannan, 2015; Kador and Chatterjee, 2021), including how encounters with curated collections promote well-being across audience groups. Falk (2021) further underscored the value of encountering objects in exhibitions and museum experiences in general, linking them to well-being across four desired overarching objectives: personal, intellectual, social, and physical. He asserted that well-being demonstrates the worth of museums to society. He made this notion explicit when he stated, "If we [museum professionals] are to be successful, we must begin with how the public and policy makers themselves define the outcomes of museum experiences, and then help these same people appreciate just how much value those outcomes are worth" (p. 8).

This brief overview highlights works that inspired the need for and development of the Dimensions of Curation Competing Values Model. The power of objects and the need for visitor-centered approaches form a continuum of practice options; the role of curatorial authority from content specialist to community collaboration, likewise, offers an array of choices; and the role of museums as sites for reflection and well-being to assemblies for civic engagement also provides options for consideration. Nearly forty years after its first edition, *Museums in Motion*, Alexander's original history of the evolution and functions of museums, looks different (Alexander, 1979; Alexander, Alexander, and Decker, 2017). Its third edition tries at the same time to honor the past iterations and to bring in newer histories, practices, and discourses providing parallels to the notion of competing values. Are we back to the question of temple or forum? Why choose one over the other? Finding the right blend or balance through intentional planning and reflection led us to the following theory and model for practice.

THEORETICAL FRAMEWORK: COMPETING VALUES

Decades ago, organizational theorists Quinn and Rohrbaugh (1981) aspired to develop an overall theory of organizational effectiveness. However, as they looked through the literature in the field, they quickly noticed contradictory positions: some publications, for instance, suggested that an organization should look inward while others recommended outward. Quinn and Rohrbaugh acknowledged that either orientation could be appropriate, depending on the organizational context, and cast these alternatives, which they initially described as recognized dilemmas, as competing values. They then placed the alternatives as endpoints on a continuum, reflecting a range of options and showing the potential for movement in between them.

An everyday example of a competing value might be the choice a new parent sometimes faces: should I go back to work or stay home with the baby (figure 1.1)? The alternatives, which some see as an either-or choice, are not the only possibilities, however. Their placement on either end of a continuum suggests the existence of other options between the two polar positions. For instance, the new parent might return part-time, work from home, or ask their partner to request parental leave—or do a combination of options as the baby grows. There is no one "correct" answer, and any of the choices will have benefits and challenges.

Faced with the recognized dilemmas, Quinn and Rohrbaugh (1981) repositioned their initial work on organizational effectiveness, publishing instead a

Stay home with baby   Go back to work

Figure 1.1. Competing values continuum. IMAGE COURTESY OF AUDREY JACOBS.

competing values framework for organizations that reflected multiple positions from literature and practice. They began the framework modeling in two dimensions. Their *x* axis represented **organizational focus,** ranging from internal to external. The *y* axis referred to **organizational power** and structure, from controlled and stable to flexible with freedom to act. When bisected, the axes delineated four organizational practices with distinct priorities and goals: internal process (internal focus + controlled power), human relations (internal focus + flexible power), rational goals (external focus + controlled power), and open systems (external focus + flexible power).

TWO-DIMENSIONAL CURATORIAL MODEL: INTERPRETIVE FOCUS AND CURATORIAL POWER (*X* + *Y*)

We saw Quinn and Rohrbaugh's framework (1981) as a way to address perceived binaries in museum curation and adapted it for our Dimensions of Curation Competing Values Exhibition Model (Love, Villeneuve, and Burns, 2020; Love, et al., 2021; Villeneuve, et al., 2021; Villeneuve, 2019). Earlier, Davies, Paton, and O'Sullivan (2013) had developed a museums values framework based on Quinn and Rohrbaugh's work that they applied to multiple museum functions including curation. In our model, which focuses exclusively on curation, practice and literature informed endpoints reflecting more traditional versus contemporary positions in the field. The *x* axis refers to **interpretive** rather than organizational **focus**. It ranges from the object on one end to the audience on the other. The *y* axis attends to who holds the **curatorial power**, from the solitary curator we've labeled the lone creative (Love and Villeneuve, 2017) to a collaborative, team-based approach. Bisected, the two axes yield four quadrants, each representing different curatorial practices (figure 1.2).

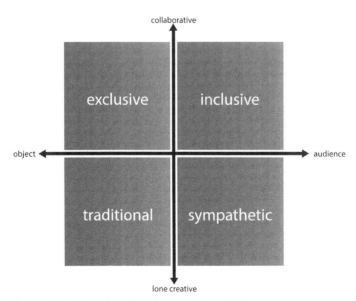

Figure 1.2. Two-dimensional curatorial model.
IMAGE COURTESY OF AUDREY JACOBS.

OBJECT INTERPRETIVE FOCUS + LONE CREATIVE CURATORIAL POWER = TRADITIONAL PRACTICE

This quadrant represents a widely recognized practice with a singular curatorial expert selecting and interpreting objects for an exhibition on a particular topic, such as the Belgian avant-garde or Ming Dynasty costumes.

OBJECT INTERPRETIVE FOCUS + COLLABORATIVE CURATORIAL POWER = EXCLUSIVE PRACTICE

In this quadrant, the interpretive focus remains on the object, but the curatorial power enlarges slightly to select individuals who can bring additional expertise to the exhibition while safeguarding the curator's role. Think, for instance, of an academic art museum welcoming a traveling exhibition on Czech scenography. The museum's curator in charge might invite a faculty member from theatre to supplement interpretation.

AUDIENCE INTERPRETIVE FOCUS + LONE CREATIVE CURATORIAL POWER = SYMPATHETIC PRACTICE

In a Sympathetic practice, the lone creative curator remains in charge of curatorial decisions but makes those on behalf of the presumed audience. An audience interpretive focus in no way diminishes the value of the objects. Instead, it increases their relevance to visitors. Although a Sympathetic approach is well-intentioned, the extent to which the exhibition resonates depends on the curator's familiarity with the community. Imagine the challenge of a solitary curator presenting an exhibition on migration in a community with large immigrant populations.

AUDIENCE INTERPRETIVE FOCUS + COLLABORATIVE CURATORIAL POWER = INCLUSIVE PRACTICE

This practice shares curatorial power with educators and other museum staff along with appropriate knowledge bearers from the community. Curators will always be essential for their content expertise, but additional voices at the table provide other types of important knowledge, such as cultural fluency or community memory. For example, a member from the local quilt guild joining the curatorial team for a textiles exhibition could provide technical expertise or help the museum connect to local objects and audiences.

FROM TWO DIMENSIONS TO THREE DIMENSIONS: ADDING CURATORIAL INTENT ($X + Y + Z$)

Quinn and Rohrbaugh (1981) added a z axis to their competing values framework addressing means versus ends. Earlier Dimensions of Curation publications by Villeneuve (2019) and Love, et al. (2021) similarly considered means versus ends to help visualize curatorial processes and exhibition outcomes but did so in tables rather than on an axis. This saved the z axis for curatorial intent, extending the model from four quadrants (two dimensions) to a three-dimensional representation (see figure 1.3). We recognize that curators make decisions about their exhibitions regarding goals, outcomes, and content. To better understand these decisions, we chose to turn to cultural policy orientations, which seem to be reflected in curatorial statements about the role of a given exhibition to the larger community or society. The cultural policy orientations *democratization of culture* and *cultural democracy* have both been used to better understand policy decisions made in and for cultural organizations including museums and the training of museum professionals (Bennett, 2006, Evard, 1997; Sandell, 2003; Gray and McCall, 2020). The democratization of culture orientation reflects a long-standing set of intentions including wide audience access and presentation of knowledge from expert sources (Juncker and Balling, 2016; Langsted, 1990; Mulcahy, 2006). Mulcahy described this orientation as "a top-down approach that essentially privileges certain forms of cultural programming that are deemed to be a public good" (p. 424). At the other end of this continuum, cultural democracy orientations embrace community-driven decision-making and action (Graves, 2005). Although these orientations are often seen as opposing, Gray and McCall (2020) underscored the potential for both when they stated, "The next state towards the establishment of a fully inclusive museum could be the creation of either cultural democracy or democratization of culture, both of which expect museums to become fully user oriented if in rather different ways" (p. 67). Table 1.1 offers several characteristics associated with each orientation.

Table 1.1. Characteristics of Democratization of Culture and Cultural Democracy

Democratization of Culture	Cultural Democracy
✓ Focus on access	✓ Focus on inclusion
✓ Cultivate	✓ Collaborate
✓ Assumes a dominant cultural viewpoint	✓ Assumes there are multiple perspectives
✓ Take art to audiences/bring audiences to museums	✓ Community-based discourse and decisions
✓ Presentation by renowned museum-based content specialists	✓ Presentation by/within culture-based specialists

In general, democratization of culture orientations are convergent, intending to disseminate valued, dominant cultural knowledge for the benefit of audiences, whereas cultural democracy approaches are divergent, recognizing and nurturing diverse meanings and community priorities.

The decision tree in figure 1.3 presents all combinations of *x* + *y* + *z*, resulting in eight distinct types of practices that we label descriptively as exhibitions that ___ (figure 1.3).

To help visualize the differences among some of these, we'll use the hypothetical example of a museum intending to curate an exhibition on migration using early twentieth-century objects from the Jewish diaspora in its collection. As you read table 1.2, think about how each exhibition might look and feel, what message each would convey, and who would likely appreciate the exhibition and who might feel turned off by it.

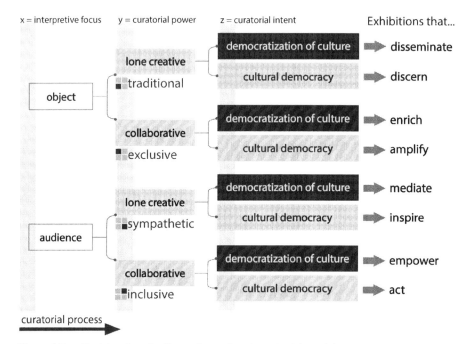

x = interpretive focus   y = curatorial power   z = curatorial intent   Exhibitions that...

lone creative
■traditional

object

democratization of culture ➡ disseminate
cultural democracy ➡ discern

collaborative
■exclusive

democratization of culture ➡ enrich
cultural democracy ➡ amplify

lone creative
■sympathetic

audience

democratization of culture ➡ mediate
cultural democracy ➡ inspire

collaborative
■inclusive

democratization of culture ➡ empower
cultural democracy ➡ act

curatorial process ➡

Figure 1.3. Decision tree for three-dimensional curatorial model.
IMAGE COURTESY OF AUDREY JACOBS.

Placements along any of the continua may move away from the polar terms defining the axes. For instance, a curator in a contemporary art museum may work closely with a living artist on the artist's exhibition and its interpretation. This would nudge the placement on the y continuum along slightly—because the curator is no longer working as the lone creative (although the artist and curator may be working very much as one). Adding an educator to the curatorial process would move the placement farther up the continuum, but it would still not be at the collaborative end of the axis where multiple knowledge bearers would be more fully involved in the curatorial process.

USING THE MODEL AND IMPLEMENTING CHANGE

We are often asked how to use the Dimensions of Curation Model. As previously stated, it can be used to examine the curatorial practices of current or previous exhibitions, think intentionally about future exhibitions, or effect curatorial change using the model as a road map. For examples, read an imagined scenario in the first articulation of the two-dimensional model (Villeneuve, 2019) or many chapters that follow.

Changes in curatorial practice will happen most readily with the support of the director or curators (Villeneuve, 2019). To start, museum staff might read this chapter and discuss the model. To increase familiarity with it, try placing current or past exhibitions in the three-dimensional model (exhibitions that ___). Many of our authors have said that they didn't fully appreciate the model until they

Pat Villeneuve and Ann Rowson Love

Table 1.2.   Examples of Different Types of Exhibitions That ___.

Curatorial Process	Curator(s) Might Think . . .	Type of Exhibition That ___
Curator works alone selecting valued objects to tell a previously established narrative of Jewish migration for the benefit of the museum public.	"We have high-quality objects from the Jewish diaspora that our audience should see, and they tell a story of migration that our public should know about."	Object Interpretive Focus + Lone Creative Curatorial Power + Democratization of Culture Curatorial Intent = **Disseminates**
Curator works alone while keeping the audience in mind and hoping to inspire them.	"This is one case, but I hope these objects from the Jewish diaspora will encourage the public to think more broadly about migration and immigration issues."	Audience Interpretive Focus + Lone Creative Curatorial Power + Cultural Democracy Curatorial Intent = **Inspires**
A curatorial team that includes curator, educator, and other appropriate knowledge bearers from the museum and community works together with the community to tell relevant and diverse stories of migration.	"There are so many migration stories that we'll need to incorporate objects from other cultural groups. We hope to embrace community voices, dignify their stories, and cause people to think deeply about commonalities among migration stories and current immigration issues."	Audience Interpretive Focus + Collaborative Curatorial Power + Cultural Democracy Curatorial Intent = **Acts**

applied it to their exhibitions. Pick an exhibition that was particularly successful—or one that didn't live up to its expectations. Identify where it fits within the model and reflect on its successes or shortcomings: What were we trying to achieve? Whom did we curate it for? Who came, and who didn't? Was it a good fit for our community? Imagine the exhibition with a different placement on the three-dimensional model: "What would have changed if the interpretive focus had been on the audience?" "How would we have benefited from more voices in the curatorial process?" Tools introduced in chapter 30 will also be helpful.

As seen in chapters in this book, the model can also be used to make intentional decisions about upcoming exhibitions as well as to think strategically about the overall curatorial schedule. Some museums may find they rely heavily on one type of exhibition that ___. Consider whether that is an intentional practice or the presumed mode of curating in the museum (Villeneuve and Song, 2017). Does it work well for the objects and audiences? Sometimes, it is appropriate to curate an exhibition that disseminates, for instance; other times, an exhibition that transforms—or any other type—might better serve audiences and the objects. Taking advantage of a repertoire of different types of exhibitions that ___ throughout the exhibition schedule may have broader appeal and bond more audiences to the museum.

A museum that typically does curator-driven exhibitions and wishes to do more collaborative, visitor-centered exhibitions (those that act or transform) may want to make physical, systemic, or organizational changes to facilitate these new practices (Villeneuve, 2019; Villeneuve and Song, 2017). For instance, the museum may need to arrange for collaborative work times or spaces. For a past example, see Czajkowski and Salort-Pons (2017).

Without strong administrative or curatorial support, it is still possible to effect bottom-up curatorial change. Begin by looking for allies in the museum or community. Then seek opportunities to try a different type of exhibition that ___. Perhaps there is an exhibition on the schedule that lacks curatorial enthusiasm or an available time slot in the education gallery. Or you might need to move outside the museum space. Maybe a new curator, local artists, community teens, or educators from the university or local schools would be open to trying something new. Mount and promote the exhibition and talk about it explicitly with the curators and director. In our experience, people recognize the changes and often become interested in other types of exhibitions. There will be successes and setbacks. Learn from them, as many of our authors have, and use them to inform future intentional curatorial practices.

REFERENCES

Alexander, E. P. (1979). *Museums in motion: An introduction to the history and functions of museums*. Nashville: American Association for State and Local History.

Alexander, E. P., Alexander, M., and Decker, J. (2017). *Museums in motion: An introduction to the history and functions of museums* (third edition). Lanham, MD: Rowman & Littlefield.

Bennett, T. (2006). Exhibition, difference, and the logic of culture. In I. Karp, C. A. Kratz, L. Szwaja, and T. Ybarra Frausto (Eds.), *Museum frictions: Public cultures/global transformations* (pp. 46–59). Durham, NC: Duke University Press.

Cameron, D. F. (1971). The museum, a temple or the forum. *Curator: The Museum Journal* 14(1), 11–24.

Chatterjee, H., and Hannan, L. (2015). *Engaging the senses: Object-based learning in higher education*. New York: Routledge.

Chinnery, A. (2012). Temple or forum? On new museology and education for social change. *Philosophy of Education Archive*, 269–76.

Czajkowski, J. W., and Salort-Pons, S. (2017). Building a workplace that supports educator-curator collaboration. In P. Villeneuve and A. R. Love (Eds.), *Visitor-centered exhibitions and edu-curation in art museums* (pp. 239–49). Lanham, MD: Rowman & Littlefield.

Davies, S. M., Paton, R., and O'Sullivan, T. J. (2013). The museum values framework: A framework for understanding organizational culture in museums. *Museum Management and Curatorship* 28(4), 345–61.

De Angelis, A., Ianniciello, C., Orabona, M., and Quadraro, M. (2013). Introduction: disruptive encounters—museums, arts, and postcoloniality. In I. Chambers, A. De Angeli., C. Ianniciello, M. Orabona., and M. Quadraro (Eds.), *The postcolonial museum: The arts of memory and the pressures of history* (pp. 1–21). Burlington, VT: Ashgate.

Dewdney, A., Dibosa, D., and Walsh, V. (2013). *Post-critical museology: Theory and practice in the art museum*. New York: Routledge.

Evard, Y. (1997). Democratizing culture or cultural democracy? *The Journal of Arts Management, Law, and Society* 27(3), 167-75.

Falk, J. H. (2021). *The value of museums: Enhancing societal well-being*. Lanham, MD: Rowman & Littlefield.

Falk, J. H., and Dierking, L. D. (1992). *The museum experience*. Washington, DC: Whalesback Books.

Graves, J. (2005). *Cultural democracy: The arts, community and the public purpose*. Champaign, IL: University of Illinois Press.

Gray, C., and McCall, V. (2020). *The role of today's museum*. New York: Routledge.

Hein, G. (1998). *Learning in the museum*. New York: Routledge.

Hirzy, E. (1992). *Excellence and equity: Education and the public dimension of museums*. Arlington, VA: American Alliance of Museums.

Hooper-Greenhill, E. (1994). Museum learners as active postmodernists: Contextualizing constructivism. In E. Hooper-Greenhill (Ed.), *The educational role of the museum* (pp. 67-72). New York: Routledge.

Janes, R. (2009). *Museums in a troubled world: Renewal, irrelevance, or collapse*. New York: Routledge.

Juncker, B., and Balling, G. (2016). The value of art and culture in everyday life: Toward an expressive cultural democracy. *Journal of Arts Management, Law, and Society* 46(5), 231-42.

Kador, T., and Chatterjee, H. (2021). *Object-based learning and well-being: Exploring material connections*. New York: Routledge.

Kletchka, D. C. (2018). Toward post-critical museologies in U.S. art museums. *Studies in Art Education* 59(4), 297-310.

Korn, R. (2018). *Intentional practice for museums: A guide for maximizing impact*. Lanham, MD: Rowman & Littlefield.

Langsted, J. (1990). *Double strategies in a modern cultural policy*. Stamford, CT: Management Consultants for the Arts Inc.

Latham, K. F. (2013). Numinous experiences with museum objects. *Visitor Studies* 16(1), 3-20.

Lonetree. A. (2012). *Decolonizing museums: Representing Native America in national and tribal museums*. Chapel Hill, NC: University of North Carolina Press.

Love, A. R., and Villeneuve P. (2017). Edu-curation and the edu-curator. In P. Villeneuve and A. R. Love (Eds.), *Visitor-centered exhibitions and edu-curation in art museums* (pp. 11-22). Lanham, MD: Rowman & Littlefield.

Love, A. R., Villeneuve, P., and Burns, W. J. (2020). Democracy in action: The *Dimensions of Curation Competing Values Exhibition Model* can help curators navigate today's changing landscape. *Museum* 99(1), 12-15.

Love, A. R., Villeneuve, P., Burns, W. J., Wessel, B., and Jiang, X. (2021). *Dimensions of Curation Competing Values Model:* Tool for shifting exhibition priorities. *Curator: The Museum Journal* 64(4), 1-17.

Mulcahy, K. V. (2006). Cultural policy: Definitions and theoretical approaches. *The Journal of Arts Management, Law, and Society* 35(4), 319-30.

Murawski, M. (2021). *Museums as agents of change: A guide to becoming a changemaker*. Lanham, MD: Rowman & Littlefield.

Price, C. A., Greenslit, J. N., Applebaum, L., Harris, N., Segovia, G., Quinn, K. A., and Krogh-Jespersen, S. (2021). Awe and memories of learning in science and art museums. *Visitor Studies* 24(2), 137-65.

Quinn, R. E., and Rohrbaugh, J. (1981). A competing values approach to organizational effectiveness. *Public Product Review* 5, 122-40.

Samis, P., and Michaelson, M. (2017). *Creating the visitor-centered museum*. New York: Routledge.

Sandell, R. (2003). Social inclusion, the museum, and the dynamics of sectoral change, *Museum and Society* 1(1), 45–62.

Simon, N. (2010). *The participatory museum*. Museum 2.0.

Van Mensch, P. (1990). Methodological museology, or towards a theory of museum practice. In S. Pearce (Ed.), *Objects of Knowledge* (pp. 141–57). London: Bloomsbury Publishing.

Villeneuve, P. (2019, June). Considering competing values in art museum exhibition curation. *Stedelijk Studies* 8. https://stedelijkstudies.com/journal/considering-compet ing-values-in-art-museum-exhibition-curation/

Villeneuve, P., and Love, A. R. (Eds.). (2017). *Visitor-centered exhibitions and edu-curation in art museums*. Lanham, MD: Rowman & Littlefield.

Villeneuve, P., Love, A. R., Aerts, P., Forero, J., and Kim, H. (2021). Considering Competing Values in a Model for Curation. *The International Journal of the Inclusive Museum* 14.

Villeneuve, P., and Song, J. (2017). Paradigms, visitor-centered museum practices, and systems thinking. In Y. Jung and A. R. Love (Eds.), *Systems thinking in museums: Theory and practice* (pp. 37–45). Lanham, MD: Rowman & Littlefield.

Weil, S. (1999). From being about something to being for somebody: The ongoing transformation of the American museum. *Daedalus* 128(3), 229–58.

Wheadon, N. (2022). *Museum metamorphosis: Cultivating change through cultural citizenship*. Lanham, MD: Rowman & Littlefield.

Part II

Two Dimensions

Traditional, Exclusive, Sympathetic, and Inclusive Quadrants

TRADITIONAL

Object (*x*) + Lone Creative (*y*) = **Traditional**

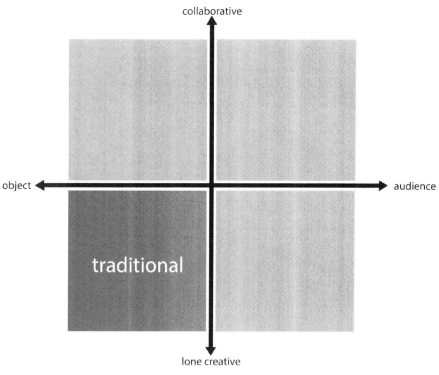

IMAGE COURTESY OF AUDREY JACOBS.

2

Queering the Museum

FROM A TRADITIONAL MODEL TOWARD A MORE INCLUSIVE PRACTICE

Kara Fedje

Queer Abstraction, an art exhibition at the Des Moines Art Center (DMAC) in Des Moines, Iowa, in the United States, from June 1 to September 8, 2019, featured contemporary LGBTQ+ artists highlighting concepts of sexuality and gender through abstract art (Ledesma, 2019). *Queer Abstraction* was the first exhibition in DMAC's seventy-year history to focus on queer subject matter, celebrate LGBTQ+ artists during Pride month, and provide a free family day devoted to LGBTQ+ families (Fedje and Ledesma, 2020). *Queer Abstraction* challenged traditional boundaries. Physically, it was installed in three galleries and was at the center of the museum where an art sculpture wall, *Deep Purple* by Tom Burr, intersected DMAC's reflecting pool and created a queerer version of Richard Serra's *Tilted Arc*. Additionally, there was a sea of blue beads strung and conceptually designed by Felix Gonzalez-Torres that hung from the I. M. Pei butterfly ceiling, ensuring visitors would enter and "queer the space." To define queer as an adjective is abstract in itself, but a person who identifies as queer may "defiantly stand to the side of normal . . . shifting in relation to the ways in which normativity is constantly and covertly reinstalled, redeployed, and defended" (Getsy, 2019, p. 65). Queer as a verb, or to "queer a space," means inevitably changing our museums so that we can offer "an opportunity to redefine the binary" (Halberstam, 2005, p. 161). *Queer Abstraction* represented queer identity, but the impact was immense, because it altered the way staff and the community viewed an art museum using an LGBTQ+ lens.

A TRADITIONAL CURATORIAL APPROACH TO MUSEUMS

Jared Ledesma, Associate Curator at the DMAC, was the source for this exhibition. Creating this exhibition was his "baby"—he curated this exhibition because of his expertise in queer art history, his understanding of queer theory and culture, and his lived experiences as a gay man. He had the autonomy to create *Queer Abstraction* because the former senior curator, Alison Ferris, trusted him to represent many of us in the marginalized queer community. His voice as a queer curator had not been heard before in a major way at the DMAC, nor had many of us queer staff been heard before. His enthusiasm for exhibiting world-class LGBTQ+ artists resonates with many of us in the museum field.

FROM A MUSEUM EDUCATOR'S PERSPECTIVE

Queer Abstraction began shifting DMAC from a traditional museum to a more inclusive space. From the beginning of this exhibition, as a queer educator, I wanted to implement hands-on visitor-centered activities for the community, but exhibition development is often limited to curators and senior administrators. In museum hierarchy, educators traditionally report to the director of education or the curators (Kletchka, 2021). Yet educators want to be a part of the exhibition creation conversation. Edu-curators can blend different languages and ideas between curator and educator in a communicative form that best supports visitors' experiences (Villeneuve and Love, 2017). These partnerships enhance visitor engagement, ultimately supporting the institution's mission and goals. As a member of the LGBTQ+ community and friend of the curator, Jared Ledesma, I helped shift the exhibition. Wanting to create a visitor-centered exhibition space, I asked the senior curator if I could create a participatory interactive. Together we selected a comment board with a table and stools nearby for people to write comments or draw ideas inspired by a prompt written on vinyl. The question was specific to the exhibition but open-ended enough to elicit a response. Ultimately, we asked visitors, "What does *Queer Abstraction* mean to you?" This simple addition was a starting place for visitor feedback. It took courage to ask for exhibition space that first day, but it takes more perseverance and grit to continue asking for museum resources.

THE MUSEUM SHIFTS

Inclusion was not always a focus at DMAC; it was a traditional art museum in the heart of Iowa. However, in 2016, DMAC began making space to grow its inclusion efforts. DMAC's strategic plan emphasized how it would provide "empathetic programs, thought-provoking exhibitions, and open conversations" (DMAC, 2019). To deploy some of these collaborative ideas before the exhibition's opening reception, Ledesma invited LGBTQ+ community members to visit the exhibition. One community member asked, "How many artists of color are in the exhibition? Why are there no bisexual artists in the show?" Museum staff needed to discuss representation further in depth. The internal and external museum groups found ways to diversify the plans of the opening reception by including vendors, disk jockeys, and artists representing more diversity. The opening celebration had more than 1,500 people in attendance. This exhibition drew more diverse visitors (in gender, sexual orientation, race, and age) than the museum's typical receptions or the demographics of the surrounding area. To expand its audience, DMAC created an exhibition that featured a marginalized group of LGBTQ+ artists that in turn attracted a new audience.

Kara Fedje

Figure 2.1. Visitors at the opening reception walk through a sea of blue beads in the *Queer Abstraction* exhibition. PHOTO COURTESY OF THE AUTHOR.

While there were many successful aspects of this exhibition, there was much to learn. A queer curator produced the exhibition and a queer educator created the programming, but DMAC still operated as a more traditional museum and needed to push toward more diverse points of view. The curator and I fulfilled the need for representation of marginalized voices, but we also needed to expand our community inclusion efforts. Changing a museum is a process, not a finite goal. To "queer a space" isn't just about changing the museum staff and exhibitions; it is about changing infrastructure to co-create museum experiences with communities.

REFLECTIONS

If community collaboration had been central earlier in the curatorial process and there was more urgency to represent LGBTQ+ voices, we might have had even more engagement. DMAC was in the process of shifting from a traditional museum to a more inclusive model and was in the initial phases of institutional change. We had an incredible art exhibition, but we also programmed for LGBTQ+ people that helped make internal staff embrace the larger Des Moines LGBTQ+ community. We intertwined families, children, people with disabilities, BIPOC, and LGBTQ+ people. We learned by doing and making sure the groundwork of collaborative programming had to be set up for the exhibit to be successful.

I collaborated with Director of Education Jill Featherstone, and together we were inspired by other institutions such as the Chicago Children's Museum to host *Entirely Kids Day: Family Equality*, a day devoted to LGBTQ+ children and families. Through research, I found material on how parents can be more LGBTQ+ friendly, a glossary for educators, a list of children's books, the value of a nongendered bathroom sign, and ways museums participate in International Family Equality Day. In July 2019, a thirty-foot pride flag greeted seven hundred children and families. Families explored the galleries, studios, and auditorium. Activities included two drag storytimes, docent-led tours, artmaking, and LGBTQ+ professional dance performances.

Queer Abstraction and the associated activities brought new audiences to the museum. DMAC was a traditional museum transforming into a more inclusive space when hundreds of LGBTQ+ people saw art in a new way—in a more "queer" way—and felt they were represented in the galleries. The process of institutional change in museums can at times be messy, challenging, and time-consuming. Despite these difficulties, museums should seek to involve the marginalized community voices from both within and outside the institution. To sustain the relevancy and viability of the institution in the community at large, the museum must change to become a more inclusive space. Museums are at a pivotal juncture as arts organizations shift from the curatorial voice to supporting community voice and agency (Janes and Sandell, 2019). Museums want to improve diversity, equity, accessibility, and inclusion practices so all people feel welcomed. Visitors and staff want to know they will have a sense of belonging in museums (Price and Applebaum, 2022). Museums take time to change paradigms (Villeneuve and Song, 2017). DMAC had not always been so inclusive but as it shifted from a traditional approach toward a more inclusive approach with queer representation in staffing, more community involvement, and more visitor-centered engagement, the museum took its first steps that would continue to impact future museum exhibitions. The Queer Abstraction exhibition went on to be displayed at the Nerman Museum of Contemporary Art in Kansas, the ideas were a presentation topic at the 2020 American Alliance of Museums conference, and the content was featured in the March 2020 issue of Museum, American Alliance of Museums' magazine (Fedje and Ledesma, 2020). More than anything, this exhibition opened new doors for inclusion work to begin at a museum that otherwise would have stayed as a traditional model of a museum.

REFERENCES

Des Moines Art Center (DMAC). (2019). We believe in the power of art [video]. https://desmoinesartcenter.org/about/#:~:text=We%20connect%20people%20and%20art,with%20a%20spirit%20of%20openness

Fedje, K., and Ledesma, J. (2020). "Abstract art concrete goals." Museum Magazine 99(2), 32–36. https://www.aam-us.org/2020/03/01/abstract-art-concrete-goals/

Getsy, D. (2019). "Ten queer theses on abstraction." In J. Ledesma (Ed.), Queer abstraction (pp. 65–75). Des Moines Art Center.

Halberstam, J. J. (2005). In a queer time and place: Transgender bodies, subcultural lives. NYU Press.

Janes, R. R., and Sandell, R. (2019). Museum activism. Oxfordshire: Taylor & Francis.

Kletchka, D. C. (2021). "The epistemology of the basement: A queer theoretical reading of the institutional positionality of art museum educators." Museum Management and Curatorship 36(2), 125–35.

Ledesma, J. (2019). Queer Abstraction [exhibition]. Des Moines Art Center.

Price, C. A., and Applebaum, L. (2022). "Measuring a sense of belonging at museums and cultural centers." Curator: The Museum Journal 65(1), 135–60.

Villeneuve, P., and Love, A. R. (Eds.). (2017). Visitor-centered exhibitions and edu-curation in art museums. Lanham, MD: Rowman & Littlefield.

Villeneuve, P., and Song, J. (2017). "Paradigms, visitor-centered museum practices, and systems thinking." In A. R. Love and Y. Jung (Eds.), Systems Thinking in Museums: Theory and Practice (pp. 37–45). Lanham, MD: Rowman & Littlefield.

3

Using Traditional Practice to Review the Chinese National Art Exhibition

Zida Wang

The *13th National Exhibition of Fine Arts, Experimental Arts Division Exhibition* displayed eighty-one Chinese experimental contemporary artworks from October 10 to December 30, 2019 (Ministry of Culture and Tourism of the People's Republic of China, 2019). This exhibition was co-hosted by the Artists' Association of China and the Silk Road Arts Center. The Artists' Association of China, an official organization, specializes in organizing Chinese national exhibitions. The Silk Road Arts Center is a private art center in Langfang City, Hebei Province, China. Langfang serves as an important satellite city for Beijing. The Silk Road Center was founded in 2017 and has an ongoing collaboration with the Artists' Association of China. This collaboration created the opportunity for the Silk Road Center to present the exhibition in its four galleries.

The exhibition's purpose was to demonstrate to the audience how Chinese experimental art flourished from 2014 to 2019. The *National Exhibition* started with a call for proposals that encouraged all Chinese artists to submit their experimental artworks to participate in the exhibition. The exhibition received around eight hundred artwork submissions. After selections, the curator of the exhibition featured eighty-one artworks from all the submissions to be presented in the galleries. These eighty-one artworks included sculptures, paintings, video installations, new media works, and large-scale public installations.

THE EXHIBITION AS AN OBJECT (*X*) + LONE CREATIVE (*Y*) = TRADITIONAL PRACTICE EXAMPLE

This section discusses how the *National Exhibition* fits the Dimensions of Curation Competing Values Exhibition Model's traditional practice. The discussion will pay attention to the objects as the exhibition's interpretive focus and lone creative as curatorial power that resulted in a traditional practice approach.

OBJECTS AS THE INTERPRETIVE FOCUS (X AXIS)

In China, the notion of experimental art is frequently employed to describe contemporary art experimentations. These experimentations include discovering new themes and forms, and using new media and materials. Experimental arts explore new results, develop new audiences, and accomplish unique goals (Qiu, 2020).

The curator designed four galleries with different themes to present these eighty-one exhibition objects. The first gallery showcased artistic experiments that used contemporary techniques to illustrate traditional Chinese culture. The calligraphy, installations, and traditional Chinese paintings on display in this gallery all entailed experimenting with textures, techniques, and content. The exhibition curator thought that by interpreting the audience through familiar traditional Chinese cultural works, visitors would make connections with the exhibition's experimental objectives.

The second gallery featured concept-based experimental artworks. The works in this gallery included photography, films, and new media pieces, along with many other works. For example, this gallery highlighted an artwork that showcased the work called *Divorced Memorial Photography*, a photo series that the artist Gao Meilin took of her divorced parents every year. Her parents reunited once a year for the artist, and she recorded these moments of the reunion. This artwork was an example of concept-based experimental work in the exhibition. The third gallery showcased multimedia presentations of experimentations in various ways. This gallery was full of new media works that express the historical movements in the past five to ten years. In particular, this gallery's interpretive labels highlighted the social changes in China from the experimental art perspective. For example, Liu Qingyuan's work *Stories on Streets: Art Moments from the 1960s to 1990s* described twenty-eight historical street art moments, including the famous art movement in China with digital print techniques.

The theme of the fourth gallery was interactions. In this gallery, the audiences could engage interactively with the artworks instead of just looking at the artworks. For example, the virtual reality work *Do the Undersea Citizens Dream of Mazu* by the artist Chen Baoyang encouraged audiences to wear the virtual reality headset and interact with the work by following the digital characters inside the virtual reality artwork, and audiences could create their own storylines through their individual interaction. In addition, the interpretive labels in the fourth gallery also involved the interaction with the audience and how experimental artworks acknowledge the interactions with them.

These eighty-one artworks included various forms of artistic experimentation that the curator considered comprehensively to strengthen connections between the objects to the audience through QR codes that focused on the object's place in contemporary art history and the artist's theory behind each piece. QR codes have been widely used in China since the development of the internet and smartphones. Therefore, the curator decided to place QR codes on all object labels so

Figure 3.1. The curator demonstrates the exhibition with the government attendees before the exhibition's opening reception. PHOTO COURTESY OF THE AUTHOR.

the visitors could use their smartphones to scan the QR codes to learn more about the objects in digital form.

LONE CREATIVE AS THE CURATORIAL POWER (Y AXIS)

In traditional practice, the lone creative curator has the power to engage in a solitary curatorial process, producing an exhibition focusing on the art objects. All curatorial decisions in the *National Exhibition* were made exclusively by the curator. The curator reported to a committee, which did not hold any curatorial responsibilities or intervene in the professional curatorial plan. A government official and several well-known experimental artists served on the committee, drawn from the ranks of fine arts university professors, independent artists, and researchers. The committee's responsibilities included ensuring the exhibition followed government policies, curatorial fairness, and transparency procedures from the selections to the presentation and the purpose as originally outlined.

The committee assigned the exhibition curator to establish the curatorial plan and follow up plans to fulfill the purpose of this exhibition. As discussed, the purpose of this exhibition was to present to the public the development of Chinese experimental art from 2014 to 2019. The curator developed the four themed galleries to properly represent the exhibition's goal and set the artworks within their contemporary art historical context. Furthermore, the curator accomplished the lone creative curatorial research with multiple stages during the exhibition curatorial

Figure 3.2. Audiences participate in the exhibition artwork *Our Sky Project*, 2018.
PHOTO COURTESY OF HU BEI.

planning stage. Object interpretation focused on developing wall texts and labels that emphasized the content of the artworks. The curator outlined the curatorial works in the following stages. First, the curator conducted the research on all objects and wrote the interpretive labels for them. Second, with in-depth studies of the objects, the curator categorized these eighty-one works into four themes. Third, the curator established a curatorial plan that reflected the purpose of the exhibition. Fourth, the curator analyzed the potential traffic flow for the exhibition in four galleries and designed the floor plans for the exhibition.

In summary, the curator independently communicated with artists, conducted research on the objects, selected the eighty-one display artworks, categorized featured artworks, categorized the galleries' themes, developed the curatorial plan, created the floor plans, and reported on progress to government officials.

TRADITIONAL PRACTICE APPROACH

In a traditional practice, the curatorial expert discriminates art historical content about chosen works. The big idea is the concept that guided every part of the exhibition design, resulting in a statement explaining what the exhibition was about (Serrell, 2015). Although the purpose of the *National Exhibition* had been finalized by the officials, it was to present to the public the development of Chinese experimental art from 2014 to 2019. The curator retained curatorial autonomy from the committee and reinforced the exhibition's big idea to illustrate to the public the experimentations of experimental art in modern China. This was a critical step to transform the official purpose of the exhibition into a coherent idea. In the process of introducing the objects to the audience, the curator used technologies like QR codes for the audience to better make connections with the art objects.

In addition, the curator independently concentrated on the artworks' research and label writings. For example, labels were written in both Chinese and English. The interpretive labels included bilingual name introductions of the artwork, the creation date, the texture, the size, the artist information, the interpretive explanations about the objects, the QR code for digital discovery, etc. As a *National Experimental Exhibition*, another experimentation trial was the label explaining why the featured artworks were considered to fit the requirements as experimental artworks. After researching all the artworks and their artists, the curator made this curatorial choice explicitly. Under each label and basic information, each label had a short explanation that demonstrated what perspectives made this artwork experimental. The explanations included the experimentations in texture, the experimentations in concepts, the experimentations in the usage of advanced technologies, etc.

REFLECTIONS

The *National Exhibition* attracted three main types of audiences and gained great success. First, local communities participated in the national exhibition of China. Second, it attracted many college art students. Third, it aroused the enthusiasm of the public for experimental arts. For example, the *National Exhibition* attracted around 200,000 visitors from October to December 2019; on the social media platform, Weibo, there were many hashtags regarding the exhibition artworks; other Chinese fine art colleges organized their students to visit the exhibition weekly. As a free admission exhibition, visitors only needed to register online to get free tickets and relevant educational programs. The exhibition had great success and many positive responses from multiple audience perspectives, especially on the side of the interactive artworks. For example, the *Our Sky Project 2019* by Hu Bei was an interactive, audience-generated video installation. This work was displayed at the fourth gallery as a crucial interactive artwork. The fourth gallery was meant to cultivate the visitors to take action to engage in the experimental artworks. Visitors watched this three-minute-long sky video and could interact with it through their smart devices.

Although the exhibition's curator retained the curatorial autonomy from the government officials, the purpose of the exhibition was established by the authorities prior to the exhibition. The curator worked independently to convert the governmental purpose and requirements into generally acceptable ideas and action plans. In the future, the curator of the *National Exhibition* hopes to have the opportunity to join the exhibition purpose decision-making process and collaborate with other museum exhibition professionals to curate other exhibitions.

REFERENCES

Ministry of Culture and Tourism of the People's Republic of China (Ed.). (2019, December 10). 第十三届全国美术作品展览/*The 13th national exhibitions of fine arts*. People's Publishing House. https://13qgmz.artron.net/

Qiu, Z. (2020, February 24). *Art Education: introduction to experimental art*. https://www.artda.cn/yishujiaoyu-c-11359.html

Serrell, B. (2015). *Exhibit labels: An interpretive approach*. Lanham, MD: Rowman & Littlefield.

EXCLUSIVE

Object (*x*) + Collaborative (*y*) = **Exclusive**

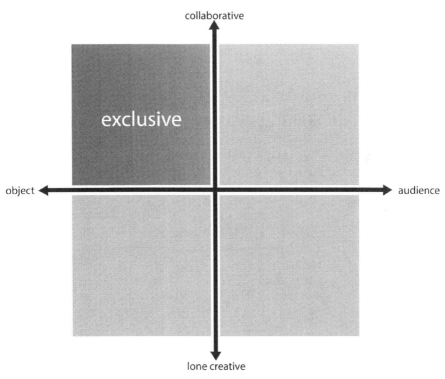

4

Iterations of Curating with Matthew Ritchie

WORKING COLLABORATIVELY DURING THE COVID-19 PANDEMIC

Stefanie Dlugosz-Acton

As the director and curator at the University of North Texas (UNT) College of Visual Arts and Design (CVAD) in Denton, Texas, United States, I have been working on a project with artist Matthew Richie since early 2020, a commissioned public sculpture through the university's *Art in Public Places* program. The commission predated my tenure, and I came into the project during the final design approval. In addition, I served as curator of the project and co-chair for the Art in Public Places Committee. These dual yet parallel roles led the project into several iterations—with the sculpture as the first—influenced by the COVID-19 pandemic, prolonged timelines, and the artist's desire to see what was possible with collaboration and conversation. The sculpture titled *Shadow Garden* installation was completed in May 2022 and dedicated in fall 2022.

This sculpture and its iterations, including an exhibition, fit into the following value model based on the *Dimensions of Curation Competing Values Model* (Object + Collaborative = Exclusive). I will discuss these iterations in more detail throughout the chapter.

The exhibition was born from limited collaborations between the artist and me and focused on his artistic practice. The emphasis of the show and the sculpture were object-based. However, it grew to include a more significant number of participants and co-creators, initially with the composer Shara Nova. It expanded to include the conductor Dr. MacMullen and her students, singers, percussionist, and other musicians. As a result of these collaborators, the exhibition shifted from object-based to experiential through the iterations. Although I believe we were inclusive/audience adjacent, at its core, there were a small number of specialized co-creators interpreting the artwork and exhibition. Even within the performances of *Infinite Movement*, many of the participants voiced that after the first performance, they did not know what we were creating until they performed it. Honestly, I was not quite sure either, as everything was so piecemeal, for practice and logistically, until more than one hundred persons were together rehearsing the week of the performance outside the exhibition space. It was unclear *what* we were creating other than that we *were* making. The theme of emergence, trust, and collaboration was clear to everyone involved in the iterations, who overheard a rehearsal, stumbled upon the exhibition, and experienced the artwork and the music.

SECOND ITERATION: TEACHING

The catalyst for this project was the commissioning of the sculpture. However, the project postponement due to the pandemic and supply chain issues gave the project more time and space to gestate, resulting in a series of iterations. The second iteration was the co-teaching of a course. In spring 2021, I co-taught a Topics in Contemporary Art Practice class with Ritchie. The class focused on the idea of emergence. It was a think-tank seminar with weeks concentrated on various theories, including isolation, asking, seeking, holding, assembly, storytelling, undoing, disturbing, community, and never knowing. We recorded the Zoom class and provided sketchbooks for their potential inclusion in the exhibition.

THIRD ITERATION: *MATTHEW RITCHIE: FLORILEGIUM*

The third iteration was Ritchie's new body of work shown in our main CVAD Gallery, *Matthew Ritchie: Florilegium* (August 24 to December 10, 2021). *Florilegium* included a three-channel video projected across a gallery wall, thirty-six paintings made by Ritchie and an oil-painting robot prototype, and a window banner that filtered and obscured light within the space. There were also maquettes of various design progressions of the sculpture *Shadow Garden* and a soundscape created with Ritchie's longtime musical collaborator, UNT alumna Shara Nova, playing hauntingly within the exhibition space.

The exhibition also included artistic outputs from the co-taught class, including a digital piece co-created by Ritchie and the students using an artificial intelligence framework and *An Artist Lecture* by Sean Lopez (UNT, 2021). These videos were projected on the side of the CVAD building to be viewed after dusk for the exhibition's duration. Ritchie said, "by developing an iterative project that explores digital and physical spaces, we have tried to engage with the students positively when social and academic interactions are being challenged and disrupted by COVID-19, climate change, and new technologies such as artificial intelligence" (UNT, 2021).

The exhibition highlighted Ritchie's deep investigation into the history of mapping human knowledge and lived experience using complex systems. As part of his ongoing exploration, *Florilegium* accentuated the looming presence of the internet and the virtual nature of communication during the pandemic. Ritchie's research for this project focused on generative adversarial networks (GANs). A GAN is a machine learning framework in which two computer networks are joined in competition. The framework created distinct variations based on similarities and differences using images as data.

Figure 4.1. Installation view of *Matthew Ritchie: Florilegium* at the CVAD galleries. PHOTO COURTESY OF COLLEGE OF VISUAL ARTS AND DESIGN GALLERIES, UNIVERSITY OF NORTH TEXAS, DENTON.

Historically, a *florilegium* is a collection of flowers of thought. Shifting between many forms of information and exploiting the GANs' unsettling power to infinitely iterate new states, Ritchie has created unique, uncanny artworks that echo the current paradox of stasis and change in which we find ourselves. Using his sketches for *Shadow Garden*, botanical drawings, and selected images from the Metropolitan Museum of Art's collection of drawings and prints, Ritchie trained multiple GANs to produce the artworks exhibited. The outcomes suggest the shadow of the ongoing pandemic and the continuing creative potential of the conditions it imposes. In contrast, the transformative energy of Ritchie's explorations represents the refusal of images—or art itself—to be contained in a single, final state.

FOURTH ITERATION: *INFINITE MOVEMENT*

The fourth iteration started as working with Nova to compose a soundscape for the exhibition that shifted to commissioning her to write music as a twenty-minute musical score for the project. Those twenty minutes turned into two operatic performances and the near hour-long world premiere of *Infinite Movement*. We created *Infinite Movement* in collaboration with UNT's College of Music Associate Professor of Choral Studies, Director of University Singers, and Kalandra, Kristina Caswell MacMullen. Dr. MacMullen conducted over eighty student choral singers (with the help of two graduate student conductors for the outdoor October 9 iteration), ten brass musicians, and one percussionist. The first performance on October 9 took place outside the gallery and exhibition in the CVAD Courtyard as a plein-air experience. Ritchie and Nova started the production by reading the paint-

Figure 4.2. Still image from *Infinite Movement* performance in CVAD Courtyard with artist Matthew Ritchie and composer Shara Nova. PHOTO COURTESY OF COLLEGE OF VISUAL ARTS AND DESIGN GALLERIES, UNIVERSITY OF NORTH TEXAS, DENTON. KIM LEESON, PHOTOGRAPHER.

ings' titles as the prelude to the performance. Although it was only twenty-five minutes long, around four hundred people sat in seats and on courtyard walls to share in the manifestation of the merging of visual art, choir, and the brass band for a never-before-seen and never-to-be-seen again experiential performance.

My colleagues and I were surprised that most of our audience for the exhibition and these iterations were the music students. They were invested as active contributors along with their friends, family, and supporters. They showed up in droves to attend the performances and then view the exhibition and artwork to make connections between them. In addition, our university president, donors, upper administrators, and deans of the colleges of Music and CVAD attended the events, showing their dedication to this project. For context, the UNT College of Music puts on over three thousand shows yearly, making the support more notable.

FIFTH ITERATION: FULL-LENGTH *INFINITE MOVEMENT*

The fifth iteration, the full-length performance, and world premiere took place on November 2, 2021, at the UNT Lucille "Lupe" Murchison Performing Arts Center in the Margot and Bill Winspear Performance Hall. It was an extended stage performance that lasted an hour and added more context. Again, the show delineated between audience and performer, with all musicians in a traditional stage sitting below screens of new GAN work by Ritchie. Again, Ritchie and Nova started the performance by reading the titles of the paintings as the prelude to the performance. Still, Ritchie had additional storytelling moments, providing further context for the work through narrative.

CURATORIAL ROLE AND DIMENSIONS OF CURATION MODEL

My role was to facilitate and determine what was best for the project while collaborating with an artist, musician, and university partners while keeping the CVAD galleries' mission, vision, and values at the forefront of the project. As curator, I saw my role as agile and responsive (within reason and the time/space/money continuum). As the pandemic situation continually changed, we accomplished the exhibition and programming with in-person and social-distancing measures and virtually continued to engage the student population at UNT and within the CVAD.

Due to its ambitious nature and the breadth and depth of the endeavor, along with the state of the world due to the pandemic, it is not the type of curatorial project I foresee repeating soon. A similar undertaking would require the amount of time, trust, and investment to be apparent from the beginning, as it was in this instance. Otherwise, the project could not have grown in the way it did. Additionally, not all artists and musicians like to collaborate. Thankfully, Ritchie and Nova had a long-standing working relationship before this project and met each other's level of dedication, grace, and tinkering desires until the very end.

REFERENCE

University of North Texas. (2021, September 8). *New York artist Matthew Ritchie explores presence of internet and virtual communication in UNT exhibit*. News. Retrieved June 1, 2022. https://news.unt.edu/news-releases/new-york-artist-matthew-ritchie-explores -presence-internet-and-virtual-communication

5

The Artist Is No Longer Present

RECONSIDERING CROSS-BORDER EXHIBITION CURATING
IN THE POST-PANDEMIC ERA

Ting Zhang

Since the COVID-19 outbreak, curators have faced unprecedented challenges internationally. According to traditional practice, before an exhibition is presented to the audience, the cultural message produced by museum, curator, artist, and artwork collectively is a kind of closed-loop relationship. Since the rise of new museology in the late twentieth century, the working structure that used to focus on object interpretation seemed to gradually switch to audiences, a more open system to engage the public and embrace more social and ecological missions.[1] In 2007, the International Conference of Museums (ICOM) museum definition took an important turn to the public at the forefront of its functions and sees the museum as a dynamic institution of people rather than a static institution of things.[2] During the pandemic, when people struggled emotionally, the healing functions of art seemed to reach a high point, fostering human connection. The policy of social distancing also reinforced a primary objective of museums: to pay more attention to and cultivate the value of local communities. However, the working structure still relies on a stable relationship within the museum circle with a focus on objects. Often, contemporary artists install their works at the museum. Resulting from the pandemic, travel restrictions prevented international artists from being present, and logistical difficulties increased rapidly. Despite statements that "economic indicators predict that the cultural sector will be one of the most affected, and probably one of the slowest to recover" (Radermecker, 2020, p. 1), a survey from Organisation for Economic Co-operation and Development (2020) said, "Cross-border cooperation and coordination with business can be key for finding the best balance between agility and risk management at the border" (p. 2). In 2021, international exhibitions could gain customs clearance due to the loosened international transportation policies, which made it possible for exhibitions to tour internationally, albeit without the artist's presence. This chapter asks whether curators can explore an alternative model to effect transnational projects while artists are isolated outside borders.

FROM EXCLUSIVE MODEL TO INCLUSIVE CURATING

I curated a project in Shanghai titled *Inclusive Break—A Time Besides Many Others* (hereafter *Inclusive Break*) by adapting international collaboration with artists' absence during the pandemic. In 2019, *Inclusive Break* was planned as a one-year Sino-German dialogic project organized by Department of Culture and Education of the German Consulate General Shanghai and Liu Haisu Art Museum (LHAM) in China. Selected artists included Chinese artists Shan Gao, Qing Kang, and Yinchen Zhou, who use art media to connect to physical materials, and German artists Nicole Wendel, Saskia Wendland, and Stella Geppert, who use their bodies to create works. The title *Inclusive Break* focuses on how artists could simultaneously experience the idea of *changeable time* in their different time zones. The curation emphasized the Dimensions of Curation Competing Values Model with an Exclusive perspective.

Exhibition planning started with a 2020 workshop at LHAM in Shanghai, with live performances by German artists and artworks from Chinese artists. However, progress was interrupted by the outbreak, and it became unfeasible to bring German artists to China. After multiple online events to maintain a year of collaboration, there seemed no way to continue the project as previously anticipated among taskforce members. To try to keep November 8, 2020, as the planned opening day, we transformed our contribution into a Shanghai-Berlin synchronized event by inviting audiences to interact with artists' materials and observe time and temporality, due to time differences. Three days before the event, according to a renewed prevention policy in Germany, the Berlin audience couldn't attend in person. In

Figure 5.1. All artists and their workshop at Shanghai, while the project *Inclusive Break— Pop Up* started in 2019. PHOTO COURTESY OF THE DEPARTMENT OF CULTURE AND EDUCATION OF THE GERMAN CONSULATE GENERAL SHANGHAI & LIU HAISU ART MUSEUM.

Ting Zhang

Figure 5.2. (Top left, bottom right, bottom left) German artists and their progress of *Inclusive Break—Pop Up* at HAUNT art space Berlin, 2020. Photograph: Birgit Kaulfuß. (Top right) Live shot capture of bilateral public interaction, 2020. PHOTO COURTESY OF THE DEPARTMENT OF CULTURE AND EDUCATION OF THE GERMAN CONSULATE GENERAL SHANGHAI & LIU HAISU ART MUSEUM.

Figure 5.3. Site photos of the progress of *Inclusive Break—Pop Up* at SLHAM Shanghai, 2020. Photograph: GUO Bin. (Middle right, bottom right) Live shot captures of public interaction in Shanghai, 2020. PHOTO COURTESY OF THE DEPARTMENT OF CULTURE AND EDUCATION OF THE GERMAN CONSULATE GENERAL SHANGHAI & LIU HAISU ART MUSEUM

response, the team developed remote artist and public interactions with objects and performances. On the date, captured by two simultaneous cameras in each city—the Berlin remote audience at 8:00 am, while on-site visitors participated at LHAM at 3:00 pm.

AUDIENCE ENGAGEMENT ENHANCES COLLABORATIVE CURATING

From this well-received event, we discovered that audiences can be key to pivoting projects in new directions. In this sense, the team hoped to connect visitors from Shanghai and Berlin in meaningful dialogue and engagement about art. The shared experience in real time led to uplifting healing, especially in a stressful social context after massive lockdowns in China. With live streaming captured by overhead cameras in real time, the absence of artists and works dissolved; the public in both locations experienced resonance and connections. Thus, we gained momentum to continue for another year of the exhibition. After a period of distant training, a group of Shanghai performers substituted for the German artists' pieces at the grand opening of *Inclusive Break* at LHAM on December 3, 2021. All the Chinese artists' works were displayed on-site; three German artists participated remotely.

PURSUING A DEMOCRATIZED CULTURE AND PUBLIC WELL-BEING

The collaboration led to ingenuity as visitors engaged with artworks in new ways. Curators had to confront the reality of systemic uncertainty. To circumvent the blocked international borders, an effective strategy maintained the focus on artworks (objects), while also exploring a participatory pattern between audience and artworks. Therefore, embedding the initiative of visitor (human) into this Exclusive structure, and transforming the internal nature of museum collection to be an external public property, to interpret the exhibition with empathy, curators should pursue a democratized culture and public well-being.

In overcoming technical barriers to cross-border exhibitions due to the pandemic, we had to alter curatorial strategies. Digitalization came first. As Radermacker (2020) stated, "Cultural institutions and industries have tried to be as responsive as possible to this growing demand by engaging in digital innovations and systematizing the use of alternative dissemination tools of cultural content" (p. 8). Some arts organizations have shifted to contactless and digital ticketing, made physical modifications to indoor spaces to allow for more social distancing, or shifted to outdoor performances or experiences when the weather allowed (Guibert and Hyde, 2021). Lehrer and Butler (2020) advocated participatory curating, urging "museums to view the current 'state of exception' not only as a constraint (which it obviously is), but as a moment to experiment" (para. 3). Enhancing the interrelationship of collaboration and codependency between curators and artists introduces a co-productive approach to exhibition production (Lai, 2021). The collaborative curatorial dimension focuses on artworks, but also moves to enhance audience interpretive focus as the projects advanced during the pandemic, both on-site and digitally.

Art historian Crimp once emphasized the importance of public intervention with the object at the venue. He noted that "whatever relationship was now to be perceived was contingent upon the viewer's temporal movement in the space shared with the object" (Crimp, 1993, p. 154). Lai also agreed that "When the display is reconfigured, both the narratives and spectatorship in the exhibition are reconstituted, with audiences re-situated in an 'interrelationship' reshaped and re-connected by ongoing spectatorial participation in the artworks and their modified sites and contexts" (Lai, 2021, p. 330).

Is going digital really the last straw? As curators, before virtual reality became our alternative sensory experience for possible future and transnational activities, a question was how can we dispel the pressure of losing physical and emotional perception of common space. Quoting economist Friedman (1962), "Only a crisis—actual or perceived—produces real change. When that crisis occurs, the actions that are taken depend on the ideas that are lying around" (p. ix). Although visiting artists were absent due to the ever-changing boundary constraints caused by COVID-19, exhibition curators pursued human connection and well-being continuously while offering physical experience and public interaction with objects. The lesson learned helped the curators to start moving from object-centeredness toward audiences.

NOTES

1. A movement of new museology had its first and international public expression in 1972 at the "Declaration of the Roundtable of Santiago (Chile)" organized by International Council of Museums (ICOM) and United Nations Educational, Scientific and Cultural Organization. In 1984, the *Declaration of Quebec—Basic Principles of a New Museology* was adopted by the 1st International Atelier Ecomuseums/New Museology by ICOM in Quebec, Canada. *Declaration of Quebec—Basic Principles of a New Museology*. ICOM. https://ceam2018.files.wordpress.com/2018/05/declarac3a7c3a3o-minom-quebec-en-1984.pdf
2. In 2007, museum was defined as "a non-profit, permanent institution open to the public for the purpose of serving and developing society, which collects, preserves, studies, communicates and presents the tangible and intangible assets of humanity and its environment for the purposes of education, research and recreation" by the International Council of Museums. *Museum definition*. https://icom.museum/en/resources/standards-guidelines/museum-definition/.

REFERENCES

Crimp, D. (1993). *On the museum's ruins*. Cambridge: The MIT Press.

Guibert, G., and Hyde, I. (2021, January 4). *ANALYSIS: COVID-19's impacts on arts and culture*. COVID-19 RSFLG Data and Assessment Working Group, Argonne National Laboratory. https://www.arts.gov/sites/default/files/COVID-Outlook-Week-of-1.4.2021-revised.pdf

Lai, M. (2021). Curating pandemic contingencies: Remote collaboration and display reconfiguration in practice. *Journal of Contemporary Chinese Art* 21(8), 313–37.

Lehrer, E., and Butler, S. R. (2020, May 4). Curatorial dreaming in the age of COVID-19. *Alliance Blog*, American Alliance of Museums. https://www.aam-us.org/2020/05/04/curatorial-dreaming-in-the-age-of-covid-19/

Friedman, M. (1962). *Capitalism and freedom: Fortieth anniversary edition*. Chicago: The University of Chicago Press.

Organisation for Economic Co-operation and Development. (2020, November 8). *Getting goods across borders in times of COVID-19*. Paris. https://www.oecd.org/coronavirus/policy-responses/getting-goods-across-borders-in-times-of-covid-19-972ada7a/

Ottone, E. (2020, March 29). *In moments of crisis, people need culture*. UN Educational, Scientific and Cultural Organization. https://www.unesco.org/en/articles/moments-crisis-people-need-culture

Radermecker, A. V. (2020). Art and culture in the COVID-19 era: For a consumer-oriented approach. *SN Business & Economics* 1(4), 1–14.

SYMPATHETIC

Audience (*x*) + Lone Creative (*y*) = **Sympathetic**

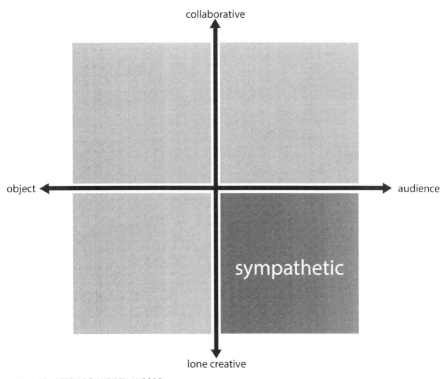

IMAGE COURTESY OF AUDREY JACOBS.

6

A Shared Body

REENVISIONING CURATORIAL COLLABORATION IN AN ACADEMIC ART MUSEUM

Annie Booth and Meredith Lynn

A Shared Body was a multimedia art exhibition hosted at the Florida State University Museum of Fine Arts (MoFA) from August 23 to December 11, 2021. Featuring projects exploring water access, the show invited visitors to consider the spiritual, physical, and ever-present connections we feel to water and what it means when those connections become strained.

Artists in the exhibition included Andrea Carlson (American, Anishinaabe), Jim Denomie (American, Ojibwe), Heid E. Erdrich (Ojibwe registered at Turtle Mountain), Courtney M. Leonard (Shinnecock), Cannupa Hanska Luger (Mandan, Hidatsa, Arikara, Lakota), Pope.L (American), Calida Garcia Rawles (American), and Sarah Sense (Chitimacha, Choctaw, American). The artists in the show push back against the violence and imposition of the historic and ongoing impacts of colonialism and racism as they reclaim, protect, defend, and dream of a future of water equity and access. *Ways of Water / Wash Over*, a commissioned poem by Heid E. Erdrich, responded to the work, providing a guiding text throughout the exhibition.

WORKING WITHIN THE SYMPATHETIC MODEL

A Shared Body typifies Sympathetic practice within the Dimensions of Curation Competing Values Exhibition Model. MoFA began discussing the project in 2019, applying to fund an external curator the following grant cycle. The global pandemic shifted our plans and funders' priorities, and in the uncertainty of that moment, we decided to refocus and curate the exhibition in-house.

Despite our small staff, MoFA has a long history of independence between units, reinforcing the curator as the sole authority. With Meredith Lynn joining the team in 2018 as Curator and Annie Booth in 2019 as Education Director, we quickly saw that by collaborating, we could embed visitor-centered techniques into the beginning of exhibition planning, addressing environmental justice more sensitively (Hammer Museum, 2021). *A Shared Body* was MoFA's first exhibition co-curated by the museum's curatorial and education specialists, with each contributing equally to the scholarship, artist selection, exhibition design, and gallery interactives, a model that is more responsive to audience experience. This represents a movement toward more collaborative curatorial processes along the continuum.

Moving forward with this interdepartmental focus, the curatorial team sought to interpret the exhibition with the audience in mind, including perspectives from the artists and experts in the field whenever possible. This decision was twofold: to inspire empathy and action within our audience by creating direct engagement with artists who have lived experience and enriching the exhibition beyond the curatorial team's perspective.

IN-GALLERY INTERACTIVES

We identified three spaces to highlight and encourage visitor interaction and engagement. The reading nook housed nonfiction, fiction, children's books, and poetry used during the exhibition's research phase. Not only could visitors learn more about the artists and topics of interest to them, but also deep perspectives on environmental justice.

The second interactive space, the reflections wall, invited visitors to respond and continue the conversations started by the artists. A visitor could select one of three prompts, respond with text or a drawing, and hang it on a hook on the wall, allowing for anyone to rearrange, sift through, and physically engage with the content created by other visitors, addressing different types of visitor engagement (Simon, 2010).

Visitors considered the following prompts:

- Share a water memory.
- What action can you take to protect our water?
- Envision a future in which we are all Water Protectors.

At the end of the exhibition, the reflections wall had over 250 responses sharing important memories, ideas for water protection, and collective dreaming for a better future (figure 6.1).

The third space was a listening station where visitors could sit and hear Heid E. Erdrich read her poem, experiencing the text in a more intimate way. The listening station also had a printed copy of the text as a takeaway, with over three hundred copies taken during the show's run.

PROGRAMMING

Programming and social media became additional tools to scaffold the exhibition, engaging and including our audiences. In addition to more traditional program-

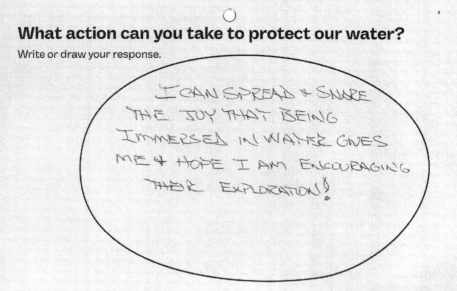

Figure 6.1. Response wall example responses. PHOTOS COURTESY OF THE FLORIDA STATE UNIVERSITY MUSEUM OF FINE ARTS.

ming, we hosted a series of events that prioritized reinterpretation of the show. For example, Heid E. Erdrich and Tacey M. Atsitty, a Tallahassee-based Diné writer, read water-related poems and responded to the exhibition. Through the workshop series *Make It with MoFA*, visitors screen printed posters and tote bags while learning about the current action surrounding Line 3, a proposed pipeline that would impact the water supply of several Ojibwe and Anishinaabe tribes in northern Minnesota.

Additional partners reflected cross-departmental and community voices. The Leon County Public Library co-sponsored a storytime, reading Carole Lindstrom's "We Are Water Protectors" and distributing 120 exhibition-themed activity bags to the museum and eight local library branches.

Structures for Change, a storytelling and performance collaborative led by Florida State University School of Dance faculty Hannah Schwadron and Irvin Gonzalez, performed in the exhibition weekly. Inspired by the artwork, Structures for Change offered an interpretation of the exhibition's themes, as visioned through the dancers' lived experiences, and guided by a vocal performer. The culminating performance was co-hosted by the Florida State University Civil Rights Institute, another project partner whose mission and ethics aligned with the exhibition (figure 6.2).

In a first for the museum, visitors were invited into the curatorial process when asked which Jim Denomie painting to acquire. Through a written survey and a social media poll, the audience voted for *Standing Rock, Bitches*, which is now accessioned into the museum's collections.

CURATORIAL CHOICE

While shifting forms during the planning phase of this exhibition, the curatorial process was explicit and transparent. We began with a very clear idea to show how artists lead conversations around environmental justice. While curatorially, power remained internal to the museum, we were conscious of our limitations as White settler scholars. To combat this, we made deliberate decisions within our interpretation, in-gallery interactives, and programming to broaden the perspectives to include the artists, scholars, programming partners, and visitors, encouraging engagement and participation within each aspect of the show.

AUDIENCE ANALYSIS

MoFA serves a broad audience in our region, attracting a local population including families with school-aged children, older adults, and university students from Florida State University and nearby universities. During the exhibition run, we received and met over sixty requests for tours from classes, student groups, and other university-affiliated entities. While the exhibition successfully engaged the curricular and academic goals of university stakeholders, it also found audiences new to the museum. The partnership with the Civil Rights Institute brought an older, more diverse, and non-university group to the museum, while the programs with the library attracted parents and young children. The response to this exhibition was overwhelmingly positive.

Figure 6.2. (Top) Structures for Change performance. (Bottom) Installation view of Mirror Shield Project by Cannupa Hanska Luger. PHOTO COURTESY OF THE FLORIDA STATE UNIVERSITY MUSEUM OF FINE ARTS.

Several of the projects in the exhibition confront potentially controversial topics, contending with the painful histories of colonialism and racialized violence. We decided that rather than use a generalized history, storytelling would enable audiences to connect to the work with empathy (Gokcigdem, 2019). Each interpretative text in the show included quotes and stories directly from the artists; for example, the discussion of Cannupa Hanska Luger's *Mirror Shield Project* foregrounded his personal experience at Standing Rock and then broadened the context to consider how access to water is used to control disenfranchised communities in the United States. The installation then positioned the visitor as an outsider as they approached the work, inviting them to exit from the perspective of the Water Protectors (figure 6.2). This approach, emphasizing personal connection as an entry point into dense and painful topics, encouraged visitors to consider their own experiences. We did not receive any feedback that visitors felt unprepared for and excluded by the subject matter.

REFLECTIONS ON THE DIMENSIONS OF CURATION MODEL

While the general upheaval of 2020 and 2021 limited our ability to work with external curators, we knew the immense value of adding voices and experiences to the in-gallery interpretation, solidifying our Sympathetic practice. By deemphasizing the institutional authority of the museum and making a platform for artists, scholars, creatives, organizations, and community members, the show was a rich and multifaceted experience for our visitors.

At MoFA, we must strike a careful balance between community engagement and meeting the scholarship needs of our university stakeholders. A university is, at its core, an institution that believes in the value of a particular kind of expertise, one that often corresponds to the traditional approach to curatorial research and practice. While we have begun a process of unpacking and subverting the inequity of such approaches to cultural production, we must also contend with the university museum as a space that, in some ways, is still limited by the ethos of the academy itself.

In the future, pursuing shifts toward cultural democracy and collaborative process on the Dimensions of Curation Competing Values continua would open projects up to shared authority at the start. Now that the exhibition has closed, it is interesting to reflect on what *A Shared Body* could have looked like if visitors, community members, and outside collaborators, each with lived experience and expertise, were involved in the initial phases of the exhibition.

REFERENCES

Gokcigdem, E. M. (2019). *Designing for empathy: Perspectives on the museum experience.* Arlington, VA: American Alliance of Museums.

Hammer Museum. (2021, March 24). *Reimagining the museum: Community, collaboration & radical inclusion.* Retrieved May 4, 2022. https://hammer.ucla.edu/programs-events /2021/reimagining-museum-community-collaboration-radical-inclusion

Simon, N. (2010). *The participatory museum.* Museum 2.0.

7

Ally is a Verb

ADOPTING A SYMPATHETIC CURATORIAL PRACTICE TO BUILD ADVOCACY
AND COMMUNITY WITHIN A TEACHING MUSEUM

Alexia Lobaina

The Rollins Museum of Art (RMA) sits on the campus of Rollins College, a private liberal arts college located in Winter Park, Florida, and one of the oldest educational institutions in the southeastern United States. As part of Rollins' cultural fabric, RMA embodies the college's teaching mission, leveraging its collection to integrate art learning into daily life for the campus and local community. In the fall of 2021, RMA presented the exhibition *Art Encounters: Ally is a Verb*, organized in two chapters, with chapter 1 opening in September 2021 and chapter 2 in January 2022. *Ally is a Verb* marked the first time a curricular exhibition was developed for the Rollins College Conference (RCC)—a seminar-based program to help transition first-year students into college life. In recent years, Rollins had incorporated the *Common Read* into the RCC program, selecting a unifying theme grounded in issues of social relevancy and analyzing it across the various disciplines represented among RCC courses.

Ally is a Verb was designed as the museum's contributing lens through which to consider the 2021 *Common Read* theme, Activism & Allyship. Serving as a resource for RCC faculty, the exhibition required engagement strategies to help students from all majors relate to and reflect upon the artists' visual stories. The exhibition asked visitors to consider what it means to be an ally, placing it in the context of an act, and featured the work of seven contemporary artists belonging to communities facing different forms of discrimination. Each work considered the artists' personal experiences, tackling issues that included racism, homophobia, transphobia, globalization, sociopolitical control, and body politics from places of vulnerability and anxiety. In this chapter, I examine *Ally is a Verb* against the Dimensions of Curation Competing Values Exhibition Model, presenting it as an

Figure 7.1. Installation view of the first chapter (fall 2021) of *Ally is a Verb*.
PHOTO COURTESY OF THE AUTHOR.

example of Sympathetic curatorial practice. I discuss interpretive methods used to advocate for visitors' experiences and the process and limitations of a singular curatorial voice, particularly when working with topics relating to social marginalization. Lastly, I consider future improvements to this curricular exhibition model, with an eye on collaborative practices.

ALLY IS A VERB: AN EXAMPLE OF SYMPATHETIC PRACTICE

From the beginning, *Ally is a Verb* was intended to serve not as a space in which to appreciate art objects but rather as a site of discussion, change, visibility, and compassion. Our curatorial team asked itself the following questions: How could we use our collection to support the conversation initiated by our college regarding the importance of activism and the process of being an ally? How would we de-center ourselves as curators to make room for the artists' testimonies and visitors' kindred experiences? While justification can be made to fit *Ally is a Verb* within a number of the models presented by the Dimensions of Curation Model, I would argue it best exemplifies a Sympathetic practice of curation. The Sympathetic quadrant is the intersection between a single curatorial voice and advocacy for audience over object.

CREATING ART ENCOUNTERS FOR THE CAMPUS AND COMMUNITY

The focus on audience (*x* axis) was key to this exhibition before it even existed; its principle objective was to translate and give shape to various social justice causes and societal inequities for Rollins College students, namely incoming students. To achieve this goal, the exhibition introductory label became a starting point, stopping visitors and asking them, first, to define what being an ally means and, second, to identify if and where they are on the road to becoming one. Once prepared with these preliminary questions, visitors were invited to "listen" to the visual testimonies of the featured artists, emphasizing listening as the first step in doing allyship work. Including a discussion stop at the beginning of the exhibition was intentional, serving as a form of diagnostic assessment for RCC faculty and connecting the exhibition to the readings students had previously completed in their RCC courses. Visitors were also provided with a Closer Look booklet to use in the gallery. The booklet included in-depth information about each artwork and posed exploratory questions, encouraging visitors to adopt the artists' stories as lenses through which to think about their own lives and beliefs.

A SINGLE VOICE SPEAKING FOR MANY

In the Sympathetic model of curation, a lone curator (*y* axis) makes object, narrative, and interpretive selections on behalf of the community being represented within the exhibition. Despite the focus being on the audience and their connection to these objects, narratives, and interpretive measures, this model runs the risk of misrepresentation and assumption-making. This concern was ever present in the development of *Ally is a Verb*, considering the diversity of marginalized groups and social issues being discussed, only two of which—out of seven—represented my own experiences and community (as curator). To avoid the problematic issue of speaking on behalf of the artists (Alcoff, 1991), we took two approaches.

First, we placed strict parameters around the selection of objects—they had to be deeply intimate works through which the artists reconciled past traumas, whether personal or communal. Second, the labels created for the exhibition drew from the artists' own words, including direct quotes pulled from artist interviews, as *Ally is a Verb* featured only contemporary works of art. By staging the exhibition as a series of intimate vignettes between visitors and artists, audiences had the opportunity to momentarily step into the shoes of someone facing discrimination and hardship, seeing them first as human and then as artist.

FURTHERING THE DIALOGUE BETWEEN ART AND COMMUNITY

At the end of the gallery, we installed a recording booth where visitors could respond to questions about being an ally, listen to the lived experiences and reflections recorded by others in their community, and share their own. The booth provided a platform for visitors to synthesize their experiences and reflect on the connections made across sociocultural differences that emphasize the universal likeness of human suffering. For those willing to add their thoughts and personal accounts, it also became an opportunity for audience inclusion as part of the exhibition. As such, the booth extended the curatorial conversation occurring on the gallery's walls by creating a space for the community to participate in shaping content and how it was interpreted. This alleviated some of the limitations brought about by the exhibition's lone curatorial voice, encouraging visitor contributions to better capture a diversity of perspectives.

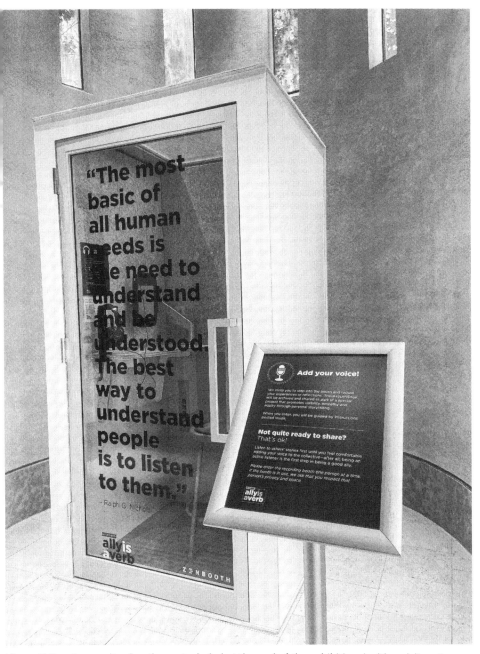

Figure 7.2. A recording booth was included at the end of the exhibition, inviting visitors to share their thoughts on the importance of being an ally, share their experiences, and listen to the experiences shared by others. PHOTO COURTESY OF THE AUTHOR.

LOOKING AHEAD TOWARD MORE COLLABORATIVE PRACTICES

Given the positive reception received by *Ally is a Verb* among faculty, students, and the general public, our curatorial team should consider several modifications to the RCC curricular exhibition in order to improve upon this exhibition model in the future. Following an Inclusive (x = audience and y = collaborative) model of curatorial practice would strengthen the goals and mission of the RCC exhibition program. Currently, the *Common Read* theme is selected by a group of students and their faculty advisor. Partnering with these students to select artwork from the collection would go a long way in diversifying the group of voices involved in shaping how these objects affect and are transformed by the chosen theme. It would also benefit student voices to have their peers—also experiencing their first year in college—co-curating to develop relatable methods to better engage other students via didactics and gallery tools. Including additional programming with ties in the community would also be worth exploring, creating added opportunities to expand the exhibition's reach beyond students in a more intentional way.

CONCLUSION

Despite the exhibition being developed specifically for Rollins RCC students, the viewership it received extended far outside the original expectations. Within the scope of Rollins courses, faculty outside the RCC incorporated the exhibition into their syllabi in discussion of topics including creative writing, sociology, gender and sexuality, Latin American and Caribbean studies, disability studies, and more. Faculty at neighboring colleges and universities also visited the exhibition with their students, representing a similar range of disciplines as those from within Rollins. The exhibition also prompted two collaborations with new cultural partners. The first was a virtual tour co-led between RMA and the Goldsboro History Museum—the second all-Black incorporated township in the United States—in honor of Black History Month and the ten-year anniversary of Trayvon Martin's murder. The second was a special lecture by LGBTQ activist Arsham Parsi, focusing on the important work of activists and allies in securing safe passage for LGBTQIA+ refugees in Iran. Also unexpected was the breadth in demographics of visitors that engaged with *Ally is a Verb* from outside the Rollins student body. Interim and summative assessments of booth recordings revealed that visitors of all ages and backgrounds shared stories and reflections. Recordings included narratives about personal experiences with discrimination, struggles with self-acceptance, and the empowerment that comes with overcoming hardship, to name a few. Of particular interest were the number of visitors who used their messages to respond to others' recordings, offering words of encouragement and compassion. As RMA continues to participate in the RCC program, we look forward to growing our approach to this curricular exhibition as a site of advocacy, collaboration, and fellowship.

REFERENCE

Alcoff, L. (1991). The problem of speaking for others. *Cultural Critique* (20), 5–32.

Alexia Lobaina

INCLUSIVE

Audience (x) + Collaborative (y) = **Inclusive**

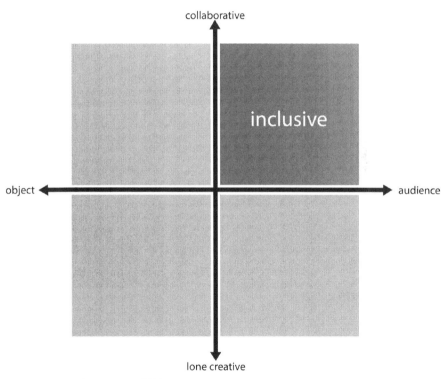

IMAGE COURTESY OF AUDREY JACOBS.

8

Art Connects

Jennifer Jankauskas and Laura Ashley N. Bocquin

The Montgomery Museum of Fine Arts (MMFA), Montgomery, Alabama, United States, strives to maintain dynamic relevance with audiences and regularly seeks new ways to engage communities through innovative exhibitions and programs. The MMFA has found through the steady expansion of programming that one crucial element to achieving these efforts is not just considering but incorporating non-institutional voices in the curatorial process.

This chapter details one such project, *Art Connects: Works from the Vault Curated by the Community*, an example of the Dimensions of Curation Competing Values Exhibition Model of an Inclusive practice Audience (*x*) + Collaborative (*y*). Conceived in 2020, the MMFA presented *Art Connects* from August 7 to September 19, 2021. Through curation, interpretation, and engagement, *Art Connects* celebrated the input of local citizens as they shaped an exhibition with their perspectives and aesthetics.

THE BEGINNINGS

Like many museums, the MMFA has increasingly turned to our permanent collection in exhibition planning for a variety of reasons including first to share with our visitors the depth of works the museum has continued to collect since its inception and second as a strategy to combat the rising costs of organizing and hosting exhibitions. With a desire to explore our collection through diverse viewpoints from our community—versus solely through the traditional curatorial voice—we envisioned *Art Connects* to be co-curated by a spectrum of community members (figure 8.1). As we planned for the exhibition, we outlined the following goals:

- to deepen audience engagement with our collection and foster dialogues among visitors;
- to allow participants creativity with their responses;

- to build trust with community members, emphasizing their value and creating sustainable relationships;
- to reach new audiences; and
- to provide opportunities for nonparticipant audience members to relate to art through interpretations and experiences of people with whom they identify.

To achieve these goals, we first met internally and cross-departmentally, relying on staff members' knowledge of and relationships with different people in the community. By collaborating with colleagues in curatorial, development, education, and special events, we were able to enlist an ethnically and culturally diverse range of participants from around our region. The final list included some long-standing supporters of the museum along with others who had not previously been involved with our institution, but with whom we wanted to build relationships: representatives from our docent volunteers, Board of Trustees, and Junior Executive Board along with local artists, educators, restaurateurs, representatives from other arts organizations and the media, government officials, and leaders in business, the nonprofit world, and the military.

Simultaneously, as project directors, we created a framework for the exhibition (Simon, 2010). This included setting a timetable that factored in potential delays from participants, determining that we would ask participants to select works from our collection that were not currently on view (to both create a truly unique exhibition and to alleviate work on our curatorial and preparatory staff by not having to replace works that were already displayed in our galleries) and identifying themes to help guide the selections. Due to the number of hoped-for participants, the project directors provided themes to reduce the likelihood of duplicate selections, to narrow the focus for participants and to make the task

Figure 8.1. Photograph of the installation of the 2021 exhibition *Art Connects: Works from the Vault Curated by the Community* at the Montgomery Museum of Fine Arts, Montgomery, Alabama. PHOTO COURTESY THE MONTGOMERY MUSEUM OF FINE ARTS.

less intimidating, and ultimately to help structure the exhibition when determining placement on the walls with easy entry points for visitors to navigate. Our guiding themes were as follows: the environment, journeys, roots and traditions, social change, spirituality, symbolism, movement, regional highlights, academic versus self-taught, three-dimensionality, abstraction, sharing a meal, heroes, patterns, and emotional expressions.

With our institutional scaffolding in place, we sent personal invitations via email to each participant.[1] The initial email clearly described the exhibition concept, assigned the participant a theme,[2] and asked each person to select a favorite work from our collection using our easily accessible online database located on our website.[3] We stressed the importance of each individual's input and asked every participant to write a personal statement of up to seventy-five words explaining their selection. Those written expressions became extended labels within the exhibition; the original statements remained in each participant's voice—we edited only grammatical errors. The clarity of the invitation was key to relaying expectations and guiding outcomes.

THE RESULTS

Our invitations were met with enthusiastic and almost universal acceptance, and at this stage, our original vision of *Art Connects* was truly realized, as we moved from working cross-departmentally within the museum to integrating and highlighting the perspectives of over fifty others from outside our organization. Community co-curators felt shared ownership of the project, and, as hoped for, their selections vibrantly called attention to a range of works that are not often on view at the MMFA. Additionally—and exceptionally—their written responses offered a plethora of perspectives through unique voices and experiences. Some were whimsical, such as the statement about Maltby Sykes's (American, 1911–1992) painting, *Still Life with Avocado*, 1954 (figure 8.2) (theme: sharing a meal), which read:

> Maltby Sykes *Still Life with Avocado* is a study of my kitchen counter. I eat a lot of avocados, and I eat them cut in half—like in this image—with a little salt and olive oil. Guacamole might be made if there is an onion and a lime on hand.
>
> I wish I could have spoken with this Alabama artist about this still life. Was Diego Rivera nearby? Was tequila and beer considered a printmaking aide? Did Cloverdale remind him of Coyoacán?

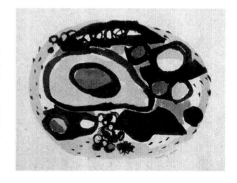

Figure 8.2. Maltby Sykes (American 1911–1992), *Still Life with Avocado*, 1954, ink and polymer on paper, Montgomery Museum of Fine Arts, Montgomery, Alabama, Gift of the artist, 1983.3.25. ©Estate of the artist. PHOTO COURTESY THE MONTGOMERY MUSEUM OF FINE ARTS.

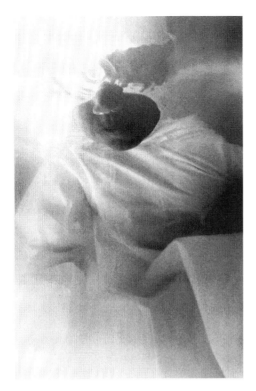

Figure 8.3. Caroline Davis, (American, born 1963), *And a Voice Came from Heaven: You Are My Son, Whom I Love; With You I Am Well Pleased*, 1998, gelatin silver print on paper, Montgomery Museum of Fine Arts, Montgomery, Alabama, Association Purchase, 2001.6.1. ©The artist. PHOTO COURTESY THE MONTGOMERY MUSEUM OF FINE ARTS.

Others were deeply personal, such as the reflection inspired by Caroline Davis's photograph *And a Voice Came from Heaven: You Are My Son, Whom I Love; With You I Am Well Pleased*, 1998 (figure 8.3) (theme: patterns), which said:

My youngest son Justin died from a massive heart attack in his sleep on October 8, 2018. Daily, I envision him drifting into my activities and conversations as I go throughout my day. I see him in my mind, in my heart, and in the faces of my grandchildren. In this photograph, the interplay of light and splashing water represents his caring and giving personality.

Son, continue to enjoy your freedom splashing as you float.

Then still, some simply stood in awe of the artwork, such as this deep consideration of the blown glass piece by Dale Chihuly (American, born 1941), *Emerald Soft Cylinder with Khiva Red Lip Wrap* (theme: three-dimensionality):

Chihuly's work mesmerizes me. He captivates my attention with his choice of bold contrasting colors and then draws me into this piece with his beautiful detail. He balances perfectly between manipulating the glass into what he envisioned and allowing the glass to take on the form it wants. Perfectly exquisite details married to his intentional imperfections create this colorful, magical piece.

These examples illustrate the nonhierarchical nature of the resulting exhibition and didactic labels. Personal selections written by community members, rather than a curator invoking art historical language, subverted the traditional model of most museum exhibition planning and execution. This approach allowed for a focus on unique interpretations and invited other viewers to construct personal connections to the art. In fact, *Art Connects* showed how people react and respond to art in diverse ways. Other avenues of inclusion incorporated an array of public programs that showcased our community co-curators, involving using several participants as exhibition narrators during a gallery walk-through at the opening and others as panelists during an informative and intimate virtual dialogue for our series *Creative Conversations*. For these reasons, *Art Connects* illustrates the two-dimensional model of the Inclusive quadrant, resulting in innovative, sustainable engagement with and through community members—in both the exhibition and associated programming—that forged new connections among a variety of works of art and diverse demographics, and creates what Villeneuve (2019, p. 2) called a "museum of mutuality."

Even more than modeling an Inclusive practice of curating, *Art Connects* (figure 8.4) fits squarely within the MMFA's mission and vision statement that aims to "provide compelling experiences centered on human creativity valued for their significant contributions to the individual well-being of its citizens and visitors and to the rising vibrance of the city, county, and region." Our expansive collaboration achieved deeper connections between the museum and our audiences—established and new—as each partner helped design the project through active participation with the result of everyone feeling ownership of and pride in the project's demonstrable success.

The MMFA views *Art Connects* as an exciting way to encourage community participation with our collection, exhibition, and educational programs. This contemporary model of working had a deeply positive effect on staff and collaborators

Figure 8.4. Photograph of the installation of the 2021 exhibition *Art Connects: Works from the Vault Curated by the Community* at the Montgomery Museum of Fine Arts, Montgomery, Alabama. PHOTO COURTESY THE MONTGOMERY MUSEUM OF FINE ARTS.

Jennifer Jankauskas and Laura Ashley N. Bocquin

and further extended throughout the community to our nonparticipant audience, bridging us all through art in new ways. Because of the profound impact felt and expressed by many, the MMFA will continue to strategically use a variety of approaches to the curatorial and programmatic planning processes, including future iterations of *Art Connects*. By shifting an exhibition's voice from one of a lone curator to that of a vibrantly varied and inclusive community, we fulfilled our aim of being a museum that does not merely exist as a space but is alive through the energy and experiences of our audience.

NOTES

1. In *The Participatory Museum*, Nina Simon outlines this theory of instructional scaffolding, as when "educators or educational material provides the supportive resources, tasks, and guidance upon which learners can build their confidence and abilities" (2010, p. 12.)
2. As project directors, we sorted participants by community role or profession and assigned a theme to each group (i.e., educators had the theme of patterns, and members of the media the theme of social change).
3. One of the built-in resources for this project is that the MMFA's permanent collection is available digitally through our website. We have approximately 95 percent of our collection available for viewing.

REFERENCES

Simon, N. (2010). *The participatory museum*. Museum 2.0.

Villeneuve, P. (2019) Considering competing values in art museum exhibition curation. *Stedelijk Studies Journal* 8, 2–11.

9

Responsive, Relational, and Disruptive

A CASE STUDY IN COMMUNITY-BASED CURATION

Marianna Pegno, Christine Brindza, Patricia Lannes, and Cecilia Garibay

The curatorial intervention *People of the West*, discussed in this chapter, is an example of the Inclusive quadrant of the Dimensions of Curation Competing Values Exhibition Model. Developed with a network of collaborators, its purpose is to address philosophical questions about representation within the permanent collection display of the art of the American West. This emerged from discussions with artists living in the region who were often left out of the dominant narrative of this genre. From these exchanges, it became apparent that the Tucson Museum of Art and Historic Block (TMA) needed to rethink its approach to curation, develop new modes of training for those facilitating conversations, and evaluate this changing practice. We learned to activate artworks in response to community inquiries, inserting them within an existing exhibition to examine and alter audiences' experiences of a work of art—and by extension disrupt the expected approach to curation as well as traditional or mythic concepts of the American West.

BACKGROUND: AN EMERGING FRAMEWORK FOR COMMUNITY-BASED EXHIBITIONS

For the past several years, TMA—located in Tucson, Arizona, United States—has engaged stakeholders to collaboratively develop a framework for community-based curation, where communities identify issues and topics that relate to them, which then inform exhibition development, collections care, and programs (Pegno and Brindza, 2021). In 2019, TMA received a National Leadership grant from the Institute of Museum and Library Services to implement *Expanding Narratives*, to create an adaptable framework and tool kit for this work, and to ultimately support other museums in building stronger external relationships. This work activates and engages staff, volunteers, artists, community members, and board members. It proposes an interdepartmental networked curatorial process embedded in community engagement, collections, education, *and* the production of exhibitions.

In this chapter, we discuss the development of *People of the West* (figure 9.1), a curatorial intervention that is part of this larger initiative. Our reflections are excerpts from an evolving process that define, test, and iterate this framework for community-based curation. We, the authors, are active participants in this endeavor. Two are TMA staff members—Christine Brindza is the Senior Curator, Glasser Curator of Art of the American West, and Marianna Pegno is the director of engagement and inclusion. Two are external consultants—Cecilia Garibay is the

Figure 9.1. *People of the West: A Rethinking of "Westerners"* is a special project that seeks to expand representation of people living, working, and thriving in this region. It is on view as part of Art of the American West in the Frank and Jean Hamilton Gallery at the Tucson Museum of Art. IMAGE COURTESY OF THE AUTHORS.

Responsive, Relational, and Disruptive

evaluation partner, and Patricia Lannes is the collaborating professional development consultant. The goal of *Expanding Narratives* is to generate shared authority among *all* stakeholders. To bring multiple viewpoints into this community-based curatorial process, conversations and/or professional development sessions were facilitated where art from the TMA permanent collection and regional identities were at the center of the conversations.

People of the West is not TMA's first attempt at community-based and co-curated approaches within exhibitions. While formally using this curatorial practice since 2019, it stems from years of commitment to working with communities. Thus, we challenge the notion of the audience as external by putting them at the core of exhibition development. Curation and exhibitions are not isolated processes of sole genius. Rather, inclusive, community-based exhibitions are the outcome of converging forces that call for new frameworks, paradigms, and norms. This process is shared with community audiences to build bridges, make connections across boundaries, and find common ground (Archer and Cameron, 2013).

INCLUSIVE EXHIBITIONS ARE RESPONSIVE, RELATIONAL, AND DISRUPTIVE

How does a Southwest museum located an hour's drive north of the United States and Mexico border, with a rapidly changing cityscape and diversifying demographic, understand, define, and exhibit the American West? If posing this question a few years ago, the response would be something like: "it consists of landscapes, cowboys, and Indigenous people." But what happens when artists who are active collaborators with the museum and living in this region, but born outside the country, ask how they fit into the narrative? This exchange presents an opportunity to be responsive, engage in conversations, and disrupt expected ways of doing business.

This vignette is a simplified example of the relational practice that can result in a community-based exhibition, whereby meaning-making flows from the interactions of the collaborators. The authors co-developed core values that drive all aspects of this work comprising professional development workshops, community conversations, exhibition development, volunteer training, and collections care. Together, these elements foster inclusive exhibitions with long-term and sustainable impact that are rooted in dialogue and relationships. It requires:

• an open system grounded in continual conversations to challenge single authority structures;
• a process driven by individual sovereignty that prioritizes that all voices are heard and come together from different perspectives;
• a commitment to working as a collective toward a shared goal;
• a flexible mindset that adjusts as the focus is fluid and is shaped by the worldviews of contributors;
• an attentiveness to learning and listening to show curiosity and a willingness to determine shared goals; and
• an empathic understanding built from collective positionalities, experiences, and knowledge.

Marianna Pegno et al.

These values aim to dismantle limited single narratives, question homogenous or binary interpretations, address the damage created by historical erasures and silences, and create space for multiple voices.

PEOPLE OF THE WEST

People of the West is a curatorial intervention within TMA's gallery dedicated to Art of the American West—one of the museum's core collection areas. It features fifteen two-dimensional portraits hung in constellations designed to draw attention to varying perspectives. Each portrait cluster includes people who are underrepresented or mythologized in popular culture within the Western narrative—thus, a viewer will encounter a cowboy and an immigrant on the same plane. This installation is the result of a series of conversations between staff and two Arizona-based artists, a refugee and an immigrant, who questioned who qualifies as a Westerner and who is missing from stories of the West told in museums.

Photographer Anh-Thuy Nguyen noted the disconnect between the West of her imagination versus reality when she arrived in Arizona: "I came to the U.S. in my adulthood. . . . The West that I always imagined and heard of did not resemble what I saw in Tucson. . . . As I transitioned into an immigrant, I questioned the meanings of the Western landscape" (AT. Nguyen, personal communication, June 30, 2021). For Nguyen, her Vietnamese self rarely occupied the American West of artists' representations (figure 9.2).

The painter Papay Solomon shared a similar frustration: "The discussion pertaining to identity has always been a difficult one for me to have, even prior to my family and I migrating to the United States, and more specifically Arizona. . . . I was not aware that I was 'Black' or an 'immigrant' until after I arrived. As a Black man, refugee, or immigrant—whatever term you'd like to use—I am often left out of the expected roll call of a citizen of the American West" (P. Solomon, personal communication, July 30, 2021) (figure 9.3).

From these discussions, a question emerged: how might we offer a new interpretation of a *Westerner* that is more inclusive and reflective of a twenty-first-century vision? The resulting exhibition contains works of art depicting a variety of individuals, including those often left out of stories of the West, such as people of color, women, immigrants, and people with disabilities. With select works, artists and cultural experts provided written responses to this phenomenon to broaden interpretative focus beyond the individual object.

People of the West is an example of using a dialogical approach for collaborative meaning making, focusing on conversation rather than traditional, didactic, one-way methods of presenting knowledge. In this example we have seen how the interpretation, as well as conceptualization of the exhibition, evolves from communities/stakeholders and curatorial authorship is shared. As evaluation findings document, this approach challenged traditional curatorial practices, leading to generative tensions. Some curators on staff were at best uncomfortable with power-sharing and at times questioned community expertise. For example, during one meeting related to *Expanding Narratives* a question emerged in response to labels authored by collaborators: "But then how do you also

Figure 9.2. *People of the West: A Rethinking of "Westerners"* is a special project that seeks to expand representation of people living, working, and thriving in this region. It is on view as part of *Art of the American West* in the Frank and Jean Hamilton Gallery at the Tucson Museum of Art. In the upper right corner, the portrait of a headless figure in a traditional Vietnamese tunic is the photographic work of Anh-Thuy Nguyen, *Boat Journey series: In transition, Saratoga #1*, 2012. IMAGE COURTESY OF THE AUTHORS.

Figure 9.3. *People of the West: A Rethinking of "Westerners"* is a special project that seeks to expand representation of people living, working, and thriving in this region. It is on view as part of Art of the American West in the Frank and Jean Hamilton Gallery at the Tucson Museum of Art. In the upper right corner, the portrait of a figure in a baseball cap against an orange background is a 2020 portrait of Ahmaud Arbery by Papay Solomon.
IMAGE COURTESY OF THE AUTHORS.

maintain academic or scholarly rigor?" This inquiry was then further explained with the following:

> As curators, we [have an] expectation that we will be the best, but when it's community—we don't want to offend, demean . . . perhaps [they don't have] the same kind of background or training. . . . So I don't know if we've resolved that. I'm going to be just blatant about it. The fear is that we tiptoe to allow these voices in, but as long as the public knows the difference, and I don't know if they always do. (Garibay Group, 2022)

Conversations between colleagues such as this can be useful in surfacing different perspectives, assumptions, and ways of working. This can lead to discovering internal roadblocks, illuminating how community-based curation can be challenging to some while perceived to undermine curatorial authority.

IT IS A PROCESS: LESSONS LEARNED AND RECOMMENDATIONS

Our evaluation partner highlighted ways that TMA staff stressed emergent frictions when traditional Western academic training bumped up against community expertise. To address this, staff and community members often considered diverse perspectives. Christine reflected that her experiences as a curator had evolved through community-based practices and relationships. She developed a sense of responsiveness that when community discussions unearthed important critical concepts, and she acknowledged the issue and found ways to make space for missing narratives.

To engage in relational and responsive practices within this disruption of the traditional curatorial model, we have identified four main elements that yield inclusive, community-based exhibitions:

- Resource these efforts through time and money: Plan exhibition timelines accordingly. This process requires time to engage in authentic and trusting conversations. Consider compensation for collaborators.
- Listen to constituents: Be responsive to emerging needs, ideas, questions, and topics that arise.
- Align goals from all stakeholders: Seek the points over convergence or overlap from different perspectives.
- Be vulnerable: Sit with discomfort and allow yourself to be changed in these moments. Know when to step up *and* step back.

The insights we have shared are part of an iterative process. Its evaluation has raised additional needs for engagement across staff to sustain this approach and align equity work across the museum. Scaling the project involves expanding the work beyond its current core team and involves more staff beyond curators. It is critical to consider how to expand efforts to include more staff, continue to engage stakeholders across the organization and community, consider what types of ongoing support and professional development museum staff will need, and remain open to where the process takes us. This can be time and resource intensive, but it is critical.

REFERENCES

Archer, D., and Cameron, A. (2013). *Collaborative leadership building relationships, Handling conflict and sharing control* (second edition). New York: Routledge.
Garibay Group. (2022). *Expanding Narratives year two evaluation report.*
Lonetree, A. (2012). *Decolonizing museums: Representing Native America in national and tribal museums.* Durham, NC: University of North Carolina Press.
Pegno, P., and Brindza, C. (2021). Redefining curatorial leadership and activating community expertise to build equitable and inclusive art museums. *Curator* 64(2), 343-62.

Part III
Three Dimensions
Exhibitions that ___

x = interpretive focus   y = curatorial power   z = curatorial intent   Exhibitions that...

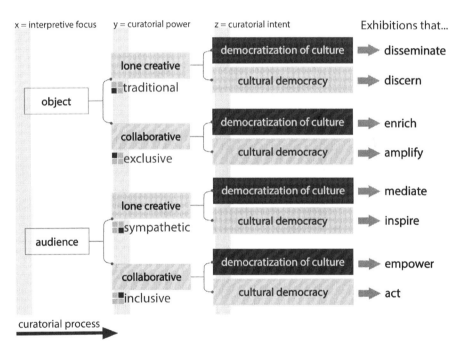

curatorial process

IMAGE COURTESY OF AUDREY JACOBS.

DISSEMINATE

Object (*x*) + Lone Creative (*y*) + Democratization of Culture (*z*) = **Disseminate**

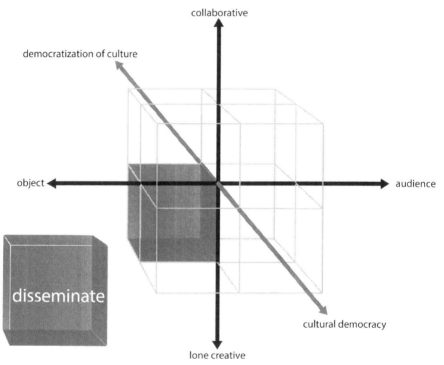

IMAGE COURTESY OF AUDREY JACOBS.

10

Traditional Practice That Disseminates

NATIVE BRAZIL/ALIEN BRAZIL ANNA BELLA GEIGER

Peter Aerts and Aline Van Nereaux

Native Brazil/Alien Brazil was the first retrospective exhibition of the work by Anna Bella Geiger, one of Brazil's most important living artists. Belonging to the first generation of conceptual artists in South America, her multi-disciplinary oeuvre draws on scientific, philosophical, and spiritual sources in which she critically examines the sociopolitical context of Brazil. Geiger has explored contemporary national debates around culture, identity, and history in her work since the early 1970s, themes that still hold relevance today. Her experimental practice includes pioneering video work, innovative printmaking, performance, installations, and painting. Featuring over 180 artworks made over six decades, it provided a comprehensive overview of the artist's oeuvre (see figures 10.1 and 10.2).[1]

AUDIENCE INTERPRETIVE FOCUS + LONE CREATIVE CURATORIAL POWER + DEMOCRATIZATION OF CULTURE = EXHIBITIONS THAT DISSEMINATE

The interpretive focus originates from the collaborative form chosen by the curatorial team and the vision they pursue. The artist and curator took the creative lead in the making of *Native Brazil/Alien Brazil*. This approach is common practice in exhibition-making, certainly when it concerns the work of living artists. It is close to the traditional role a museum fulfills—disseminating knowledge to democratize culture. When conceiving a traditional exhibition, it is the artist and curator that own the knowledge, envisage a narrative, create the concept, and define the context in which to position the exhibition. *Native Brazil/Alien Brazil* portrayed Anna Bella Geiger as a pioneer of contemporary art in Brazil, continuously injecting the Brazilian contemporary art scene with challenging points of view on art and society. The artist's changing views of the world were shown with an emphasis on her multitude of practices. The artist's extensive and versatile body of works was

Figure 10.1. Anna Bella Geiger, *Circumambulatio*, 1972.
PHOTO COURTESY OF MARTIN CORLAZZOLI.

Figure 10.2. Anna Bella Geiger, *Circumambulatio*, 1972.
PHOTO COURTESY OF DIRK PAUWELS.

Figure 10.3. Anna Bella Geiger, *Native Brazil/Alien Brazil*. PHOTO COURTESY OF DIRK PAUWELS.

missing from the broader perspective on contemporary art. This void needed to be filled in a way that resonates today, in close dialogue with the artist. The selected works and exhibition design immersed the audience in contemporary themes like colonialism, emancipation, and feminism. The retrospective exhibition challenged the audience to change their European perspective on contemporary art to a wider point of view (figure 10.3).

AN EXPLICIT CHOICE: TRADITIONAL PRACTICE WITH AN EXHIBITION THAT DISSEMINATES

The chosen exhibition approach was intended to take visitors on a journey of discovery through the work of an artist of irrefutable influence on contemporary art in South America. The artist and curator opted to offer an extensive range of background texts to enable visitors to reconstruct for themselves the relevance of today. It is often assumed that exhibitions that show unknown artists, with complex and layered work, are automatically aimed at art-savvy visitors, historians, and professionals. These artists are rated as less attractive to nonspecialist visitors and leisure seekers. Yet conceiving a retrospective is always a balancing act. Curators and artists want to avoid a didactic, stale, retrospective exhibition. For a living artist, it is a search for balance between the historical framework and the current zeitgeist, the general overview of the artist's work, and an eye for precision. The work may have been created over decades, but its present interpretation and presentation should be fresh. In the work of Anna Bella Geiger, wording and language are essential elements. Each piece of work that contained Brazilian (Portuguese) text was translated into Dutch, English, and French (figure 10.4). Exhibition booklets of Geiger's milestone exhibitions were also translated and made available.

Figure 10.4. Anna Bella Geiger, room view of *Native Brazil/Alien Brazil*.
PHOTO COURTESY OF DIRK PAUWELS. GRAPHIC DESIGN JAN & RANDOALD.

When the translations became visually disruptive for the exhibition design, the creatives sought ways of making them subtly available to the visitors with the input of the mediation team. This resulted in a very complete and precise presentation with which artists and curators could fully identify. It was up to the visitor to find the access points to the artist's work using comprehensive booklets. However, the necessary visual literacy and academic knowledge cannot be expected to be acquired by every visitor. Artists and curators go through a process of reflection as solitary experts without the need for input from other voices. Creating a rewarding experience for different visitor types is often seen from a curatorial perspective as synonymous with dumbing down or as holding the audience by the hand. "Don't underestimate the intelligence of the audience" is an often-heard quote. Alternative ways to collaborate are welcomed as long as it does not impact the choices the curator and artist envisage. More time for debate inspires a deeper common understanding of visitor preferences. In the case of *Native Brazil/Alien Brazil*, the mediation team would have needed several weeks to create different narrative options, in collaboration with the creative team.

INTENDED AUDIENCE

The democratization of art and culture implies inclusiveness. When different audiences' needs are neglected, these visitors may not only feel unwelcome; they may experience exclusion. Visitors have different needs and motivations to which museums can respond in different ways. However, this also involves a balancing act. For many S.M.A.K. visitors, it is their first contact with contemporary art.

Peter Aerts and Aline Van Nereaux

An exhibition that demands a lot of effort to access risks becoming a turnoff for first-timers because they can't find an entry point to the work or the mediation language is complex and too high in volume. For an academic audience, the thorough introduction to the life, work, and meaning of the work of Anna Bella Geiger was exactly made to measure. Even though all visitors are always warmly welcomed, the leisure seeker on a rainy Sunday afternoon might have been lost in the translations. The sense of pleasure to be had in making great intellectual efforts mainly applies to one type of visitor: people who inform themselves thoroughly, read articles, and regularly visit galleries and museums. The introduction to Anna Bella Geiger's work included a language barrier, for which only some were prepared to read the thirty-seven pages of transcripts while looking at the work. More time to discuss adapted mediation with different audiences' needs in mind could have closed this gap.

AUDIENCE RESPONSE

To the audience of connoisseurs and art press, Anna Bella Geiger immediately struck a chord. It was an exclusive occasion to see an extensive overview of her work for the first time in Europe. The detailed background information was regarded by the curatorial team as an obvious necessity to interpret the work correctly and added an intellectual challenge. The traditional approach of disseminating the artist's oeuvre brought a degree of selectivity in audience appraisal. For an unprepared leisure seeker, combining text and images was an exhausting experience. At worst, this type of visitor may have felt unskilled or not smart enough. The huge volume of information and high degree of complexity may tire first-time visitors instead of enthusing them. Mediation approaches can lead to inclusion or exclusion. The museum may strive to be open and inclusive but still come across as exclusively for experts. A first-time negative experience may brand the museum as "not for me" with a loss of goodwill with few chances of winning back a lost soul. The key lies in recognizing the different needs of different audiences on which to build other relevant narratives than the sole academic. Efforts to listen to different voices in the creative process will add to the impact on audience attraction. It's not that there's no room anymore to create strong monographic exhibitions that disseminate an artist's work, where the knowledge and decisions lie in the hands of a single-minded creative team. Approaches can be weighed with a strategic mindset in the totality of the exhibition year plan. The more awareness grows of the different needs of different audiences, the better curators can direct their efforts toward the most relevant mediation approach for each exhibition and the museum visit as a whole.

REFLECTIONS ON THE USE OF THE MODEL

If we genuinely want to be inclusive, we have to reflect strategically on exhibition-making concerning different audience needs. An integrated team shares the responsibility to connect with multiple audiences. The one-size-fits-all approach will make museums lose relevance with a risk of becoming niche institutions alienated from the general public. The curatorial approach by and for experts still has a future when it is one of the approaches among others. The uncovering of visitor insights will lead the team to different options. Disseminating the work of an artist will remain an essential task of a museum. The oft-heard fear that exhibitions will be converted into bite-sized entertainment because the public no longer wants to be intellectually challenged ignores the possibilities of planning and collaboration. It becomes crucial for museum staff to share a common understanding of how to regain relevance and impact. Cross-discipline or integrated planning will be the way forward when organizations want to resonate with different audiences. Contemporary art exhibitions are primarily about artists bringing their practice, with precision, to an interested public. The creative team setting the direction can still focus on one particular audience with their knowledge and expertise, while other team members can highlight unheard audience voices during the planning process. It is desirable that work that is less accessible is not only disseminated to connoisseurs but also captures a less initiated audience. The awareness of different needs, a mutual understanding of the process, shared responsibility and control, and close collaboration is the road to explore toward more inclusivity.

NOTE

1. This exhibition took place at S.M.A.K. Municipal Museum of Contemporary Art Ghent Belgium (May–November 2021) working in cooperation with the Museu de Arte de São Paulo Assis Chateaubriand.

11

Something's Off

RECONSIDERING TRADITIONAL PRACTICE

Michelle Sunset

Something's Off: Paintings by Harold Garde and Ron Kroutel began like many exhibitions at the University of Wyoming Art Museum (UWAM) in Laramie, Wyoming, United States. I, the curator, was solely responsible for developing the exhibition (with oversight from the director and chief curator) and chose to focus primarily on the objects and artists. *Something's Off* began through conversations with artist Ron Kroutel, whose creative process reminded me of Harold Garde, an artist whose works we hold in our permanent collection. Both are process-focused painters who work on a large scale. We put the two artists' works in conversation with each other, privileging the artists' voices for the benefit of visual arts students on campus, as well as the general audience we expect. *Something's Off* featured nine paintings and was on view June 12 to December 23, 2021, in one of UWAM's smaller galleries. The works of both artists entice viewers to take a closer look at the details to discover what is being presented. They both employ familiar objects and imagery, but through either unusual composition or abstracted brushstrokes, they disturb or disorient the viewer.

EMPLOYING THE MODEL

When analyzing *Something's Off* through the Dimensions of Curation Competing Values Exhibition Model, the exhibition fit best into the Disseminate category. In considering the interpretive focus, the model provides possibilities along the continuum in between object and audience. While I would like to argue that this exhibition was curated *for* a very specific audience (painting students), ultimately the interpretive focus was the objects. I considered the paintings themselves to hold valuable insights for our audiences to uncover. I also privileged the voices of the artists, including their artist statements and direct quotes in relation to the works on object labels. The approach to curating this exhibition from the outset did not include participatory or constructivist museum elements (Samis and Michaelson, 2017; Weil, 1999, Hein, 1998; Hooper-Greenhill, 1994).

The next consideration in terms of the model is the curatorial power. *Something's Off* was developed during 2020 amid the COVID-19 pandemic, when collaborative work faced more roadblocks than ever as our team worked largely remotely with some individuals simultaneously caring for their children. The museum's education team was spread thin by the necessity of developing new virtual programs and the additional staffing each of these programs required due to the nature of the technology. This exhibition was also not the largest we had on view at the time. While I loved it, I knew it would not receive as much time or attention as some of the larger exhibitions we showed simultaneously, so the curatorial power was more on the individual side of the continuum. I worked closely with the artists to collect their thoughts and writings on the artworks and also with UWAM's director and chief curator for text editing and overall approval, but the vision was largely mine. The *Something's Off* exhibition skewed far to the left, favoring the museum's authority as opposed to the right side where museums relinquish authority.

Finally, the exhibition fell more in line with the concept of *democratization of culture* than *cultural democracy* because UWAM had insider knowledge about the paintings through contact with Kroutel and Garde that we wanted to share with our visitors. These curatorial decisions were not necessarily made explicitly or intentionally. Several factors contributed to this; as previously noted, pandemic conditions made collaboration more difficult. Additionally, UWAM has a small staff and produces a large number of exhibitions. Because this was not a headlining exhibition, it did not initially receive the same level of attention and planning as some other shows in terms of including educators and other stakeholders in the process.

A SHIFT

While installing this exhibition, everything shifted when the education team decided to use *Something's Off* as the focus of UWAM's Museum Assessment Program for education and interpretation through the American Alliance of Museums. As I sat with the education team of four in the partially installed gallery space, we began to have deep conversations about the artworks and my rationale for the inclusion and placement of works while digging into the didactics I chose to provide. Through our conversations, I gleaned much insight into what others found interesting about the exhibition, and we collectively developed an interactive participatory element called "Speed Stories." Because each of the paintings featured familiar elements, but in unusual ways, we realized that to make the works more engaging for our audiences—especially younger—we needed to actively invite storytelling into the space. The low-tech interactive was simply a provided sheet of paper with instructions to list out ten things seen in one artwork and then write a quick story about the work including those elements listed.

The simple inclusion of this activity and the perspectives of my education colleagues shifted the entire exhibition experience. It occurred too late in the

Michelle Sunset

process to completely upend the intentions and design of *Something's Off*, but in using the Dimensions of Curation Model as more of a continuum than of strictly parceled categories, it seems fair to assess that we shifted *Something's Off* from pure Dissemination to somewhere closer to Empowerment. On the continuum of interpretive focus, where we began as strictly object-centric, the inclusion of an activity that engaged an open-ended and fairly accessible skill—storytelling—we created another access point for visitors to construct personally meaningful knowledge about the artworks. The participatory nature of this activity also shifted the balance from object toward audience, though there is still room to grow in that direction.

An additional shift occurred in curatorial power. By including educators, with their expertise in learning theory and visitor behavior, the power became more collaborative. The Speed Stories additionally shifted the authority, as we placed a box in the gallery, asking visitors to share their stories with us thereby giving them the authority to tell us what is happening in an artwork of their choosing. To

Figure 11.1. Students writing Speed Stories in *Something's Off* exhibition, summer 2021.
PHOTO COURTESY OF THE UNIVERSITY OF WYOMING ART MUSEUM.

Something's Off

Figure 11.2. Ron Kroutel (American, b. 1935), *Green Wall*, 2009, oil on linen.
PHOTO COURTESY OF RON KROUTEL.

our delight, during a time of pandemic-hindered attendance, we received around forty stories. One story written in response to Kroutel's painting, *Green Wall*, reads:

> There's a disconnect, between me, myself, and I. Somehow all three are entangled and just out of reach. There's a break in time and space, between the thicket. There's a house in the dark of the woods, only ever found if you're lost. Don't go in. Once you do you've started the game, where you're trapped with your opponent. Don't go. Take flight into the shifting skies. Relish in the cold wind whipping through you. That house is not home. If you are lost in the forest, stay that way. Better to hold yourself than be held hostage.

Michelle Sunset

The creative and exciting stories infused visitors' voices in the gallery; however, there is still great opportunity for this exhibition to be more firmly collaborative, as there were no outside voices involved in interpretive planning or decision-making. The shift did not alter the relationship between the exhibition and its underlying cultural policy or philosophy. Although the museum offers free admission and included interactive components, *Something's Off* was not driven by the community, so the approach remained "top-down" from the museum to the visitors (Mulcahy, 2006).

REFLECTING ON THE MODEL

Using the Competing Values Model to review the curatorial process for *Something's Off* showed how a lack of intentionality in the beginning allowed UWAM to fall into the habit of curating an exhibition that disseminated information. Reviewing the exhibition's intention after collaboration between the curator and education staff highlighted areas where the exhibition could shift in its curatorial focus and power. While the co-editors of this book explicitly stated that the model does not judge, I found their means and ends table (see chapter 1) to be particularly illuminating. Given the cross section of power, focus, and intent, *Something's Off* was designed to Disseminate, a far less satisfying result than exhibitions designed toward the other options of Enrich, Inspire, or Act. Had we employed the model from the start of the exhibition, I would have opted to curate an exhibition that falls further into the category of Empowerment. Determining this desired outcome from the beginning of the project would have helped us to prioritize the audience as our interpretive focus with greater collaboration throughout the planning phases. In future exhibitions, using the Competing Values Model will allow for greater intentionality throughout interpretive planning and exhibition development processes. We would determine the desired outcome of our exhibitions and work backward to ensure that curatorial practices and process align with the intended outcome.

REFERENCES

Hein, G. E. (1998). *Learning in the museum*. New York: Routledge.
Hooper-Greenhill, E. (1994). *The educational role of museums*. New York: Routledge.
Mulcahy, K. V. (2006). Cultural policy: Definitions and theoretical approaches. *The Journal of Arts Management, Law, and Society* 35(4), 319–30.
Samis, P., and Michaelson, M. (2017). *Creating the visitor-centered museum*. New York: Routledge.
Weil, S. E. (1999). From being about something to being for somebody: The ongoing transformation of the American museum. *Daedalus* 128(3), 229–58.

DISCERN

Object (x) + Lone Creative (y) +
Cultural Democracy (z) = **Discern**

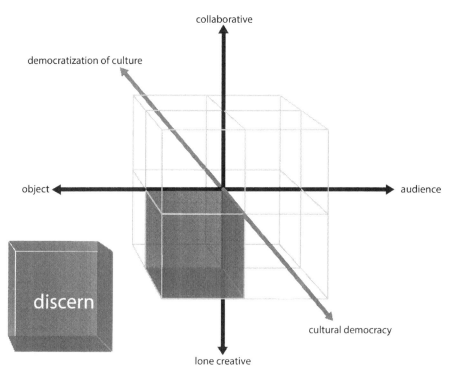

IMAGE COURTESY OF AUDREY JACOBS.

12

Discerning the Cryosphere

HUMANS AND CLIMATE IN ART FROM THE FRANCES LEHMAN LOEB ART CENTER, VASSAR COLLEGE

Elizabeth Nogrady

In Poughkeepsie, New York, United States, the Frances Lehman Loeb Art Center of Vassar College held the exhibition *Cryosphere: Humans and Climate in Art from the Loeb* from January 17 to May 22, 2022.[1] On view in the Loeb's interdisciplinary Focus Gallery, the exhibition brought together approximately twenty works depicting the "cryosphere," a term defined as "the part of the earth's surface where water exists as ice; the entire region of the natural environment that is below 0°C, especially permanently" (Oxford University Press, n.d.). Included were works in a variety of media that ranged in date from the 1800s to today, created in Asia, Europe, North and South America, and Antarctica. Walking into the exhibition, visitors found themselves surrounded by depictions of the cryosphere featuring snowstorms, icicles, glaciers, ice sheets, and frozen bodies of water. Accompanying each work was an interpretative text that incorporated the perspective of geologist Jill Schneiderman, a Vassar professor and co-curator of the exhibition. With this approach, the exhibition harnessed the cross-disciplinary ethos of a liberal arts college and, through art, raised problems on an issue that concerns us all: climate change.

Though intimate, the show—comprised of objects from the Loeb's permanent collection—addressed several key themes. One was geological phenomena of the cryosphere. A glacier, for instance, can include a horn (a peak formed when the heads of three or more glaciers meet) as is visible in the painting *Sunrise on the Bernese Alps* (1858) by Sanford Robinson Gifford or a crevasse (a deep fissure caused by stresses due to movement on the glacier's surface) as seen in a photograph by Joseph Tairraz (1870).

Figure 12.1. Installation shot, *Cryosphere: Humans, Climate, and Art from the Loeb.*
PHOTO COURTESY OF THE FRANCES LEHMAN LOEB ART CENTER, VASSAR COLLEGE.

Figure 12.2. Sanford Robinson Gifford (American, 1823–1880), *Sunrise on the Bernese Alps,* 1858, oil on canvas, 9 × 15½ in. (22.9 × 39.4 cm), Gift of Matthew Vassar, 1864.1.36.
IMAGE COURTESY OF THE FRANCES LEHMAN LOEB ART CENTER, VASSAR COLLEGE.

Figure 12.3. Taguchi Beisaku (Japanese, 1864–1903), *Braving Heavy Snow, a Japanese Officer Scouts Enemy Territory,* 1895, woodblock print; ink and color on paper, 13¾ × 27½ in. (34.9 × 69.9 cm) Gift of Justine Lewis Keidel, class of 1937, 1987.20.6.
IMAGE COURTESY OF THE FRANCES LEHMAN LOEB ART CENTER, VASSAR COLLEGE.

Also on view were examples of *snowfall* and *snowpack,* evident in an 1895 woodblock print of a blizzard during the First Sino-Japanese War by Taguchi Beisaku and a 1970s photograph of layers of fallen snow creating a cornice by Robert Gambee.

Another cornerstone of the exhibition was the North and South Poles, captured in the commanding black-and-white drawing *Hunters and Walrus* by Inuit artist Oshutsiak Pudlat from around 1980 and Ronald B. Kitaj's haunting silkscreen *With Scott to the Pole* from the series *In Our Time* from 1969. Linking the cryosphere to the museum's backyard were images of New York's Hudson Valley, where Vassar is located. These included a nineteenth-century wood engraving of iceboating on the Hudson River and a 1936 lithograph *Winter in the Catskills* by Doris Lee, who was a member of an artists' colony in Woodstock, New York. As this imagery made clear, geological proxies for climate (e.g., tree rings, ice cores) exist alongside germane written materials and visual art. Through works like these, it is possible to observe the strong link between changes in the Earth's temperature and our daily lives.

Undergirding any exploration of the cryosphere, including this exhibition, is human beings' effect on the planet, in particular our role in climate change. Even though most of the works were not created with the climate crisis in mind, when seen together they show how difficult it can be to reconcile our long-held perceptions (and memories) of ice, snow, and winter with the current realities of our planet. What such an exercise makes clear is that neither the visual language of art nor science alone can confront the complexity of the climate crisis (Newell, 2019). Instead, thinking must expand beyond discrete disciplines as humanity employs every possible means—scientific, artistic, and beyond—to address our geological moment in time.

Discerning the Cryosphere **81**

DISCERNING THE CRYOSPHERE IN THE DIMENSIONS OF CURATION MODEL

In the Dimensions of Curation Competing Values Exhibition Model, this project most aligned with exhibitions that Discern. Its genesis began with an exercise in close looking, in particular a visit to the Loeb's study room by a seminar taught by Professor Schneiderman. In advance of the museum visit, I worked in my role as the Loeb's Andrew W. Mellon Curator of Academic Programs to select works from the collection featuring the cryosphere. Meanwhile, students read an article titled, "Can Art Put Us in Touch with Our Feelings About Climate Change?" (Gergis and Whetton, 2017). As is typical in the Discern category, the works themselves were the impetus for the show, prompting the project to fit the Traditional quadrant of the two-dimensional model. In addition to stimulating thought-provoking conversation on art and climate change, the objects were united visually, demonstrating how artists from across time and geography found solutions to depicting snow and ice—often through the absence of color or by employing the blank page.

From this starting point, we evolved the course content into an exhibition for the public. The endeavor leaned somewhat Exclusive in the two-dimensional model, as it was based on the collaboration of its curators, trained in geology and art history, respectively. Yet each brought specialized knowledge to the project, which presented art historical information alongside scientific data. At times, this led to compromise in both object selection and text. Through this process, we hoped to create a traditional museum-going experience for visitors as we invited them to look closely, while also providing an opportunity to discern information about climate change in a manner apart from conventional scientific presentations. One example was the wall label for Alison Murphy Conner's photograph from 1981 of Paradise Bay, Antarctica, that shows an ice shelf, a permanent floating slab of ice attached to a coastline that mitigates sea-level rise. As noted on the label, a 2021 study by scientists at the University of Reading determined that if global temperature rises to 4 degrees Celsius (7.2 degrees Fahrenheit) above preindustrial levels, about 500,000 square kilometers (193,000 square miles) of Antarctic ice shelves could collapse into the sea (Gohd, 2021). The choice to invite visual discernment as an inroad to this scientific content was meant to be explicit to visitors, who were informed of the approach through the show's didactics. More implicit perhaps was the third dimension, or Cultural Democracy aspect, of the project: while *Cryosphere* might inspire or further climate activism among visitors, we intentionally grounded the presentation in specific art objects and the geological phenomena they reveal.

AUDIENCE RESPONSE TO *CRYOSPHERE* AND CURATORIAL REFLECTIONS

The exhibition was aimed at the Loeb's communities—which includes undergraduates, faculty, campus staff, and Poughkeepsie residents, as well as visitors from the wider Hudson Valley and beyond. The strongest response came from campus, where the issue of the climate crisis, and climate activism, is paramount. A review in the student newspaper, *The Miscellany News*, suggested the reporter did indeed glean the project's Cultural Democracy: "The art in *Cryosphere* serves as not just a historical record of what we're losing, but as a heartening reminder of what we still have. In this way, it serves as a call to action: to preserve and protect as much of it as we can" (Saini, 2022, p. 1). It was also visited by the education seminar Science, Spirituality, and Peace Education: Addressing Climate Change, and earth science majors attending a "GeoTea" event. Marketing to the general public and partnerships with community groups unfortunately suffered due to the curbing of large programs because of the global pandemic. Were we to do this project again, this avenue would be the primary area of additional outreach.

The key means of campus engagement was interdisciplinary programming. Programs included screenings co-organized with Vassar's office of Creative Arts Across Discipline of the short film *Supersymmetry* by film professor Denise Iris, described in its promotional material as "a requiem for the Arctic" (personal correspondence). Another was a campus visit by artist Christina Seely, whose work is intimately bound to both the Arctic and the climate crisis. Seely gave a public talk and screening of her film *Dissonance*, as well as a workshop for studio art students; the program called Science Technology, and Society; and the office of religious and spiritual life. Supporting these events were funds from the dean's office, specifically the Jill Troy Werner '71 Endowment for Research and Teaching on Climate Change and Sustainability, as well as cross-promotions courtesy of the Vassar College Libraries. These organic connections show that *Cryosphere* addressed issues that have permeated every corner of the college, and are acutely current.

Nevertheless, a traditional approach worked well for this exhibition: it offered viewers an opportunity for discernment that in turn opened the door to a geologist's deep knowledge of our planet, as well as, for some, an invitation for climate action. As noted by the student reporter, "One part of what can make the climate crisis feel so daunting is the perception that only people with specific scientific knowledge are equipped to handle it. However, *Cryosphere* challenges that assumption" (Saini, 2022, p. 1).

NOTE

1. Portions of this text were adapted from *Cryosphere: Humans and Climate in Art from the Loeb* by Jill Schneiderman and Elizabeth Nogrady (2022).

REFERENCES

Gergis, J., and Whetton, P. (2017, May 3). Can art put us in touch with our feelings about climate change? *The Conversation*. https://theconversation.com/can-art-put-us-in-touch-with-our-feelings-about-climate-change-77084

Gohd, C. (2021, April 11). Over a third of Antarctic ice shelf could collapse as climate change warms the earth. *Space*. https://www.space.com/antarctic-ice-shelf-collapse-as-earth-warms

Newell, J. (2019). Creative collaborations: Museums engaging with communities and climate change. In Leal Filho, W., Lackner, B., and McGhie, H. (Eds.), *Addressing the challenges in communicating climate change across various audiences* (pp. 143–57). Cham: Springer.

Oxford University Press. (n.d.). Cryosphere. In *Oxford English Dictionary*. Retrieved August 1, 2022. oed.com/view/ Entry/276568

Saini, N. (2022, February 3). Cryosphere exhibit provides chilling portrait of a warming planet. *The Miscellany News.* https://miscellanynews.org/2022/02/02/arts/cryosphere-exhibit-provides-chilling-portrait-of-warming-planet/

13

Discerning with a Good Voice

HÓWAŠTE AT THE HERITAGE CENTER

Ashley Pourier and Audrey Jacobs

In the homelands of the Oglala Lakhóta, present-day South Dakota, United States, The Heritage Center at Red Cloud has served a local creative community since 1968. Jesuits Father Theodore Zuern and Brother Clair M. Simon established the contemporary Native art and history museum that has since been stewarded by Red Cloud Indian School, a Lakhóta-Catholic K–12 school and parish organization. The Center celebrates Native art and provides economic resources for regional artists, especially those of the Očhéthi Šakówiŋ (the Lakhóta, Nakhóta, and Dakhóta nations; pronounced oh-CHET-tee shah-KOH-ween). Building on this long tradition, the Center began planning a deeper level of support for community artistic development in an exhibition that articulated the contemporary influences of deep-rooted traditions.

The *Hówašte* exhibition grew from an intensive residency that worked with a team of culture bearers and artists. Hówašte (pronounced HO-wash-tay) means to speak with a good or beautiful voice in Lakhóta. The residency and resulting exhibition developed around five culturally specific art forms that the Center identified as holding special significance and that are known historically to the Oglala Lakhóta. Although the co-authors of this chapter received a great deal of input from the artists and mentors, interpretive materials still fell within our purview to create. The curator, Ashley Pourier, an Oglala Lakhóta (pronounced oh-GLA-la lah-KOH-ta) citizen, born and raised in the area, chose the art forms to highlight the artists and their mentors. Ashley, jointly with Audrey Jacobs, the Museum Educator, a non-Native White transplant to the area, developed the interpretation. Through our reflection on this exhibition's development, we will describe factors that make this exhibition one that discerns.

FROM ARTS INCUBATOR TO EXHIBITION

In December 2018, the Center chose community-recognized, promising artists who expressed a desire to bring their artistic production to a professional level. Art has long been an economic driver in this region (First Peoples Fund, 2013). Many artists in the area work in small economies of scale, having not enough time or materials to invest in larger, resource-intensive projects. This program emerged from a mission-driven museum store program that acted as a local economic engine for the community and highlighted the work of local artists who supply the center's shop. The residency aimed to bring emerging artists—locally called kitchen-table artists—from subsistence art production to aesthetically and conceptually elaborate production. We asked artists to imagine and cultivate a dream project that could speak to the influence of their heritage in their artwork. The projects required months of dedicated work, learning more about their art form from expert culture bearers, researching, planning, and constructing the artworks. The artists all participated in the documentation of their work and artistic journeys, and some helped with educational programming associated with the exhibition. The Center funded their time, their mentors' time, and their supplies. Artists also received assistance in sourcing materials and accessing the Center's extensive historical collection of Lakhóta art.

The resulting exhibition included five thoroughly researched, culturally grounded, contemporary artworks and aimed to satisfy an array of goals. For its artists and mentors, the project provided for their activities economically, logistically, and professionally. For the artworks and cultural history, the exhibition accomplished the goal of documenting current practices in these culturally specific art forms. For the audience, the exhibition emphasized cultural understandings about the history and contemporary growth of these art forms. The exhibition ran in the Center's gallery from September through December 2019. Although the COVID-19 pandemic delayed plans to travel in 2020, the Center plans to travel the exhibition in the future. With an accompanying educational resource, the exhibition will travel to nontraditional gallery spaces in rural communities to provide wide access to the cultural and historical knowledge contained in the artworks.

DESIGNING AN EXHIBITION THAT DISCERNS

Exhibitions that Discern emphasize the institution's curatorial control and focus on the artwork while opening avenues for participation through a Cultural Democracy stance. This exhibition supported artists in residence and their mentors and, in that sense, included a high degree of collaboration with community. Indeed, the Center's activities rely on close-knit community ties with local artists, culture bearers, educators, and young people. The residency, however, was designed and developed in-house, and curatorial decisions for the exhibition were retained by the curator. The exhibition and educational materials focused on material, creation processes, and cultural importance of the art forms created for the exhibition.

CURATORIAL FOCUS ON THE OBJECT

The exhibition centered on the interpretation of the artworks and their production, with a culturally informed art history and object-centered focus. Western aca-

Ashley Pourier and Audrey Jacobs

demic boundaries around fine art and craft (such as the practices highlighted in this exhibition) set apart aesthetic systems that do not employ these taxonomies (Leuthold, 1998) in ways that obscure the social, cultural, and historical construction of what makes creative expression art (Auther, 2010). This project set out to elevate perceptions of art forms historically connected to Oglala Lakhóta culture and to document and celebrate current practices among Oglala artists. The Center chose several important art forms (porcupine quillwork, beadwork, quilting, and hide production), and the five resulting artworks included a star quilt, a women's breastplate, a men's breastplate, a leader shirt, and a trade cloth dress. The project, concentrating on the intricacies of inherited practices and contemporary expression, drew on the notion that heritage takes a long view on cultural development, supporting all forms of human expression (Graves, 2005). The project highlighted the creative expression of Indigenous art forms with an eye to reinforcing and boosting local audiences' knowledge of these art forms.

LONE CREATIVE CURATION

Hówaste included input from stakeholders and experts in the cultural arts, yet decision-making and leadership remained with the curator, Ashley Pourier, and the Center's staff. The artists poured their creative expression into their artworks and generously discussed their artwork in conversation but preferred not to be involved in interpretation and exhibition design decision-making. By following the artists' processes, we gained valuable insight to better represent the artists and artwork in an exhibition format. Curatorial research, for this exhibition, emphasized the artists' own thoughts about their work in combination with traditional research and culture bearer knowledge. Navigating between collaboration and lone-creative values, this curatorial process shed light on the entanglement of the two; yet, because we ultimately made interpretive decisions, the exhibition itself belongs closer to the lone-creative end of this continuum. The nature of collaboration in this respect falls more securely within a combination of Cultural Democracy and Lone Creative curation.

CULTURAL DEMOCRACY

In this exhibition, Cultural Democracy takes on notions of advocacy and collaboration. The project sought to challenge prevailing notions of the Eurocentric divide between contemporary art and culturally based craft, often termed traditional craft. This important communication goal aligns with the principles of Cultural Democracy, in seeking to overturn hierarchical conceptions of fine art. *Hówaste* also involved an intense amount of participation through the residency program. Our approach highlighted the often-hidden cultural participation of artists through background activities rather than the public spotlight (Graves, 2005). We did this through videos, written interviews, and inclusion in educational programs. Pourier noticed that the artists' insights and artisanship connected with visitors. The star quilt (see figure 13.1) dealt with the Native women–led work on ending violence against women regarding missing and murdered Indigenous women, a movement energizing and offering hope to many

Figure 13.1. Kristina Iron Cloud sewing *MMIW Star Quilt.*
PHOTO COURTESY OF THE HERITAGE CENTER AT RED CLOUD INDIAN SCHOOL, INC.

people in the Očhéthi Šakówiŋ. The quilled leader shirt received admiration for its technical skill, down to the brain-tanned and smoked hide (a soft leather making process using emulsifiers in animal brain), that the artist had spent countless hours preparing (see figure 13.2).

Figure 13.2. Michael He Crow tanning hide. PHOTO COURTESY OF THE HERITAGE CENTER AT RED CLOUD INDIAN SCHOOL, INC.

Ashley Pourier and Audrey Jacobs

CONCLUSION: BUILDING DISCERNING EXHIBITIONS ON COMMUNITY PROGRAMS

We developed an exhibition that Discerns based on the immense and careful learning we had undergone during the artist residency. The exhibition presented details, techniques, material, and principles that we had received throughout the year of supporting artists. In this case, the artists we worked with did not want to have a heavy hand in the design of exhibition or education materials; they preferred to offer their insight through conversation and art making and leave the interpretive decisions to the museum. Our curatorial process was therefore collaborative in its sourcing (Cultural Democracy) rather than its methodology (Lone Creative). By taking a Cultural Democracy approach to curation in combination with Lone Creative decision-making and object-focused curation, we organized the artists' experience and expertise in a way that highlighted the art form.

REFERENCES

Auther, E. (2010). *The hierarchy of art and craft in American art.* Minneapolis: University of Minnesota Press.

First Peoples Fund. (2013). *Establishing a creative economy: Art as an economic engine in Native communities.*

Graves, J. (2005). *Cultural democracy: The arts, community and the public purpose.* Champaign: University of Illinois Press.

Leuthold, S. (1998). *Indigenous aesthetics: Native art media and identity.* Austin: University of Texas Press.

ENRICH

Object (*x*) + Collaborative (*y*) + Democratization of Culture (*z*) = **Enrich**

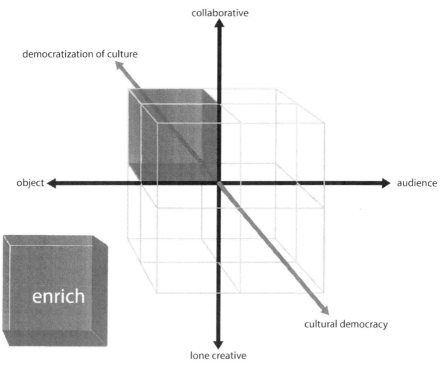

IMAGE COURTESY OF AUDREY JACOBS.

14

Not Just Dissemination, an Enriched Experience

MING DYNASTY COSTUME EXHIBITION

Xiaonan Jiang and Xuejing Dai

The *Ming Dynasty Costume* exhibition in Shandong Museum, Jinan, China, displayed the costumes of the Chinese Ming Dynasty (1368–1644). During the exhibition from September 29, 2020, to February 28, 2021, the museum attracted Chinese traditional costume fans from all over the country. Visitors commented that it was a visual feast being exposed to the essence of Ming culture. Curators of the exhibition focused on object interpretations and adopted collaborative curatorial practices, aiming to provide the public with an opportunity to appreciate the treasure of Ming costume culture and further inspire modern costume design.

OVERVIEW OF THE EXHIBITION

The *Ming Dynasty Costume* exhibition was curated in response to the social trends toward the innovation of Chinese traditional culture. Inspired by the establishment of the Chinese Han Dynasty Costume Day, Shandong Museum and the Confucius Museum made joint efforts to showcase their relatively abundant collections of Ming dynasty costumes. The co-curated exhibition featured thirty-two pieces of Ming official costumes, auspicious costumes, and daily costumes, together with relevant artworks such as clothing accessories, calligraphy, paintings, and furniture during the Chinese Ming dynasty. Curators considered the Ming costume as the epitome of Chinese history and etiquette culture. They hoped the illustration of the costume culture would encourage the public to examine the history, explore the relevance between the past and the present, and thus build their confidence in Chinese culture.

ANALYSIS OF EXHIBITION CURATORIAL PRACTICES

Through the lens of the Dimensions of Curation Competing Values Exhibition Model, we analyze the curatorial practices of the *Ming Dynasty Costume* exhibition, focusing on its interpretive focus, curatorial power, and curatorial intent.

OBJECTS AS THE INTERPRETIVE FOCUS

Museum objects convey vast interrelated ideas and embody social, cultural, and educational values (Carr, 2004; Paris, 2002; Schultz, 2018). To fulfill the objects' function as knowledge resources, curators of the *Ming Dynasty Costume* exhibition added special features to the exhibition halls, such as the specially designed background colors and glass showcases.

The exhibition included three main sections: official costumes, auspicious costumes, and daily costumes. Curators used three distinct colors as the background language to emphasize the theme of each section. The first exhibition area centered on official costumes; red, favored by Ming officials, was adopted as the main tone. Red highlighted the solemnity of the displayed costumes and demonstrated the Ming dynasty's strict hierarchical culture reflected by the ornamental pattern of the official costumes. The topic of the second area was Ming costumes for auspicious occasions, such as seasonal festivals, birthdays, feasts, and weddings. The main color of this area was bright yellow to set off the elaborate embroidery patterns on the clothes. The detailed interpretive labels introduced the exquisite workmanship embedded in the specially designed clothes. It also informed visitors of the rich cultural connotations in the patterns of auspicious birds and animals, such as kylin, phoenix, and crane, which symbolize fortune and prosperity in Chinese culture. The third section displayed Ming clothes for daily life with moon white as the background color. The pastel color set the tone for a relaxed and graceful atmosphere of daily life. The daily life clothes featured the pursuit of fashion instead of social status differences, ranging from relatively simple designs in the early Ming dynasty to the diversified ones in the middle and late Ming, from Taoist robes and shirts for men to jackets and skirts for women.

Curators were concerned about how to better display the Ming costumes considering their large sizes. Rather than hanging the clothes, they specially designed six glass showcases. The cases can be tilted forty-five degrees so that visitors can have a clear full view of the costumes on display (figure 14.1). Meanwhile, as the Ming costumes are regarded as cultural relics with a long history of over six hundred years, the cases can protect the costumes from the influences of temperature and light. Enlarged digital copies of the costume patterns were also provided beside the objects for visitors' examination. *Knowing Where They Came from, Knowing Where They Go* was an extension part of the exhibition, displaying replicas of Ming dynasty costumes and modern fashion clothes that extracted elements from Ming costume designs. Curators called this section "an exhibition in the exhibition," presenting how Chinese traditional clothes can be activated when innovatively combined with the popular colors, innovative fabrics, advanced garment technology, and aesthetic design at present.

Figure 14.1. The specially designed glass showcases. PHOTO COURTESY OF XUEJING DAI.

Museum objects are a form of documents to be studied (Latham, 2012) as they contain information and knowledge for visitors to explore. The exhibition's unique characteristics of displaying objects served for object interpretation and fostered visitors' object observation and active label reading.

COLLABORATION AS THE CURATORIAL POWER

In 2012, Shandong Museum worked with academic researchers and community members on its exhibition *Confucius Costume Collection*. With the experience in collaboration, the museum set up a curatorial team for the *Ming Dynasty Costume* exhibition. The curatorial team consisted of curators and professionals from the two museums' collection management departments, social media departments, education departments, and design departments. Each museum professional was responsible for their areas of expertise. The museum also invited Chu Yan, a famous fashion designer, to make replicas of Ming dynasty costumes and discuss the relevance between Ming dynasty costumes and the current fashions (figure 14.2). Dong Jin, a folk researcher in Ming dynasty costumes, also joined the team and helped with object display.

Besides collaboration with experts in relevant fields, the museum made efforts to involve multiple voices from the community. During the process of exhibition planning, the museum invited the public online to offer suggestions for curation and welcomed the participation of online netizens through social media including WeChat, Weibo, and TikTok. Dong Jin, the folk expert in Ming dynasty costumes, also launched an online discussion through his social media about the exhibition curation and the development of related culturally creative

Figure 14.2. The Ming Costume Show on the opening day of the exhibition.
PHOTO COURTESY OF XUEJING DAI.

products. The participation of diverse individuals in decision-making contributed to a robust exhibition; it also propelled the exhibition into a popular cultural event.

DEMOCRATIZATION OF CULTURE AS CURATORIAL INTENT

Curators regarded the *Ming Dynasty Costume* exhibition as an opportunity to disseminate knowledge related to Chinese traditional culture. As the biggest museum in Shandong Province, the state of etiquette in ancient China, Shandong Museum took advantage of its special collections and used the Ming costume as the epitome of Chinese history and etiquette culture. For object interpretations, curators and costume experts held authority and transmitted their knowledge to visitors through walk-and-talk lecture tours and explanatory panel texts.

Through introducing facts concerning collections and decoding objects from curators' perspectives, the museum educated visitors about Chinese traditional culture and elevated their aesthetic appreciation. This convergent curatorial intent was the explicit democratization of culture, holding that museums possess the knowledge and provide access to education that the public benefits from.

OBJECT (X) + COLLABORATIVE (Y) + DEMOCRATIZATION OF CULTURE (Z) = EXHIBITION THAT ENRICHES

The *Ming Dynasty Costume* exhibition was an enriched experience for both visitors and curators. Visitors cherished this visual feast as it brought to the public the ancient costumes that usually appeared in movies. While wondering at the delicate patterns and exquisite craftsmanship of the Ming dynasty costumes, visitors—

especially costume fans—discussed the meaning of beauty and explored the roots of Chinese etiquette behind the costume culture. In 2020, the Chinese Association of Museums awarded the exhibition as one of the Top Ten National Exhibitions, commenting that it enriched the cultural life of the public by connecting ancient and modern costume aesthetics. The exhibition curators acknowledged their responsibility to disseminate knowledge, and they felt that the collaboration with the public enriched their curatorial practices. Multiple voices inspired curators to explore more possibilities to venerate Chinese ancestors, enhance the public's beauty appreciation, promote the etiquette culture unique in Shandong Province, and achieve positive social effects through a cultural renaissance.

REFLECTIONS

As costume exhibitions are usually held every five years in Shandong Museum, museum professionals are exploring diverse curatorial practices for future exhibitions. Relevant visitor studies showed that 78.4 percent of the visitors accessed the exhibition information via new media, thus curators plan to further explore the potential of new media to involve visitors in label writing. Curators also felt that it was a missed opportunity not to include some visitor-centered approaches, and there was no engagement of Chinese traditional costume fans in the exhibition. Some visitors expected a more dynamic exhibition with hands-on experiences, such as putting on replicas of some traditional costumes. In the future, curators will conduct pre-exhibition surveys to identify visitors' needs and interests. The data collected will help the museum to target audiences and provide evidence for shifting interpretive focus from objects to visitors for a more inclusive exhibition.

REFERENCES

Carr, D. (2004). Reading beyond the museum. *The Journal of Museum Education* 29(1), 3–8.
Latham, K. F. (2012). Museum object as document: Using Buckland's information concepts to understand museum experiences. *Journal of Documentation* 68(1), 45–71.
Paris, S. G. (2002). *Perspectives on object-centered learning in museums.* New York: Routledge.
Schultz, L. (2018). Object-based learning, or learning from objects in the anthropology museum. *Review of Education, Pedagogy, and Cultural Studies* 40(4), 282–304.
Shandong Art Museum. (n.d.). *The Ming Dynasty Costume Exhibition.* http://www.sdmuseum.com/Uploads/sdbwgshuzizhanting/specialmingfu/home.htm

15

SKIN, a Multisensory Art Exhibition for Children Aged Eight and Older and Their Families

Stefanie Metsemakers and Gerd Dierckx

Can you live without touching?
Does your skin always stay the same?
What does your skin say about you?

In *SKIN*, a multisensory art exhibition for children aged eight and older and their families, visitors discovered how wondrous our skin is as a sensory, communicative, and protective organ and investigated the values we attach to skin color. The exhibition was held at the Bonnefanten Museum in Maastricht, The Netherlands, between April 13, 2021, and January 23, 2022. It was a collaboration between the Bonnefanten's collection and the exhibition of the same name by *Rasa*, a Belgian organization that has been developing and presenting traveling exhibitions of contemporary art for young people for almost thirty years.

SKIN showed works by contemporary artists with a particular focus on skin, including Célio Braga, Berlinde De Bruyckere, Jalila Essaïdi, Margi Geerlinks, Bart Hess, Elke Lutgerink, Carla van de Puttelaar, Renee Verhoeven, and Eline Willemarck, interspersed with artworks from the Bonnefanten's collection by Marlene Dumas, Ferdi, Bruce Nauman, L. A. Raeven, and Luc Tuymans. The exhibition invited visitors to explore, experience, and engage in philosophical questions. By looking, feeling, and discussing, visitors could gain a deeper understanding of the art. Beyond its role as an exhibition, *SKIN* functioned as a laboratory and experimental place to explore together. Rather than highlighting the physical aspects of skin, the exhibition questioned the importance of our skin philosophically.

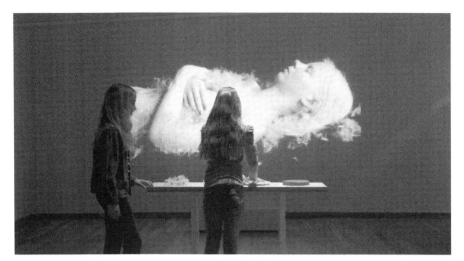

Figure 15.1. Video *Snow White* by Carla van de Puttelaar with bowls of materials used in the artwork in front of the screen. PHOTO COURTESY OF STRICTUA.

The content and visual aspects of the thirty-one artworks related to the themes of skin as a sensory organ, skin as protection and reflection (blushing, goose bumps, turning pale), skin and sensuality/touch (pleasure, pain, and other perceptions), skin in the future, skin transformation, marks on the skin (wrinkles, spots, freckles), skin as a canvas (tattoos, paintings, makeup), skin as metaphor, and skin color in all its shades.

Most of the artworks were presented in "labs" with three layers of content and scenography (exhibition design): (a) the artwork, which visitors experienced aesthetically; (b) research/behind the scenes: visitors discovered the artist's creation process; and (c) experiment: visitors explored related themes through play and the senses (figure 15.1). In the Dimensions of Curation Competing Values Exhibition Model, *SKIN* is an exhibition that Enriches.

EXHIBITION OVERVIEW

Besides an introductory text, the exhibition and the theme of skin were introduced by a short inspirational video in which children addressed the themes in the exhibition through philosophical questions such as: *Does touching yourself feel the same as being touched? Can you tell from the outside what you look like on the inside? What shades of color can you find in yourself?* This first exhibition space included an indoor barefoot path with different textures to make visitors aware of their senses and attune them to the experience. The textures were inspired by the skin of several brightly colored flower-, plant-, and animallike sculptures by the artist Ferdi, displayed around the barefoot path (figure 15.2).

In the adjacent spaces, the artworks were presented in different ways: with videos or materials that showed the artist's creation process, for the artworks

Figure 15.2. First space in the exhibition *SKIN* with three artworks by Ferdi, *Damsel Dragonfly*, *Green grass of home*, and *Vulva Pseudodomestica*, surrounded by the barefoot trail. PHOTO COURTESY OF BONNEFANTEN MUSEUM.

by Bart Hess, Berlinde de Bruyckere, and Jalila Essaïdi; interactively, by allowing visitors to touch works by L. A. Raeven, Célio Braga, and Eline Willemarck; or by encouraging visitors to experiment with and investigate the artworks by Renee Verhoeven, Bruce Nauman, Carla van de Puttelaar, and Margi Geerlinks. For instance, *Je suis le monde (Nino)*, a photo by Margi Geerlinks of her son Nino showing their origins in his skin, was combined with "skin" jackets in different shades commissioned by *Rasa* from Eline Willemarck. Young visitors could put them on and experience briefly how it felt to have a different skin tone, mirroring themselves, the other, and the artwork (figure 15.3). How did they feel in a different skin?

Stefanie Metsemakers and Gerd Dierckx

Figure 15.3. On the right, the work *Gulden Snede* by Eline Willemarck. Visitors were allowed to see, feel, and combine pieces of casts of the skin of the artist's boyfriend. On the left, the photographic work *Je suis le monde (Nino)* by Margi Geerlinks (not visible in the picture) combined with "skin" jackets in different shades made by Eline Willemarck commissioned by the curators. Young visitors could wear these and experience what it feels like to have a different skin (shade) for a moment.
PHOTO COURTESY OF STRICTUA.

The exhibition concluded with an interactive project space that sparked communication among visitors and between visitors and artists. Seated at long tables with mail slots, visitors could write a card to the artist of their preference. These cards were forwarded to the artists.

Additionally, in a life-size projection of her TED Talk, Angélica Dass tackled the theme of the diverse beauty of humanity as shown in her photo project *Humanae*. She inspired visitors to draw their own skin color on the wall with colored pencils and give it a new name in a collaborative wall drawing. By inviting visitors to search for their own skin color and give it a name, we showed the richness of skin tones and drew attention to the narrow pigeonholes or labels that are too often used.

SHARING CURATORIAL POWER

The basis of the Bonnefanten exhibition was shaped by *Rasa*. Every exhibition by *Rasa* is an all-encompassing project that grows organically from thematic research. First, *Rasa* selects a theme. Then it talks to the visitors—children—about what this theme means to them. The children's ideas nuance and enrich the exhibitions being created. *Rasa* also involves artists and experts on content, such as philosophers and a dermatologist, in their conversations. This interaction helps to imbue the objects with meaning. As such, the Interpretive Focus (*x* axis) of *SKIN* was on the Object.

With attention to the complete artistic process and experience, *Rasa* then selects works of art and contacts the artists. They discuss how to exhibit the work and help visitors to understand it. This draws artists into the process of creating the exhibition. Ultimately, the artworks are exhibited at children's eye level in a setting with a clear design, encouraging them to look, play, and investigate.

Artistic quality, power of expression, and sensory appeal were a priority for the curators both when selecting the works and developing the setting. The images shown were not merely child-friendly; they challenged perceptions and stimulated reflection. While avoiding extreme violence or strong sexual connotations, the curators did not limit themselves to images that were merely sweet or affirming. Children feel the big themes in life keenly. It is not necessary to simplify art. Real art for grown-ups also strikes a chord with young viewers. Interesting artworks open up many avenues of exploration. The important thing is for the child to feel drawn to one of those avenues to set creative thinking in motion (Dierckx, 2021).

The explicit curatorial choices were made by the curators of *Rasa* and the Bonnefanten, taking into account the contributions to the content by artists, experts and children, so the Curatorial Power (*y* axis) lies with the Collaborative. This made *SKIN* an example of Exclusive practice.

AN EXHIBITION THAT ENRICHES

The purpose of creating an exhibition in the Bonnefanten with *Rasa* for children and their families was to make contemporary art and the museum more accessible to this particular audience. The presentation of artworks in interactive labs shifted communication from a knowledge-driven model to an inquisitive lab approach. By raising philosophical questions and using a multisensory approach, the curators encouraged children and their families to experience art with their own hearts, souls, minds, bodies, and all their senses, based on their own qualities and uniqueness. The exhibition targeted all children, including those who rarely—if ever—get the chance to engage with contemporary art. Thus, it leaned strongly toward Democratization of Culture on the *z* axis. To conclude, *SKIN* was an exhibition that Enriches.

Visitors appreciated seeing the artworks in a beautiful, playful, and stimulating setting. Some families visited the exhibition multiple times, focusing on different aspects each time. Some used the philosophical questions to discuss the artworks and the related themes. Others hardly read anything and were drawn to the tactile materials. Yet others wanted to know everything about the artist's creative process.

The specific educational approach in *SKIN* created multiple channels for adults and children to communicate directly with each other. Philosophizing sparked off a thought process that generated further reflection, even after the exhibition. The invitation to visitors to share their experience of the artworks or their ideas about the theme with the artists or with other visitors was very meaningful: for visitors, as they reflected on themselves and what they had experienced, and for the curators, as it gave insights into what the audience had gained from the exhibition. The act of leaving a physical trace on the wall of the museum (in the final exhibition space) engendered a sense of well-being and involvement among the visitors.

This is exactly what we are striving for in our search for dynamic new ways to reach our audience. The collaborative method used for *SKIN* gave us meaningful insights into the interests and needs of our audiences. We learned the best way to present our objects and the context needed to connect to their world of experience, in this case for children and their families. This helped them engage more profoundly with the objects and appreciate them more, which increased the relevance of the objects and thus of our collection and our museum. This more visitor-centered approach is an important step toward making the museum (even) more part of the community. Ultimately, the stimulating theme of *SKIN* and the multilayered approach to presenting the artworks, always prioritizing the audience, were what made the exhibition work.

REFERENCES

Bonnefanten. (2022, May 6). *SKIN*–Bonnefanten, Maastricht.
Dierckx, G. (2021). *Eyes for art: Exploring visual art with children*. RASA.

AMPLIFY

Object (*x*) + Collaborative (*y*) + Cultural Democracy (*z*) = **Amplify**

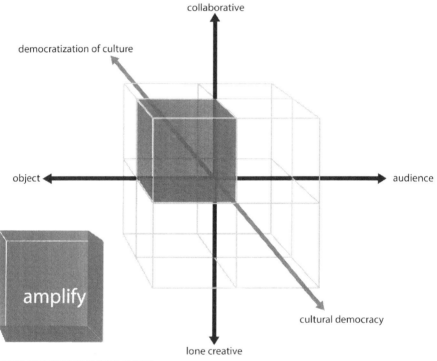

IMAGE COURTESY OF AUDREY JACOBS.

16

Challenging Romaphobia

THE CASE OF A ROMANIAN CARNIVAL MASK AT MUCEM

Julia Ferloni and Emilie Sitzia

The exhibition *Barvalo* (which means *rich* and by extension *proud* in Romanes) will be held at Mucem (Museum of European and Mediterranean Civilizations) in Marseille, France, from May 10 to September 4, 2023. *Barvalo* deals with Romani cultures in Europe and the anti-Gypsyism Roma have been facing for centuries. The exhibition is being co-created by nineteen collaborators of Roma, Sinti, Gitanx, Voyageurs, and non-Romani origins, representing different nationalities and sociocultural backgrounds, with most co-creators having never taken part in a museum project. In this way, *Barvalo* aims at auto-representation by a minority, an unusual practice in French museums. To complement the exhibition, the collated survey[1] "Romani Professions and Know-hows in Europe and the Mediterranean" was launched in 2019. It involved the *Barvalo* experts in a research project in which they proposed subjects and engaged in fieldwork, retrieving objects and documentation to be included in the museum's collections as well as the exhibition.

For this exhibition, the institution's permanent collection is serving as the starting point, with collection objects reevaluated by the communities in a collaborative process (beyond standard consultation processes). In this chapter, we will take a carnival mask (see figure 16.1) as our focus, as in many ways its exhibition histories embody issues of collecting, interpreting, and exhibiting racist heritage. This short account will thereby add to discussions on the need for community involvement in the reinterpretation and presentation of such problematic heritage.

On a wider level, this study also allows us to understand how Mucem is striving to move from being a folklore museum to a museum of civilizations, from a museum exhibiting the Other to a museum discussing with the Other and othering processes. This is a gradual, recent, and ongoing evolution, witnessing a move from a comparative and encyclopedic perspective focused on objects, objective facts, and academic

Figure 16.1. *Mascà de bàdànàrità* (*mask of a "Gypsy woman"*), 1992, Romania. Metal string, cardboard, hair, cotton, paper, elastic, satin. 61 × 42 × 14 cm. inv. DMH1992.43.13.5 ©Marianne Kuhn/Mucem. PHOTO COURTESY OF MUCEM.

knowledge to an amplifying model conveying values and situated knowledge linked to the source community. In highlighting this shift, we align this practice with the model Object (x) + Collaboration (y) + Cultural Democracy (z) = Amplify.

In the following, we will show how one particularly problematic type of object, so-called "Gypsy"[2] women masks, were subject to two very different curatorial positions. A Mucem exhibition in 2014 thus offers an example of a Lone Creative curatorial approach (Villeneuve and Love, 2017) that focused on masks as documents of a popular practice using ethnography as an academic disciplinary backbone for the curatorial methodology. With *Barvalo* in 2023, we see the institution's shift toward a collaborative process working with the impacted communities and its core aspirations of Cultural Democracy; that is, working with communities and knowledge bearers.

THE PROBLEMATIC OBJECT: A MASK OF A "GYPSY" WOMAN

When Mucem was founded in 1999, it inherited the collection of the Musée des Arts et Traditions Populaires that encompassed about one million objects focused on French folklore. To help the new museum open up to the European and the Mediterranean areas, the European collections of the Musée de l'Homme were added. These included 33,000 objects collected by European anthropologists in the twentieth century, mostly to document social rural practices. Therein, eighty-nine objects related to mostly Eastern European Roma groups were identified.

These objects linked with previous museum curators' special interests in the theme of seasonal, agricultural, or folk festivals. The museum had twice sent a team to Romania to document a specific masquerade—once in the 1950s and again in 1992. Research conducted recently by Mucem about its Romani collections stated that the mask shown in figure 16.1 was acquired along with another during the 1992 mission that had been organized to update knowledge on this carnival and the twelve-days seasonal cycle (Danet, 2021). These were purchased and labeled as two "Gypsy" costumes.

A TRADITIONAL CURATORIAL APPROACH

Originally, these kinds of masks were treated in a traditional curatorial manner, as shown by the 2014 exhibition. It had developed out of a collated survey, which, starting in 2008, had been associated with the European Research Project *Carnival King of Europe*. This survey explored contemporary carnivals and masquerades in Poland, Morocco, France, Bulgaria, and the Netherlands, and was led by a Mucem curator, Marie-Pascale Mallé. Later, the survey resulted in the 2014 Mucem exhibition, *Le Monde à l'Envers* (the World Upside-Down), which later traveled to Binche, Belgium. As part of this exhibition, the curator, a trained ethnologist, documented a carnival in Jambol, Bulgaria, featuring masked men disguised in a satirical Roma woman costume, not unlike the mask purchased in 1992 by the Musée de l'Homme.

In 2008, the aim of the survey was not to question the caricatural and insulting manner in which objects were used in carnivals to stigmatize a vulnerable minority.[3] It documented as exhaustively as possible a popular and social European practice: masquerades. However, by 2014, there was a demonstrated awareness of the questionable nature of such representations. That exhibition devoted a section to "The Other," displaying another "Gypsy" woman mask, on loan from the exhibition's partner museum (Binche's Musée International du Carnaval et du Masque, Belgium [International Museum of Carnival and Mask]), beside a Romanian Roma bear showman costume. One entry in the catalog particularly addressed Roma representation in the Bulgarian carnival,[4] a sign of the gradual evolution of the institution's positioning and processes (Strahilov as cited in Mallé, 2014).

COLLABORATION AND CULTURAL DEMOCRACY

In contrast, the exhibition *Barvalo* seeks to break with that traditional process and, following Koke and Ryan (2017), to share curatorial authority. In doing so, the institutional curators recognize their expertise limits and invite experts to contribute. The Mucem curators are thus seeking to engage in a culturally democratic and community-driven approach, opening up objects to new interpretations and sharing institutional power (Ferloni and Sitzia, 2022).

As one specific example, in February 2020, Cristian Padure, a Romanian linguist teaching Romanes at Bucharest University, joined *Barvalo*'s exhibition design seminars. He was confronted with the "*mascà de bàdànàrità*" (Mask of "Gypsy" Woman) and, being of Roma origin, was determined to challenge the prejudice against Romani women this mask conveyed. When invited to take part in the collated survey "Romani Occupations and Know-How," he offered to do fieldwork and research the stereotypical *drabarimos* (fortune teller) profession. Figure 16.2 depicts an interview he conducted with Romanian *drabarni* Craciun Floarea.

Figure 16.2. The fortune teller (*drabarni*) Craciun Floarea, Bucharest, May 2021. The tarot cards were purchased for Mucem's collections. ©Cristian Padure/Mucem.
PHOTO COURTESY OF CRISTIAN PADURE/MUCEM.

Julia Ferloni and Emilie Sitzia

In his fieldwork report, Padure stated that he intended "to bring to light the essential role played by Roma women in safeguarding the mental and emotional health and also the well-being of individuals living in a community before the advent of psychotherapy . . . but also after it" (Padure, 2021, p. 3). He also stated that he wanted "to draw a parallel between the approach and the solutions employed in magic practices and those put forth by psychotherapy," thereby challenging the stereotype of the Roma fortune teller (p. 3). It is on such a critical approach that the *Barvalo* participatory process is based. Highlighting Romani opinions, particularly with satirical installation "Musée du Gadjo,"[5] shows the underlying racism of such objects and returns the voice of the minority community concerned; in short, it aims to Amplify.[6]

As another manifestation of its community-driven approach, *Barvalo* aims to attract a public beyond its usual upper-middle-class, educated, and older audience with targeting specifically Romani publics. The exhibition team intends to elicit a reflective audience response and challenge stereotypes and prejudice about Roma populations. It also takes its audience into account to make sure it communicates its message efficiently and clearly. To achieve this, the Mucem team has worked to integrate interpretative planning (Wells, Butler, and Koke, 2013) throughout the process. When conceptualizing the exhibition, the curatorial team wanted to assess existing knowledge and stereotypes and thus, in 2019, they invited a sample of Mucem's visitors to share their representations of Roma and their opinions about what an exhibition devoted to this cultural group would/should include.

Overall, this exhibition intends to showcase the views of the people affected by its subject while allowing the museum to find, in agreement with them, the best way to convey its message to visitors. Perhaps more significantly, this exhibition project has led to institutional change. In particular, Mucem has modified its collection management policy and its approach toward the management of racist heritage.

NOTES

1. A collated survey is a process of constructing a museum's study material: ethnographic surveys are commissioned to observe a social fact, in light of which material and immaterial testimonies are collected in the form of filmed interviews, photographs, or objects, all of which are then systematically analyzed before entering a museum's collection.
2. Gypsy is a stereotypical and insulting term. We use the word in quotation marks to report it's historic use.
3. At the time it was not common practice to involve minorities in such exhibitions in France. The practice and urge for participation and auto-representation has developed a lot in the last five years.
4. Nevertheless, while mentioning that Roma took part freely in the masquerade (sometimes endorsing the mocked and stigmatizing costume of the "Gypsy"), the article never mentions the Romaphobic nature of Bulgarian carnival.
5. The Gadjo (pl. Gadje) is the Other, the non-Roma in Romanes. This installation by French Gitano artist Gabi Jimenez aims at challenging stereotypes by having regular visitors exhibited as "exotic" populations (as Roma were in ethnographic museums), thereby feeling what it is like to be "the Other" (Mirga-Kruszelnicka, 2023).
6. The selection of this approach was explicit and is the subject of two doctoral studies.

REFERENCES

Danet, E. (2021). *Le patrimoine romani au sein de la collection Europe du Musée de l'Homme en dépôt au Musée des Civilisations de l'Europe et de la Méditerranée* (Mémoire de Master 2). Ecole du Louvre, Paris.

Ferloni, J., and Sitzia, E. (2022). Quand le musée de société donne du pouvoir: Enjeux de la construction participative d'expositions au Mucem. *Culture et Musées: Le Musée de société aujourd'hui. Héritage et mutation 39.*

Koke, J., and Ryan, K. (2017). From consultation to collaboration. In P. Villeneuve and A. R. Love (Eds.), *Visitor-centered exhibitions and edu-curation in art museums* (pp. 47–55). Lanham, MD: Rowman & Littlefield.

Mallé, M.-P. (Ed.). (2014). *Le monde à l'envers. Carnavals et mascarades d'Europe et de Méditerranée.* Flammarion/Mucem.

Mirga-Kruszelnicka, A., Dallemagne, F., Ferloni, J., Maggiore, A., and Steinberg, J. (2023). Le musée du Gadjo, ou le renversement du regard–réflexion critique sur la pratique ethnographique et la muséologie. In F. Dallemagne, J. Ferloni, A.Maggiore, A. Mirga-Kruszelnicka, and J. Steinberg (Eds.), *Barvalo.* Mucem/Anamosa.

Padure, C. (2021). *From magic to psychotherapy: Mission report of the collated-survey "Romani occupations and know-how in Europe and the Mediterranean"* [Unpublished manuscript]. Mucem archive, Marseille, France.

Padure. C. (2023). Enquêter sur le travail de l'argent et les pratiques divinatoires en Roumanie. In F. Dallemagne, J. Ferloni, et al. (Eds.), *Barvalo* (pp. 60–64). Mucem/Anamosa.

Villeneuve, P., and Love, A. R. (Eds.) (2017). *Visitor-centered exhibitions and edu-curation in art museums.* Lanham, MD: Rowman & Littlefield.

Wells, M., Butler, B. H., and Koke, J. (2013). *Interpretive planning for museums: Integrating visitor perspectives in decision making.* New York: Routledge.

17

Lock & Key *Creative Expression Lab*

A CURATED SPACE DURING THE PANDEMIC

Ashley Hartman, Melanie Rosato, and Nancy Ariza

This chapter describes the exhibition *Lock & Key* and Creative Expression Lab (CEL) as an example of the three-dimensional model where Object (*x*) + Collaborative (*y*) + Cultural Democracy (*z*) = Amplify. It will provide an overview of the exhibition and will describe how this exhibition connects to the Dimensions of Curation Competing Values Model. It summarizes curatorial choices, addresses the intended audience, and discusses its connection to CEL, a socioemotional learning program designed for K–6 visitors during the pandemic.

OVERVIEW OF THE EXHIBITION

Lock & Key: Our Household Objects took place at the Everhart Museum in Scranton, Pennsylvania, United States. Due to the pandemic, the museum simultaneously held an in-person and virtual exhibition. Objects included paintings, furniture, textiles, kitchen tools, and leisure items representing the idea of home from different eras and cultures. The exhibition inquired into how societal expectations influence what we put in our personal spaces and how objects in the home reflect traditions and family history.

Permanent collections objects were curated to provoke nostalgia and inspire visitor engagement. In particular, kitchen objects promoted reflection toward family traditions and cultural roots. Because the kitchen is often a communal space used to pass down generational knowledge in the home, objects were displayed to highlight cross-cultural comparisons in the kitchen. For instance, there was emphasis on how food preparation in Asia and Africa takes place close to the floor, whereas in Western culture food preparation involves standing.

One installation included twenty-seven spoons spanning different time periods and cultures. Spoons included materials, designs, and engravings that embodied cultural significance, such as Indigenous heritage or African ancestry. In CEL, we inquired into social and emotional themes by asking visitors to consider positive memories about using spoons with important family members or friends. Visitors described how spoons were used to hold and transport nutrients, to help sick or hungry individuals, and to nurture loved ones. We also facilitated a discussion contrasting wooden spoons used for utility to gold, silver, or bronze spoons that emphasized wealth and social status through ornate design features (see figure 17.1).

Dower chests, or hope chests (see figure 17.1) were included due to their significance as objects in families, offered as gifts symbolizing life and love. Sentimental objects were stored inside, serving as conversation pieces about their origin and family histories. Textiles and quilts prompted reflection about the changing roles of women over time, values relating to women's domestic roles in the home, and societal and family expectations about women in the workplace (see figure 17.2).

Figure 17.1. *Lock & Key* objects: (top left) *Afternoon Tea*, ca. 1920, Francis Coates Jones (1857–1932), Gift of Louise Chubb, 0.67. (Top right) *Spoons* from the Collection of the Everhart Museum. (Bottom left) *Dower Chest*, 1787, American Artist, Gift of Mrs. J.L. Robertson, 46.102; *Patchwork Quilt*, ca. 1890, American Artist, Gift of Mrs. Clancy, 51.58 (Bottom right). *Clothesline* from the Collection of the Everhart Museum. COURTESY OF THE EVERHART MUSEUM OF NATURAL HISTORY, SCIENCE AND ART, SCRANTON, PENNSYLVANIA.

Ashley Hartman, Melanie Rosato, and Nancy Ariza

Figure 17.2. *Lock & Key* textile. *Patchwork Quilt*, 1890, American Artist, Gift of Arthur T. Gregorian, 51.211. COURTESY OF THE EVERHART MUSEUM OF NATURAL HISTORY, SCIENCE AND ART, SCRANTON, PENNSYLVANIA.

CREATIVE EXPRESSION LAB

CEL offered K–6 visitors a space to express imagination during the pandemic. Gallery tours emphasized discussions about family life and experiences at home during COVID-19. Saturday artmaking workshops took place weekly. Virtual programming incorporated asynchronous age-appropriate engagement and interpretive resources, videos, and artmaking tutorials. Museum educators distributed art materials to families. Similarly, Sandell (2003) underscored the importance of social inclusion and enhancing confidence, self-esteem, and creativity in the museum.

CONNECTION TO THE COMPETING VALUES MODEL

The Competing Values Model is a tool for defining intentional curatorial practices. The model encompasses eight exhibition types demonstrating a range of practices with different interpretive intentions, emphases in curatorial power, and curatorial intent focusing on different objectives and audience appeal. Each approach emphasizes the potential to achieve different goals, attract, and accommodate specific visitor audiences.

OBJECT FOCUS (X AXIS)

Lock & Key had an Object interpretive focus. Objects were grouped together in ways to encourage the visitor to derive personal meanings and connections with their own family life, heritage, generation, or culture to promote exploration of interrelated or abstract ideas similar to Paris (2002). CEL educational discussions were centered around observing, inquiring, and responding to authentic experiences with the objects, as informed by Paris (2002) and Simon (2010). Similar to experiences noted by Carr (2003), the spoon installation, for instance, provoked curiosity and exploration. In the gallery, children sat on socially distanced circular mats during object discussions. Museum educators and graduate art therapy students brought in antique, wooden, and nontraditional kitchen objects to touch and experience. Visitors explored memories of nurturing, safety, being cared for, relationships, and generational traditions. Visitors created clay spoons, collaged spoons, and assemblages using miscellaneous mixed-media objects on kitchen serving platters in CEL.

COLLABORATIVE CURATORIAL POWER (Y AXIS)

This exhibition's curatorial power (y axis) was Collaborative. Divergent perspectives visualized the focus on object interpretation. It required a team approach, integrating interdisciplinary perspectives to contribute toward the experience. Community members associated with the ArtsEngage! grant participated, including the museum, university, schools, mental health referring agencies, and the Office of Youth and Family Services. Gallery tours and workshops were facilitated collaboratively by a supervising art therapist, art therapy graduate students, and museum educators. This shared authority was intended to allow personal interpretation and create meaningful experiences for visitors.

CULTURAL DEMOCRACY CURATORIAL PRACTICE (Z AXIS)

The z axis in the model focuses on curatorial intent. The desired outcomes of the exhibition are usually reflected through the exhibition narrative, interpretive texts, catalogs, websites, press releases, programming, and other explicit materials. Cultural Democracy focuses on collaboration, multiple perspectives and cultural views, community-based discourse, partnering opportunity for social action, and social justice. We considered that it would have been a disservice to visitors to curate with the intention to impress the viewer through overly formal language or unattainable concepts. We endeavored to relate to the personal lived experiences of visitors, emphasizing natural curiosity. Accessible use of language was intended to provide visitors with a sense of belonging.

This exhibition was an example of a community-driven Cultural Democracy approach (Graves, 2005). It embraced diverse points of view and shared decision-making. It promoted social action through offering a space for social engagement outside the school setting for children who were experiencing social isolation. The program was developed to reach children with exceptionalities and children from diverse backgrounds needing extra support and resources due to poverty, trauma, or other factors associated with mental health. These collaborative curatorial activities explored how exhibitions might use digital offerings with

Ashley Hartman, Melanie Rosato, and Nancy Ariza

programming (Kidd, 2017; Rodney, 2018). The intention was to use the museum as a community learning institution during the pandemic.

CURATORIAL CHOICE AND INTENTION

The exhibition choices were explicit and implicit. Text panels and objects were grouped by theme, catering to all ages for the general public. Minimal context was provided, promoting visitor interpretation around big ideas. These intentions aligned with constructivist approaches to museum practices that emphasize the development and construction of individualized interpretations (Hein, 1994, 1998; Hooper-Greenhill, 1994). Thematically arranging objects with cultural and historical significance alongside presumably mundane objects was done with the distinct intention to combat elitism. CEL accommodated visitors from the community representing diverse backgrounds in regard to (dis)ability, developmental ability, religion, gender, sexuality, ethnicity, race, indigenous heritage, and socioeconomic status. Visitors included 667 adults, 106 seniors, 140 students, 158 children ages six to twelve, and 116 children ages five and younger during the exhibition. A total of 388 users accessed the exhibition through the Culture Connect App.

CONCLUSION

The collaborative nature of exhibitions that Amplify may foster opportunities for promoting the health and well-being of visitors through programming and interdisciplinary cooperation. Although the intended audience for *Lock & Key* was K–6 children, the exhibition interpretive focus leaned toward the object. However, object-based inquiry questions in the gallery addressed multifaceted themes relevant to visitors' family histories and personal lived experiences. These collaborative curatorial activities offered visitors opportunities for self-directed engagement resulting in personal meaning making (Kidd, 2017; Rodney, 2018). Without the connection to CEL, the exhibition may have followed a more traditional practice of Lone Creative curatorial power and Object interpretive focus. Without an emphasis toward Cultural Democracy, it may have aligned with Exclusive practice. We encourage museum practitioners to consider how museum education or therapeutic arts programming may enhance exhibitions to meet the divergent needs of the general public.

REFERENCES

Carr, D. (2003). *The promise of cultural institutions*. Lanham, MD: AltaMira Press.

Graves, J. B. (2005). *Cultural democracy: The arts, community, and the public purpose*. Urbana: University of Illinois Press.

Hein, G. E. (1994). The constructivist museum. In E. Hooper-Greenville (Ed.), *The educational role of the art museum* (first edition, pp. 73-79). New York: Routledge.

Hein, G. E. (1998). *Learning in the museum*. New York: Routledge.

Hooper-Greenhill, E. (1994). Museum learners as active postmodernists: Contextualizing constructivism. In E. Hooper-Greenhill (Ed). *The educational role of the art museum* (first edition, pp. 67-72). New York: Routledge.

Kidd, J. (2017). *Museums in the new mediascape: Transmedia, new participation, ethics.* New York: Routledge.

Paris, S. G. (2002). *Perspectives on object-centered learning in museums.* New York: Routledge.

Rodney, S. (2018). *The personalization of the museum visit: Art museums, discourse, and visitors.* New York: Routledge.

Sandell, R. (2003). Social inclusion, the museum and the dynamics of sectoral change. *Museum and Society* 1(1), 45–62.

Simon, N. (2010). *The participatory museum.* Museum 2.0.

MEDIATE

Audience (*x*) + Lone Creative (*y*) + Democratization of Culture = **Mediate**

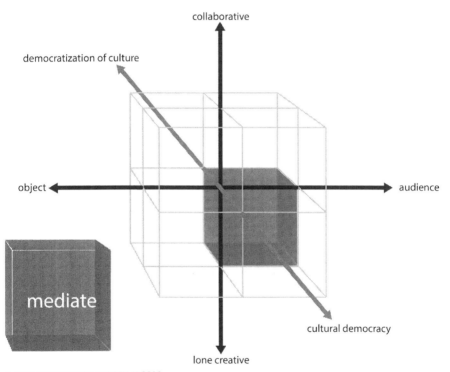

IMAGE COURTESY OF AUDREY JACOBS.

18

The Same Four Walls

INSPIRATION AND REFLECTION DURING A GLOBAL PANDEMIC

Lesley Marchessault

In October 2021, Provincetown Art Association and Museum installed an exhibition titled *The Same Four Walls: Intimate Interiors from the Permanent Collection*, curated by Lesley Marchessault. Culled from the museum's own collection of over four thousand pieces, the exhibition focused on work that depicted scenes and activities associated with solitude and confinement. Of the thirty-six pieces in the exhibition, thirty were two-dimensional (paintings, drawings, prints, and photographs) and six were three-dimensional mixed media (bronze sculptures, wooden printing block, and a silhouetted image on vellum made out of salt). All were selected because they either represented a scene of domestic interior space, mimicked solitary artistic progress, or paid homage to a household item (such as a measuring cup) with which we all became more intimate during lockdown (the exhibition was conceived of as the world passed the one-year mark of a global pandemic). After so many months of solitude, I sought to unite visitors through shared visual imagery and forge connections with others by highlighting common experiences. I placed significant emphasis on artistic creation by selecting works that either illustrated the artists' domain or highlighted a particular practice. Viewers were encouraged to ruminate on their experience with being alone in their spaces, to ask themselves whether creativity flourished or was stifled, and to consider whether their relationships with their most intimate surroundings changed or intensified. Wall text and a curatorial statement in the exhibition brochure identified these meditative points and asked viewers to use the works as a catalyst to examine their contemporary creative output. The intent was to have the viewer reflect upon their own practice while noting the role contented home life plays in that practice, for better or for worse.

Figure 18.1. A view of the exhibition, *The Same Four Walls: Intimate Interiors from the Permanent Collection*, on display at Provincetown Art Association and Museum, in October 2021. PHOTO COURTESY OF JIM ZIMMERMAN/PROVINCETOWN ART ASSOCIATION AND MUSEUM.

USING THE DIMENSIONS OF CURATION COMPETING VALUES EXHIBITION MODEL

Assigning *The Same Four Walls* its proper place on the Dimensions of Curation Competing Values Exhibition Model's z axis (representing curatorial intent) proved difficult. The x and y axes are straightforward enough; x = Audience Focused and y = Lone Creative Power. Initially, I supposed *The Same Four Walls* to find its home on the z axis on the Democratization of Culture side, because it followed a more traditional curatorial practice of a curator selecting work autonomously and asked viewers to meditate on their experience, using the works as catalysts for thought. While I maintain this view, I would also add that it skews toward Cultural Democracy in that it only fulfills its purpose as an exhibition when the audience's reaction is included in its final reporting. Cultural Democracy in this sense encourages action by using the meditative thought as the catalyst; by the viewer examining their own experiences, they are spurred to continue, enhance, or fully alter those experiences. In other words, putting significant emphasis on the visitor's personal takeaways shifts the z axis toward Cultural Democracy, as it encourages future action as a result of present meditation.

SPECIFIC CURATORIAL CHOICES

I selected works to represent a wide range of lifestyles that may have occurred during the lockdown months. Some pieces depicted quiet solitude in a home such as a chair in front of a fireplace, a solitary figure reading. Others showed a kitchen in disarray, the scene jumbled, harried, and full of clues that life was bustling just on the outer edges of the canvas. Still other works were meant to evoke not the realities of the pandemic, but rather an expression of artistic practice. For example, one large format work features a woman lazily gazing at the viewer, her veined hand resting languidly from its ninety-degree bent wrist above. Dark shadows appear on the sides of her nose and the left side of the face, and a shadowy bookshelf barely reveals its hazy existence in the background. Upon first glance, this piece appears to be a painting, but closer inspection reveals it is in fact a photograph. In order to achieve the painted effect, the artist applied paint directly on the model before photographing in dramatic lighting, leading to the final painterly impression. (If painting on and then photographing yourself doesn't seem like an activity you would've done during lockdown, what is?) This piece was added to evoke memories in the viewer of the activities they embarked upon during lockdown—or the artistic rules they may have tried to bend or even break.

Although I had solitary freedom to select the works in the exhibition, the true goal of the show was only fulfilled once viewers interpreted the works as they related to their own lives. Works in the exhibition were certainly heralded for their artistic integrity and quality, but the show sought neither a formal reading of the works nor a didactic approach to their success. By removing the emphasis from the curatorial hand deeming what is or is not of import, the implication lies instead with the viewer making the singular choice: what is important to me here, and how do I interpret it? I would posit, however, that an exhibition of this nature in a formal setting such as a museum could not promote sole Cultural Democracy, since the selection of the works came from a singular museum employee, a human with preconceived learned notions and background. When the pieces the viewer sees in the exhibition are chosen for them, I would argue that true Cultural Democracy is impossible.

VISITORS AND THEIR REACTIONS

Although presented as part of the museum's schedule for all visitors, the exhibition was primarily conceived of for artists. In my daily activities, I work closely with members of the museum and hear feedback from artists lamenting the loss of inspiration during lockdown. I decided to challenge creative types to look inward and dissect if their surroundings may have had an impact on the creative process, in an effort to identify and extract the blockage. Because *The Same Four Walls* took place in the off-season winter months, the primary visitors were the museum's members. Provincetown is heralded as the oldest continuous arts colony in the United States, and that distinction is embedded into the cultural identity of its townspeople, many of whom identify as artists and are members of the museum. The audience response was extremely positive. Respondents remarked on the "very timely theme" saying the exhibition was "current and very intriguing." One observer said, "the work you picked made for a really thought-provoking exhibit in the context of the last 20 months." Visitors said they sought the quiet meditation of walking through a museum after being alone in their homes for so long. Despite its capacity limit of five hundred, the museum capped its admission numbers at fifteen people per one-hour time slot due to the pandemic. Many visitors said they saw the museum as a safe, viable place to take in a cultural experience and reignite their own inspiration.

REFLECTIONS

The Same Four Walls—or really any exhibition of this nature—that truly exists only to serve as a catalyst for human thought, reflection, and interaction, would indeed benefit from collaborative curation. As stated, the singularity of one curatorial approach limits the pieces selected to that one person's background or interpretation of the theme. Bringing in diverse voices would amplify a range of experiences and therefore engage a wider audience. Similarly, if the works from the collection were displayed alongside works created by artists during their quarantine time, we could make comparisons between the circumstances in which the work was created.

19

SCREEN IT

A MEDIATION-DRIVEN APPROACH TO ART, TECHNOLOGY, AND AUDIENCES

Pieter Jan Valgaeren

In addition to the practical and technological challenges of curating digital art (online and offline), curators must attend to the screen culture context of younger audiences with their own backgrounds, concerns, and vocabulary. Young people often have different expectations and needs than typically delivered by the average object-focused and top-down curated exhibition or festival. Although I am biased by a traditional background, curating digital art has shifted my practice over the years from a traditional Lone Creative curator with an interpretive focus on the object to a team-based and community-driven perspective. Based on the concept that art can lead to social change when implemented in the educational system, participation in the SCREEN IT festival—an example of a Dimensions of Curation exhibition that Mediates—provided insights on Cultural Democracy and inclusiveness. This chapter discusses the opportunities for art festivals, in particular digital and technology art festivals, to work with a strong mediation focus.

A FESTIVAL NEEDS A COMMUNITY

The Stadstriënnale Hasselt-Genk started at the turn of the millennium as a project to bring a more international approach to the local art scene in a suburban area known as a former coal mine region. Supported by a wide range of cultural institutions and museums dealing with fashion, heritage, design, and contemporary art, each edition focused on joining forces, attracting (new) audiences, and revitalizing the local art scene. To achieve these goals, I developed *art=time* as a central concept to move toward *edu-curation* (Villeneuve and Love, 2017) and mediating as presented in Dimensions of Curation Competing Values Model.

Figure 19.1. (Top) Aram Bartholl's Obsolete Presence. (Bottom) Anna Riddler's Mosaic Virus, gallery view. PHOTO COURTESY OF THE AUTHOR.

ART = TIME

In my model, time is centered in a triangle with the artist, the intermediary, and the audience at each corner, with each having their own use and context of *time*. First, there is the concept of the amount of *time* the artists have to live and learn: time to train themselves and create (reflective) works. Second, there is the *time* of the intermediary (museum, gallery, director, curator or mediator/interpretation specialist). This is the time they have to educate themselves, read, visit shows and studios, and map audiences. Third, there is the *time* for the audience to interact with art. This is the time to train their eyes and their brains, not only with knowledge about the art that triggers their interest, but also to reserve mental time for art, which can impact their personal existence.

In this model, a good exhibition concept finds itself in the middle of the triangle, creating stories to attract people toward art and artists and having all of them engage with each other. Best practices, in my view, are these where edu-curation is happening without the audience even knowing it. A well-defined theme or question, rooted in the daily lives of the targeted audience, is used as an impetus to "buy time" and interact with prospective audiences. Living in the "Age of I" where artists emancipated from schools and movements and audiences from religion, state, or common narratives, art can capture our vision and freeze our worldview for a second. As intermediaries, we should foster this moment to show how art can expand, enlarge, broaden, and brighten society.

MAPPING THE DIGITAL–EDUCATIONAL PERSPECTIVE

The SCREEN IT festival (October 2019–February 2020) consisted of two major exhibitions and seventeen parallel events (lectures, solo shows, pop-up projects, interactions in the city). The central exhibitions showcased the work of thirty-seven artists, mixing up older and referential media artists and young, upcoming artists who mostly produced new works for the festival. By bringing in works of pioneers such as Wolf Vostell, Nam June Paik, Tony Oursler, or Bill Viola, younger visitors had the opportunity to get in touch with the artistic approach versus technology from the early days. It also gave an older audience a reference, as new media art might not appear as attractive to them. Mapping fifty years of screen culture, the exhibitions aimed at giving an overview of trends from the past but more importantly they examined how contemporary art and screen culture are dealing with such contemporary themes such as artificial intelligence, privacy, fake news, gender, screen culture, censorship, or blockchain. Our goal with SCREEN IT was to present the pulse of generation(s), looking through the eyes of today's people. Therefore, we created an interactive and multilayered #-driven matrix and two central interpretation lines linking the object to our expected audiences and their interactions.

The festival theme naturally linked to all surrounding grade schools for audience development. Their curricula emphasize contemporary issues such as digital literacy, machine learning artificial intelligence, sexting, etc. Although there are trainings and tools at hand to address these themes, a lot of them hardly connect

Figure 19.2. (Left) visitors to Stadstriënnale Hasselt-Genk. (Right) selfie AR project.
PHOTO COURTESY OF THE AUTHOR.

to the (visual) world of students. We created a matrix with the following hashtags: #blockchain #screenaddiction #selfie #privacy #fakenews #onlinedating #sexting #gaming #AI #censorhip #gender #internetaesthetics. By mapping these topics with our educational team in a matrix of # buzzwords beforehand, I could focus on selecting works that could be flanked by at least two of these #, thus creating the narrative and framework of the festival.

The first interpretation line was the formal concept of screen as work of art, in all its different sizes, techniques, and historical features. It was stunning to see how the different age-groups had totally different responses and interaction toward the presented technology (from wooden cabinet televisions to slide projectors to interactive television or virtual reality glasses). For example, a toddler stepped out of her pram to swipe on a wall where Rodney Graham was slowly projecting the same image, apparently hoping to see a different picture, while an older couple responded aloud while wearing virtual reality sets.

Secondly, the idea of *impact* served as a mediation line. While the traditional media still works from a one-to-many model, our current screen culture works with the one-to-one model. It creates a more personal interaction between sender-receiver, which is one of the most interesting features of digital art. Dries Depoorter created a white, Japanese Zen-inspired booth in which you could charge your cell phone, but only if you kept sitting in front on a chair with your eyes closed and the phone lying in front of you.

MAKING DIGITAL ART TANGIBLE

From the beginning, I was intrigued by participatory art works and projects that could attract people to the festival and create co-ownership. We addressed these questions of ownership and participation by programming three sorts of artworks/projects within the central exhibitions or in parallel events.

The first approach used existing artworks that demanded a certain form of participation or action from the audience, as directed by the artist. Artist Tom Galle worked with the meme "Netflix and chill," online slang for a consensual night of fun. He created a physical room in a container on the festival site with a bed and television, towels and slippers with Netflix logos, and a refrigerator. Visitors had to book the room for a night through Airbnb to experience it.

A second approach used participative creative adaptations based on an existing artwork. The students of the art academy (four to eighteen years of age) worked with an augmented reality app based on the notion of *selfies*. After taking a selfie, they create a classical self-portrait by painting or drawing that they later could animate and make come to life with an augmented reality app. *TV Garden*, Nam June Paik's take on screen culture in the 1970s and 1980s, was the inspiration for *Villa Basta*, a platform for youth aged twelve to eighteen. With the permission of the Nam June Paik Foundation, they were able to reenact the work in a contemporary 2.0 version. Their versions were placed around the city in glass containers. Immediately passersby started to take pictures of themselves being broadcast in the screens, just as Paik predicted almost fifty years ago.

A third wave of participative projects, in which the concept of screen itself was central, came nearly by itself. University design students came to the festival with the idea of turning their bikes into screens. Using hardware that was integrated into the wheels of their bikes and hacking the software that was delivered with it, they drove their bikes through the city projecting screen-based poetry or art works that were featured in the festival. The same grassroots approach came from the *Quartier Canal* project. In this (post-)industrial part of the city, there is a workshop that restores all sorts of screens. Residents were invited to come over to start re-using the screens as landmark beacons during workshops. These evenings became meetup points that supported the cohesion in the neighborhood.

CONCLUSION

A festival is always a roller coaster for an ad hoc team led by the vision of a curator, presenting the results of months of research, discussions, scenography headaches, and mediation debates. In the moment it opens, you can see the dynamics and impact. I'm particularly proud of the result of the teamwork and the sacrifices they made thinking outside the box. Our methodology was untested for us and fairly new to the audiences. With a young and dynamic team, we created a local impact, due to off-cultural track locations, but one that counted. Colleagues and artists from London, San Paolo, Berlin, and Paris visited and could hardly believe the art/artist selection we showcased, but I felt most satisfied and surprised with the results of the parallel projects. Biking with the students and scratching foil from the broken screens with the people of Quartier Canal gave me goosebumps. Or the moment a six-year-old girl guided me through their class presentation of selfies, paintings, and augmented reality made me consider again what presenting art is all about, creating those magic moments of connection between people. Although the festival started as an exhibition that Mediates (Audience Focus + Lone Creative + Democratization of Culture), I now more than ever believe in a model that starts from mediation, with a team supporting the curator to link the curatorial practice and research toward an audience that embraces it. In approaching access for all audiences (democratization of culture), the ownership felt through participation starts to move the festival to more cultural democracy approaches.

REFERENCE

Villeneuve, P., and Love, A. R. (Eds.). (2017). *Visitor-centered exhibitions and edu-curation in art museums*. Lanham, MD: Rowman & Littlefield.

INSPIRE

Audience (*x*) + Lone Creative (*y*) + Cultural Democracy (*z*) = **Inspire**

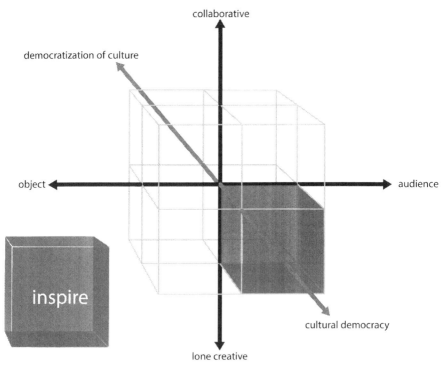

collaborative

democratization of culture

object ← → audience

cultural democracy

lone creative

inspire

20

The Boneyard

INSPIRING THROUGH IN-GALLERY ARTIST DEMONSTRATIONS

Courtney Taylor, Andy Shaw, and Grant Benoit

In January 2020, Louisiana State University (LSU) Associate Professor of Ceramics Andy Shaw submitted an exhibition proposal with the subject line "collection of ceramic demonstrations." Looking back through the lens of the *Dimensions of Curation Competing Values Model*, Shaw's vision for *exhibition as demonstration* was clear from the outset. He proposed an exhibition drawn from LSU School of Art's teaching collection, or *boneyard*, of bisqueware works created over years of visiting artist demonstrations.[1] Shaw envisioned an exhibition that focused as much on demonstrations as objects. Interpretation and engaging visitors in a creative process would be as important as viewing artists' creative output. He was driven by his deep appreciation for, and desire to share, the generosity of craft demonstration traditions. LSU Museum of Art educator Grant Benoit and curator Courtney Taylor shared this drive and saw this project as an opportunity to experiment with exhibition practices. First, they wanted to infuse the gallery with more energy by making art-making experiences central to the project. Second, they sought to collaborate from concept through installation and facilitation to align their practice with *edu-curation* models (Villeneuve and Love, 2017).

The Boneyard captured and shared the energy and legacy of ceramics demonstrations through display of approximately two hundred bisque works from LSU School of Art's teaching collection and the creation of new works by visitors and visiting artists. The exhibition also featured rotating displays and a demonstration studio that were activated by LSU master of fine arts students, local artists, visiting artists, as well as visitors. These interfaces allowed museum visitors to join in the boneyard tradition—to share in the openness of craft demonstration traditions, exchange with artists, and explore their own creative processes (Villeneuve, 2017).

The Boneyard: The Ceramics Teaching Collection was on view at LSU Museum of Art in Baton Rouge, Louisiana, United States, from July 2021 to February 2022.

As a case study for the Competing Values Model, *The Boneyard* aligns most closely with exhibitions that Inspire. As co-curated by Andy Shaw, Grant Benoit, and Courtney Taylor, curatorial authority (*y* axis) was retained by the institutional curators with traditional "expertise." But the interpretive focus of the exhibition firmly centered the audience (*x* axis)—objects were selected, displayed, and interpreted to support visitor interest, engagement, and individual meaning-making. Curatorial Intent included Democratization of Culture (*z* axis) through a design that supported broad access but waded into the Cultural Democracy realm of the axis through inclusion of diverse perspectives in programming and creation and display of new objects.

APPLYING THE COMPETING VALUES MODEL: A REFLECTION

CURATORIAL POWER

The co-authors acted as co-curators, making decisions together and leading aspects of the project according to our respective strengths. Despite internal collaboration between the museum and the school of art, the exhibition was conceptualized internally, maintaining institutional control. Authority was shared in a limited way. Visitors and visiting artists (including student, community-based, and nationally recognized ceramic artists) facilitated in-gallery programs and created new works, acting as *contributors* or *collaborators* according to Simon's (2010) levels of participation. Inclusion of community knowledge bearers, such as local ceramicists, K-12 art teachers, and university students, in our conceptualization and design phases moved our approach further along the Competing Values Model's Collaborative, Inclusive, and Cultural Democracy dimensions. The exhibition design included three display cases rotating thematic groupings, groupings of works by individual artists, and works made in the in-gallery studio space, respectively. Planning for and building additional, and more flexible, furniture earlier in the exhibition process would have better supported sharing authority through inclusion of more community-created works or community-curated groupings.

INTERPRETIVE FOCUS

Shaw's vision of inviting community(ies) into a ceramics studio set us on a path for centering the visitor from the outset by emphasizing a collection of demonstrations rather than a collection of objects. There were three priorities for our first curatorial meeting: (a) learn more about the objects in the collection from Shaw's point of view, integrating Benoit's insights as both an artist and museum educator; (b) conceive exhibition themes and outcomes, considering what we would like the visitor and their takeaways to be; and (c) conceive programming featuring student, community, and nationally recognized visiting artists as facilitators. Our intent to blur the boundary between exhibition and programming and support individual meaning-making through spatial and programming design quickly came into focus. Our approach invoked Villeneuve's (2017) notion of an exhibition as an "interface rich in challenges and educational resources visitors may choose from to support their individualized meaning-making" (p. 131).

The exhibition could be entered, engaged, and appreciated from any starting point, in keeping with Hein's (1995) elements of the constructivist exhibition. Though appreciated in terms of material, form, and artistic intent, the bisque objects were instrumentalized to support visitors' own pathways toward making meaning. Objects were selected and displayed not for mastery or canonical status—indeed these were unfinished works—but for how they might teach, demonstrate, or draw the interest of visitors and highlight underrepresented perspectives. (Again, the exclusive nature of the curatorial team admittedly created a Sympathetic approach that would have benefited from more inclusivity.) Unfinished wood furniture paralleled the unfinished state of the bisque works while remaining inviting to visitors. Aside from three text panels introducing exhibition concepts, all individual object interpretation was opt-in. iPads near display cabinets and cases allowed visitors to learn about individual objects or groupings based on their own interests. In keeping with Supported Interpretation principles, we presumed no specialized knowledge from the visitor and assumed diverse audiences would be reading texts (Villeneuve, 2017). Keeping the visitor in mind, we sought to create a space that supported interaction and exchange—deep looking, pointing, and comparing; reading and discussing; sharing and exchanging with diverse demonstrating artists; and joining in making as often as possible.

We developed three zones—a zone primarily for looking, a zone for learning, and a zone for making. The "looking" zone had our showstopping installation of the *Boneyard*, an open storage bulk display that mimicked the way a teaching collection would be displayed in a university studio. Strategic groupings and cabinet

Figure 20.1.   The gallery design for the "bulk" display of the School of Art's *Boneyard* collection sought to mimic a university studio's display by making the collection available for close looking, but also inspire comparison of similar objects or study of individual objects. PHOTO COURTESY OF LSU MUSEUM OF ART. PHOTOGRAPHS BY CHARLES CHAMPAGNE.

design broke viewing into smaller areas and prompted comparison across like forms or deep looking at individual objects. Across from this bulk display, two modular display cases rotated objects to highlight different themes and artists. Pulling pieces for these "focus" displays mimicked the way professors pull from the boneyard. The "learning" zone encouraged a longer stay and visitor exchanges. Cases featured bisque and glaze-stage, "before and after" works, or groupings of vessel forms to encourage comparison. A materials and tools case displayed each clay body at various firing stages, for example. These display cases were attached

Figure 20.2. Just across from the display featured in figure 20.1, modular units allowed multiple object rotations such as this one featuring innovative forms; pulling groups of works and returning others to the main display cases simulated the way instructors might pull pieces to teach specific techniques, and rotations kept the gallery fresh.
PHOTO COURTESY OF LSU MUSEUM OF ART. PHOTOGRAPHS BY CHARLES CHAMPAGNE.

Courtney Taylor, Andy Shaw, and Grant Benoit

Figure 20.3. Pictured here is the "teaching zone" with a nook for study of ceramics books nestled between displays comparing vessel forms (at right) and processes and surfaces (at left). The shelf on the extreme right featured varied clay bodies at different stages of shrinkage and firing alongside tools. PHOTO COURTESY OF LSU MUSEUM OF ART. PHOTOGRAPHS BY CHARLES CHAMPAGNE.

to a seating area with books on ceramics theory and practice as well as stories for young learners.

The "making and sharing" demonstration zone featured a wheel, table, drying racks with works made by visitors, and "please touch" objects. Works made by demonstrating artists were featured in a third rotating display. At all moments from conception to exhibition installation and program facilitation, a focus on audience was equally if not more important than a focus on objects.

CURATORIAL INTENT

Though never explicitly or formally articulated, our curatorial intent was to In-spire—to inspire a passion for making, an appreciation for clay, and for creative community. We sought to place visitors, students, local makers, and national ceramic artists on an equal footing by displaying their work together. Though not enacted as fully as they could have been, these efforts contributed to a Democratization of Culture with creation of an open and inviting space that inspired visitor action. We moved further toward the Cultural Democracy dimension by blurring the boundaries between exhibition and programming and focusing on introducing diverse perspectives of demonstrating artists, including their newly created works, and inviting community making and display. Our focus on ceramics demonstration and making was perhaps not conceptually activist, but a key strategy was to amplify the perspectives of diverse makers. Knowing that works created by visiting artists would add to LSU's teaching collection, we invited leading ceramic artists who were also historically underrepresented, focusing on artists of color and women. While these are not radical or groundbreaking elements of exhibition and programming practice, these efforts do invite social change by inducing new perspectives, by changing gallery representation, and by adding to the "canon" of artists included in LSU's teaching collection.

CONCLUSION

Despite the pandemic suppressing visitation, we saw success in attracting new visitors *and* deepening engagement. Making rotating displays and an in-gallery studio integral to the exhibition and interpretive design (rather than an add-on pop-up program) was a generative experiment that we hope to expand upon. These audience-focused efforts contributed to longer visits and deeper inter-action with and participation in the exhibition and programming. We missed an opportunity to lean further into experimentation with community-curated displays and the formal incorporation of artwork created by participants into gallery displays. Managing (perceived) traditional public expectations for a polished aesthetic and an informative experience with more inclusive, participatory, collaborative exhibition models is a delicate balancing act. The Competing Values Model recognizes that each exhibition will land differently on each axis and that there is value in each model depending on content and context. Experimenting outside traditional practices builds confidence and competence to conceive and execute exhibitions with greater intentionality and move toward more inclusive and socially activist dimensions.[2]

NOTES

1. Bisque refers to the state achieved after a wet clay form is completed and fired once. What remains is a porous, unglazed object. Traditionally these are displayed on shelves surrounding a teaching studio and referenced year after year by professors and students. Shaw's concept was inspired by Clare Twomey's *Factory: The Seen and Unseen*, Tate Exchange, United Kingdom, September 28 2017–October 8, 2018. http://www.claretwomey.com/projects_-_factory_the_seen_the_unseen.html
2. This project was made possible only thanks to the coordination, design, and creativity of many contributors, chief among these are Olivia Peltier, Jordan Hess, Sarah Amacker, Travis Pickett, Kyle Peruch, Kyra Jackson, Mark Shumake, and Rod Parker, as well as the many artists who generously agreed to have their work included in this unconventional project and/or demonstrated in the galleries.

REFERENCES

Hein, G. (1995). The constructivist museum. In G. Anderson (Ed.), *Reinventing the museum: The evolving conversation on the paradigm shift* (pp. 123–29). Lanham, MD: AltaMira Press.
Simon, N. (2010). *The participatory museum*. Museum 2.0.
Villeneuve, P., and Love, A. R. (2017). *Visitor-centered exhibitions and edu-curation in art museums*. Lanham, MD: Rowman & Littlefield.
Villeneuve, P. (2017). Supported interpretation: Building a visitor-centered exhibition model. In P. Villeneuve and A. R. Love (Eds.), *Visitor-centered exhibitions and edu-curation in art museums* (pp. 127–38). Lanham, MD: Rowman & Littlefield.

21

There Is No Planet B!

AN AUDIENCE PARTICIPATION PROJECT MEANT TO INSPIRE

Aline Van Nereaux

The Municipal Museum of Contemporary Art in Ghent, Belgium, or S.M.A.K. (Stedelijk Museum voor Actuele Kunst), has been developing an outreach program called *S.M.A.K. Moves* since 2015. With this program, the museum aimed to involve difficult-to-reach audiences who do not find their way to the museum individually or who would not typically seek artistic experiences. *S.M.A.K. Moves* started with some small pilot projects involving groups of teens (sixteen- to twenty-year-olds) and grew into an intensive collaboration throughout following school years. The yearly program is built around multiple contact moments between the museum and the participating schools involving discussions in classrooms, exhibition tours, co-creative work sessions with artists, and a public exhibition of their projects in the museum. Each year more than two hundred teens make their first steps into the museum and discover what art can mean through workshops in collaboration with artists. The museum believes that public engagement projects—in this case with young people—should be taken as seriously as professional artist projects. Both the process and the results carry weight.

There Is No Planet B! is one of these projects (figure 21.1). It started against the backdrop of the museum's twentieth-anniversary exhibition *Highlights for a Future*, wherein the museum tried to find answers to how young people see the future. The result was a science fiction film with an interwoven mockumentary that was shown to students, parents, and guests at a local cinema. What started as a participation project not only became an artistic project in the form of a film but also an exhibition in the museum consisting of several scale models, costumes, and props, plus a sneak preview of the film, *There Is No Planet B!* (figure 21.2). If we look at the *Dimensions of Curation Competing Values Exhibition Model*, we can state

Figure 21.1. Installation view exhibition *There Is No Planet B!*
PHOTO COURTESY OF DIRK PAUWELS.

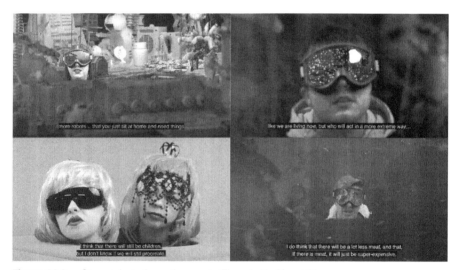

Figure 21.2. Screenshots from the movie *There Is No Planet B!*
PHOTO COURTESY OF S.M.A.K.

that this project, the exhibition and the movie, can be determined as an example of exhibitions that Inspire.

AN AUDIENCE INTERPRETIVE FOCUS (*X* AXIS)

The main curation and interpretive focus in *There Is No Planet B!* is the Audience. The starting point of the project was global climate change protest actions by young activists. At some point, there was a protest action happening in front of the museum, where Youth for Climate, a Belgian climate action movement inspired by Greta Thunberg, planted a tree in the nearby park.

At the same time, it was clear that these movements were not for everybody. For instance, for someone from a more vulnerable background, climate change protests are not at the top of the priority list—they often have other things to worry about. This is why they didn't show up at the protest actions, even though climate change may affect them more than privileged youth. *There Is No Planet B!* was the fifth collaboration of the *S.M.A.K. Moves* outreach and inclusion program in partnership with the Centrum Leren Werken (Center for Learning to Work) in Ghent, a school for young people with disrupted school experience. At the start, the project team did a survey among these students to find out what their affinity was with the subject of climate change. The result indicated most of the participants of the survey never heard of climate change protest actions. From this point onward, it was the intention of the project leader to explicitly include video interviews about their future as a component of this participatory project. The first questions were about how young people thought of preserving their future and what they think their city will look like in the future.

LONE CREATIVE CURATORIAL POWER (*Y* AXIS)

The creative project leader set the curatorial goal and intention to include the voices of these students that were absent during the protest actions. How the voices of these students could be highlighted was thought up by this one person who, as a creative director, premeditated every aspect of the project beforehand. This means the students only had to perform their parts. For example, the inspiration for the look and feel that the film would exude, namely Afrofuturism, was not chosen by the participants, who were not even familiar with this movement themselves. The students were tasked with writing out a screenplay for the film but were left in the dark about the plan for editing the film. Assisted by artists, the lone creative project leader created the outline with a clear vision of the outcome and therefore had to limit the influence of participants regarding the final product to ensure the quality of the project.

CULTURAL DEMOCRACY (*Z* AXIS)

Although coordinated by the project leader, this project reflected a Cultural Democracy position by providing students with a platform for sharing their stories, actions, and hopes for the future. Without their input, there would have been no end result. The film reflected on the community with the participation of young people showing their vision of the future, within the previously defined constraints and expectations of the project leader. The result departed from the theme of social activism, namely to make the voice and opinion of the young participants audible for their peers and a wider public through the presentation of the film and the accompanying exhibition. Throughout the film, the different visions the young people hold for the future were also discussed, embracing diverse points of view.

EXPLICIT CURATORIAL CHOICES

In this project, the role of the project leader paralleled that of an artist or curator. The audience was given a voice and participated in the project, but the final result was predetermined by one individual making all the decisions assisted by a team of artists.

The creative power of the resulting film and exhibition relies, however, on the unscripted elements such as their thoughts and stories, together with elements such as characters, costumes, props, and twists in the scenario. Because of the many moments in which the participants' input played a role, we can speak of a full-fledged co-creative process that was inspiring for the participants. The curatorial choice to allow audience input only within certain limits was thus explicit. The participating youth didn't experience the constraints and framework as something they had to follow or had no impact on. However, the complexity of the production sometimes alienated them from the purpose. We learned that it was important to clearly communicate the expected results the curator had

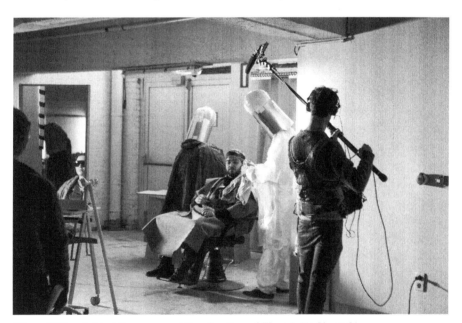

Figure 21.3. Behind the scenes of the shooting of *There Is No Planet B!*
PHOTO COURTESY OF OLIVIER DONNET

Aline Van Nereaux

in mind to avoid unpleasant surprises for the audience. In *There Is No Planet B!* the students were assigned to write a science fiction film scenario, thinking that they would film this story in its entirety. However, the curator filmed the process of the brainstorming sessions instead. Throughout the process, the students couldn't foresee the end result. This created surprised looks at the premiere of the film. They had not expected this outcome, although they were genuinely impressed with the professional result that made them feel proud of having contributed to a professional film.

AUDIENCE RESPONSE

The expectation of S.M.A.K. was that the exhibition would appeal primarily to a young audience. Because the exhibition was included in the larger exhibition throughout the museum, the project was visible to everyone. The public's reaction to the exhibition was predominantly positive. They were pleasantly surprised that the museum organized such participatory projects and impressed by the quality of the presentation, both in terms of content and visually.

The space designed by architect Olivier Goethals, in consultation with the project leader, also gave the exhibition a dynamic dimension. It gave a view of props, models, and excerpts of the video interviews within the feature film. Because of the limited co-creation sessions and the scheduled opening during the summer holidays, the exhibition part of the project was created without the input of the Centrum Leren Werken pupils and their teachers.

Figure 21.4.   Participants during the premiere of *There Is No Planet B!* at a local cinema.
PHOTO COURTESY OF TITUS SIMOENS.

REFLECTIONS ON THE USE OF THE MODEL

Even with participation projects engaging with co-creation sessions, it's helpful to go through different impacts that might be generated. *There Is No Planet B!* would not have been possible without the input and participation of the audience. It was always the intention to inspire participating students. If we look at the Dimensions Model, it could also possibly be an exhibitions that Acts if there had been a focus on a more broad collaborative power where multiple perspectives from the audience were brought together. Not only would the film and the exhibition have looked different, but possibly the impact on the audience would have been different. Thus for both the participating and visiting audiences, it is possible that this would have had made participants feel more engaged in the project for longer in different phases, which in turn could have produced the effect that they would indeed visit the exhibition at the museum. The survey afterward showed that the project left a positive impression on the participants and visitors. When asked if they would show the film to their friends, almost 50 percent of them said yes. The students also stated that there was an educational process: "I learned to be patient" (a film process often involves waiting) or "It was fun to work with everyone." The most striking aspect was that they felt more connected to the environmental issues than before, which is enough encouragement for the museum to initiate similar projects in the future.

Aline Van Nereaux

EMPOWER

Audience (*x*) + Collaborative (*y*) + Democratization of Culture (*z*) = **Empower**

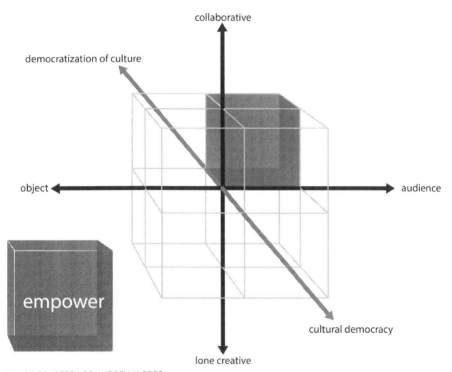

IMAGE COURTESY OF AUDREY JACOBS.

22

EmPOWER

LEARNING FROM OUR YOUNGEST COMMUNITY MEMBERS
AT THE CLYFFORD STILL MUSEUM

Nicole Cromartie and Bailey H. Placzek

Museums that align themselves with the professional standards of our field strive to be inclusive and provide their communities with physical and intellectual access to their collections (American Alliance of Museums, 1993). The Clyfford Still Museum (CSM) operates within the distinctive circumstance of stewarding a single-artist collection owned by the City and County of Denver, Colorado, United States, and by extension, its residents. This makes it particularly pertinent for the museum to think creatively about ways to engage its community.[1]

After opening in 2011, CSM staff co-developed the museum's school program with Denver-based teachers, collaborated with local artists on public programming, and in 2019, decided to plan an exhibition *with*, and not just *for*, young children from around our area. This project, *Clyfford Still, Art, and the Young Mind* (March 11–August 7, 2022), is CSM's first experiment collaborating with our community. CSM's director of education and programs Nicole Cromartie and associate curator Bailey Placzek partnered with schools and early learning centers from across the Front Range region to collaborate with children ranging in age from six months to eight years old. These 269 young children became *Young Mind*'s co-curators and assisted with every aspect of its development, from object selection to interpretation and design.

In CSM's brief ten-year history, we had never before designed programming for very young children. *Young Mind* signals to our community a new commitment to young children and their families. We realized that by planning for young children, we were creating a better experience for everyone (Kanics and Nesbitt, 2022).[2]

Figure 22.1. Young children pose in front of *Clyfford Still, Art, and the Young Mind*'s title wall.
PHOTO COURTESY OF THE CLYFFORD STILL MUSEUM.

CURATORIAL APPROACH ON THE DIMENSIONS MODEL

X AXIS: INTERPRETIVE FOCUS

Existing research on aesthetic preferences and visual development in very young children ages zero to eight years guided our approach to designing the exhibition's initial through lines and gallery themes (Danko-McGhee, 2000).[3] Researchers have shown that abstract art is not only developmentally appropriate for children, but also offers rich benefits in their growth. With this as a foundation, we identified key ideas and goals before embarking upon a collaborative process for the exhibition's development. *Young Mind*'s central idea is that young children are equal stakeholders who bring valuable perspectives that help reframe CSM's collection, exhibitions, and the holistic museum experience. We sought to expand adults' understanding of what young children are capable of, question what it means to be an art "expert," and model ways that *all* visitors can engage with abstract art. Our plan to center young children in both the exhibition's content and interpretation to achieve these goals places it within the audience realm on the Dimensions of Curation Competing Values Exhibition Model's interpretative focus *x* axis.

Y AXIS: CURATORIAL POWER

The research on aesthetic preference in early learners served only as a point of departure for the exhibition's development. We planned to conduct new research with young children in our community on their preferences of and perspectives on the work of Clyfford Still. We sought to share power and curatorial authority with our young co-curators by inviting their participation and expertise during every phase of the exhibition's creation, and we approached each partnership with complete trust, openness, and a willingness to change.

Once we began the collaborative work, the project progressed in ways we never anticipated. It soon became clear that this exhibition was more about *the process* than the final product. To begin, we identified eight schools in our area to reach a diversity of children and ensure that we would benefit from teachers' rich knowledge and experiences. Then, we broke down the exhibition's development into distinct phases and tasks to allow for varied input and consideration of our partners' schedules and curricular goals. We employed different methods during every research session depending on the children's ages and assignments. For example, six- and seven-year-olds voted on their favorite works for one gallery, while we gauged infants' preferences for another gallery by tracking eye movement, vocalizations, and pointing. This process positions the project toward the collaborative end of the Dimensions of Curation Model's *y* axis, as the input of our young co-curators determined the exhibition's final content, goals, and outcomes.

Dialogue and regular check-ins with thought partners from the early education field and other museums also shaped the project's course. One year into the show's planning, our colleagues at the Denver Museum of Nature and Science introduced us to the *Spectrum of Public Participation* (figure 22.2) (Roth, personal communication, April 9, 2021).[4] *The Spectrum* helped us frame the work we had already engaged in with our co-curators and influenced how the project evolved as we moved into subsequent planning phases (International Association for Public Participation, n.d.).[5] For example, we categorized our collaborations during

INCREASING IMPACT ON THE DECISION

	INFORM	CONSULT	INVOLVE	COLLABORATE	EMPOWER
PUBLIC PARTICIPATION GOAL	To provide the public with balanced and objective information to assist them in understanding the problem, alternatives, opportunities and/or solutions.	To obtain public feedback on analysis, alternatives and/or decisions.	To work directly with the public throughout the process to ensure that public concerns and aspirations are consistently understood and considered.	To partner with the public in each aspect of the decision including the development of alternatives and the identification of the preferred solution.	To place final decision making in the hands of the public.
PROMISE TO THE PUBLIC	We will keep you informed.	We will keep you informed, listen to and acknowledge concerns and aspirations, and provide feedback on how public input influenced the decision.	We will work with you to ensure that your concerns and aspirations are directly reflected in the alternatives developed and provide feedback on how public input influenced the decision.	We will look to you for advice and innovation in formulating solutions and incorporate your advice and recommendations into the decisions to the maximum extent possible.	We will implement what you decide.

© IAP2 International Federation 2018. All rights reserved. 20181112_v1

Figure 22.2. IAP2's Spectrum of Public Participation was designed to assist with selecting the level of participation that defines the public's role in any public participation process. The Spectrum is used internationally, and it is found in public participation plans around the world. INTERNATIONAL ASSOCIATION FOR PUBLIC PARTICIPATION WWW.IAP2.ORG

Nicole Cromartie and Bailey H. Placzek

the object selection phase under "empower" (we hung the objects selected by our co-curators in the exhibition), but the development of *Young Mind*'s label text fell more under the "consult" category (each label in the exhibition begins with a quote from one of the young co-curators, but the authors of this chapter selected the quotes and wrote the supplemental text).[6] We found it useful to recognize that a project can move back and forth along the collaboration spectrum and still ultimately be categorized as Inclusive based on its audience-centric interpretive focus and collaborative structure.

Z AXIS: CURATORIAL INTENT

Since we designed the exhibition's framework around sharing information about the aesthetic preferences of young children with our audiences, the exhibition falls within the democratization of culture area of the Dimensions Model's z axis. Our foundational intentions for *Young Mind* paired with its inclusive development process attest to the project's capacity to Empower visitors of all ages. We explicitly expressed to our partners our expectations for each collaboration, and this transparency extended into the exhibition's final design by clearly acknowledging our young co-curators' contributions and incorporating photo and video documentation of the collaborative process in the galleries. As a result, children who visit the exhibition see other children's work on the gallery walls and in American Sign Language interpretive tools, read their words in bilingual exhibition labels, hear their voices in a child-led audio experience, and are encouraged to play. By affirming the young co-curators' roles in these ways, we hope that all children who experience the exhibition feel a vested sense of ownership in our collection and belonging at the museum.

Likewise, adult visitors see our co-curators' confident and intuitive responses, reinforcing that there are no wrong answers when interpreting Still's work. Children's quotes invited them to engage in new ways of looking at art with their family, validated their own responses to Still's abstractions, and demonstrated the simple *joy* found in art experiences—a critical outcome for us all to recognize in a post-pandemic world.

AUDIENCE RESPONSE

We wanted to convey our commitment to the community by collaborating with young children, and in so doing, bring new audiences into the museum and translate "inclusive ideals into concrete practice" (Karkruff, 2014, p. 46). The students we worked with for the exhibition brought their families and friends to see and celebrate their work, and many of them are first-time visitors to CSM.

Lydia, a first-grade student and one of *Young Mind*'s most enthusiastic co-curators, had never previously visited the CSM.[7] Her mother, Sara, shared that while she and her family had visited the neighboring Denver Art Museum, she had never heard of the CSM before this project. After visiting the exhibition, we spoke with Lydia about how she felt about our work together (Lydia K., personal communication, April 13, 2022).

Bailey: *Why do you think Clyfford Still made abstract paintings?*

Lydia: *So you could see your own thing in them.*

Bailey: *How do you feel having played such a big role in bringing this exhibition to life?*

Lydia: *It feels good. Proud, happy, and excited.*

Nicole: *Are you more interested in visiting art museums after this project, or do you feel the same?*

Lydia: *Yeah, I want to go to more. And more in different places, like instead of Denver like maybe somewhere in New York.*

Figure 22.3. First-grade co-curator, Lydia from Montclair Elementary in Denver, CO, poses in front of the QR codes for the Clyfford Still, Art, and the Young Mind child-led audio and American Sign Language experiences. Lydia served as one of the hosts for the English version of the audio guide. PHOTO COURTESY OF THE CLYFFORD STILL MUSEUM.

This conversation illustrates a six-year-old's profound grasp of Clyfford Still's abstract art, pride in her contributions to a museum exhibition, and newfound interest in traveling to visit other art museums. Lydia now knows that art museums are places where she belongs and that her voice matters (Donahue, 2022).

REFLECTIONS

During this process, we discovered that inclusive exhibition practice yields many unintentional outcomes. Embracing a genuinely collaborative development process requires a massive time commitment, ample institutional support, a willingness to fail, creativity, and attentive organization. The activities and methods we used during research sessions with our partner classrooms were experimental, and we had no way of knowing what responses—if any—we would get from our co-curators. We found ourselves evolving the goals of the entire show as a result of each partner interaction. Our collaborators also pointed out some inherent challenges of our museum and collection not easily addressed in the scope of a single exhibition project.[8] Plus, most of the exhibition's development took place during the COVID-19 pandemic, further complicating the process. Though this may sound like a somewhat chaotic and frightening way to approach museum curation, it was exhilarating and enlightening.

We will continue to frame our exhibition development intentionally on the Spectrum of Public Participation and make our decisions transparent to our audiences. We've assembled an evaluation team who are using observations, surveys, and interviews during the run of *Clyfford Still, Art, and the Young Mind* to determine the impact of this new curatorial model on CSM and our visitors.[9] These findings will inform future collaboration and community empowerment strategies. We are eager to resume the rush of learning sparked by our work with these young children. Our continued care of these partnerships is vital to our success as an institution, the advancement of our city, and the well-being of its citizens. We have to ensure that each and every community member—no matter their age or background—knows that this collection, this museum, is theirs.

NOTES

1. When American abstract expressionist artist Clyfford Still died in 1980, he bequeathed three thousand artworks in his collection—nearly all of his life's work—to a US city that would build a museum dedicated exclusively to the study and display of his art. Still's widow, Patricia, selected Denver to receive the collection in 2004. The CSM staff works to display and care for the collection, but all of the artwork is owned by the City and County of Denver.
2. This idea reflects the underlying principles of universal design as outlined by architect Ronald Mace, which emphasizes the importance of considering a wide variety of users and types of learners when designing systems, products, and environments. "Benefits and Drivers." Centre for Excellence in Universal Design. https://universaldesign.ie /what-is-universal-design/benefits-and-drivers/. For discussion about how these ideas are applied in museum environments with young audiences in mind, see Kanics and Nesbitt (2022).
3. The literature review in Dr. Kathy Danko-McGhee's book *The Aesthetic Preferences of Young Children* (2000) was formative in our thinking for this exhibition.
4. The Denver Museum of Nature and Science created their own version of the chart to inform how they approach authentic community engagement at their museum.
5. There is no date listed for this publication on the website; this date range was shared via E. Ernst, personal communication, April 26, 2022.

6. Sample label for PH-247, the largest painting in our collection: *"Three 'Big Blue' paintings put together equals a megalodon . . . that's a prehistoric shark." —Bodhi and Lydia, first grade / Our co-curators were fascinated by PH-247, lovingly referred to as Big Blue. They laid down in front of it to get a new perspective; related its size to large animals; wondered aloud how much paint and time it would take to create; and pointed out the many different blues.*
7. Lydia selected objects for gallery 9, was quoted in wall text, served as one of the hosts of the audio experience, and participated in a press interview with a local journalist.
8. Some examples include the fact that many of our built-in displays are too high for very young children to experience; we do not have comfortable, private spaces for nursing; and deep-seated perceptions about the appropriateness of modern art museums for young children prompted difficult internal conversations and an overall organizational culture shift.
9. The *Clyfford Still, Art, and the Young Mind* evaluation team includes Laureen Trainer of Trainer Evaluation and Dr. Lori Ryan of University of Colorado, Denver's School of Education and Human Development.

REFERENCES

American Alliance of Museums. (1993, revised 2000). *Core standards for museums*. https://www.aam-us.org/programs/ethics-standards-and-professional-practices/core-standards-for-museums/

Danko-McGhee, K. (2000). *The aesthetic preferences of young children*. Lewiston, NY: The Edwin Mellen Press.

Donahue, M. (March 14, 2022). Kids curated the Clyfford Still Museum's latest exhibit and proved they understand abstract art better than adults. *Denverite*. https://denverite.com/2022/03/14/kids-curated-the-clyfford-still-museums-latest-exhibit-and-understand-abstract-art-better-than-adults/

Hegert, N. (April 8, 2022). Review: Pint-sized art critics weigh in on Clyfford Still. *Southwest Contemporary* 5. https://southwestcontemporary.com/review-pint-sized-art-critics-weigh-in-on-clyfford-still/

International Association for Public Participation. (n.d.) Public participation pillars: Internationally recognized principles for making better decisions together. https://cdn.ymaws.com/www.iap2.org/resource/resmgr/Communications/A3_P2_Pillars_brochure.pdf

Kanics, I., and Nesbitt, K. (2022). Using the goals of universal design to improve exhibitions for kids. *Exhbition* 40 (1), 77–83.

Karkruff, X. (2014). "Queer matters: Transforming the museum through ally practice." Master's thesis, University of the Arts. UArts Library Catalog.

23

Anybody Home?

Roselyne Francken and Tammy Wille

In early December 2022, *Anybody Home?* opened at the MAS (Museum aan de Stroom) in Antwerp, Belgium. As a semipermanent collection presentation, the exhibition will be on display for several years. An end date has not yet been set and is dependent on audience response, among other factors.

Anybody Home? delves into the meaning of *home*, emphasizing feeling rather than form. Formulated as a question, the exhibition title alludes to the often elusive and indefinable nature of home. Its manifold theoretical dimensions and lived realities can be presented only in a reduced form. In an effort to reach beyond these unavoidable restrictions, we encourage visitors to take the objects on display and the presented testimonies and stories as a point of departure for reflective exercise and dialogue.

Anybody Home? is conceptualized as a family exhibition. To help ensure its accessibility, recognizability, and relevance to both children and adults, its curation is supported by multiple collaborative and participatory projects.

As elaborated in the following, *Anybody Home?* meets the specifications of "an exhibition that empowers" in the Dimensions of Curation Competing Values Exhibition Model; it is built on collaboration in its curatorial process as well as its presentation (*y* axis) and audience focus (*x* axis). Its overall mission and intent are oriented to Democratization of Culture (*z* axis).

CURATION AND PARTICIPATION

From the onset, it became apparent that the exhibition's curation would require multiple backgrounds or fields of expertise. Knowledge of and research into the collection as well as an understanding of the presentation and translation of (potentially loaded) themes, such as home or the lack thereof, to the exhibition's broad target audience proved essential. A co-curatorship was set up between members of the MAS public and education and the collections teams, authors Tammy Wille and Roselyne Francken.

Soon after, the MAS project team joined forces with Ghent theater collective Studio ORKA. Multilayered and emotion-focused narratives with frequent humorous undertones, appealing to children and adults alike, are ORKA's forte. The collective is renowned for its site-specific productions.[1] In close cooperation with ORKA, under direction of its head writer and co-founder, Martine Decroos, the concept for the *Anybody Home?* exhibition was further elaborated and different themes delineated. ORKA was tasked with the creation of fictitious audio stories, an interactive visitor guide that offers a playful alternative to the exhibition texts, and the production of interviews. To guarantee a well-integrated end result, a concept design for the exhibition space was developed by the collective's in-house scenographer (exhibition designer) and co-founder, Philippe Van de Velde. The scenographic design is aimed at visually supporting and complementing the exhibition narratives.

The curatorial team set up a consultation trajectory with Antwerp families to further ensure the exhibition's accessibility to children ages six to twelve and its relevance to adults, as well as a broad recognizability of the treated topics. The panel was constituted of ten families representing different ages, household compositions, and heritage and cultural backgrounds. Meetings with the family panel were organized on a regular basis and ranged in form from philosophy sessions to craft assignments.

A cooperation was established with nonprofit organization Recht-Op, which strives to raise awareness about poverty and its alleviation through policy changes. In the framework of its socio-artistic *Right to Culture* project, Recht-Op initiated a parallel trajectory about home in the Antwerp Luchtbal area. Over the course of a year, several families were introduced to the MAS and the exhibition concept and took part in workshops supervised by artist Clara Luyckx. As a collaborator of das Kunst, a nonprofit cultural organization for arts experiences for children and teenagers outside formal education settings, Luyckx was engaged to distill the participating families' input into a work of art. The artwork, as the end result of this project, is shown at the MAS.

For a few of the collection pieces selected for presentation, which are considered historically or culturally sensitive heritage,[2] efforts were made to contact representatives of the communities involved or heritage institutions in the respective countries of origin with regards to their description and/or display. This is an ongoing process for the MAS that goes beyond the framework of this specific exhibition.

EXHIBITION OVERVIEW

A solitary artwork created by Studio ORKA, a model house carved from a tree stump with extensive roots, takes up the central position in the first section of the exhibition space. It serves as an introduction. Curious visitors might be tempted to peek inside. Anybody home? This creation touches on different

Roselyne Francken and Tammy Wille

themes that are closely linked to home including rootedness or connectedness, shelter, and, on a more implicit level, privacy. The use of the tree, as a living organism, can be interpreted as referring to the potential growth of a home or the changes that occur in its context.

The first chapter of the exhibition is devoted to a theme that several of the panel families highlighted as a requirement for home—a feeling of safety and protection. "Home protectors" from the MAS collection, the majority of which are associated with religion, are shown in close proximity to a small selection of miniature houses and houseboats. Without placing focus on the possible physical forms of a home, these models illustrate the theme of protection as its shielding outer layer. Visitors can make their own "protector." There is a display case at hand where they can leave their creations and, at the same time, their marks.

The second chapter treats the topic of feeling at home beyond the limits of one's house. How important is a sense of belonging in, or connectedness to your current neighborhood, village, city, or country? Through a call for submissions posted on the MAS website and spread via our school network, photographs were gathered taken by children from their bedroom window. These photographs capture a little slice of the outside world that seeps in. A compilation of these *Room with a View* images, each with a short quote by its photographer, is included in the exhibition.

The third chapter focuses on home rituals that are often, to greater or lesser extent, part of domestic routines (e.g., hosting visitors). Hosting and hospitality are embodied by a table with objects and tableware that were seemingly left behind after a dinner party. Visitors can pull up a chair and listen to stories about the party and its guests, written by Studio ORKA.

The fourth chapter is centered around the animals we share home with, visible as well as invisible to the naked eye. The audience is encouraged to critically consider why some are mostly welcomed into our homes, while others are shunned or even feared.

The fifth chapter revolves around privacy and, closely linked to the former, keeping up appearances. The starring role is attributed to a nineteenth-century dollhouse that is used to represent the unreal ideal of the "perfect home" and the real sense of pressure that often lies in its wake. The accompanying text offers critical contextualization.

The sixth chapter is devoted to the memory of home. Photographs of people showing an object that reminds them of home and that they hold dear fill this part of the exhibition space. This theme could potentially stir deep-rooted emotions. To add a lighter note, we then encourage visitors to think about: "What if your home or the objects in it were to also remember you?" Collection pieces play the part of *tsukumogami*, vengeful spirits from Japanese storytelling that reside in household objects. If they have been ill-treated, they are likely to pull pranks on their owners.

The concluding part of the exhibition is designed as an intimate movie theater. The interviews shown here, with people living in different home contexts in and outside Antwerp, are of key importance to the overall exhibition. Inter-

Figure 23.1. *I am not really happy with this view, because I often hear people quarreling. And I often hear the noise of traffic jams and honking. But at nighttime, I like that there are trees. That calms me down.* [own translation from Dutch] Lina Amajoud, student at elementary school Crea 16 in Antwerp. PHOTO COURTESY OF LINA AMAJOUD.

Figure 23.2. Nineteenth-century dollhouse that once belonged to the Antwerp-based trading family Kreglinger. Collection of the city of Antwerp, MAS, MFA.1962.066
PHOTO COURTESY OF BART HUYSMANS.

viewees share their thoughts on the meaning of *home* and what they believe to be indispensable for feeling at home. Some of the interviews were conducted spontaneously, for example with passersby in a park, while others are the result of scheduled times, for example in a nursing facility.

CONCLUSION

Different collaborative initiatives and participatory projects have played a formative role in both the curatorial process and final presentation of the *Anybody Home?* exhibition. Valorization of the displayed objects remains a significant goal. However, the importance attributed to personal stories and testimonies, as well as

Figure 23.3. Passerby Orlando Verde being interviewed by Studio ORKA at Park Spoor Noord in Antwerp. PHOTO COURTESY OF FREDERIK BEYENS.

the incorporation of interactive activity stations, were expected to tilt the balance toward a public-oriented as opposed to an object-oriented result. Textual guidance on three levels—texts about the themes and collection pieces, the aforementioned interactive visitor booklet, and questions on the walls that concisely capture the essence of each chapter—reinforced this aim. Accommodating visitor-centered interpretative practice also influenced the object selection process. Certain collection pieces, such as the dollhouse, were chosen to take on a metaphoric role to spark dialogue and reflection, allowing them to surpass their historical function.

Developed through collaboration, visitor-oriented, and aiming for broad accessibility by gaining input from a community-based family panel, *Anybody Home?* is situated in the Empower field of the presented three-dimensional Curation Model.

NOTES

1. *Inuk*, a Studio ORKA play that was staged on the grounds of a residential youth care facility, treats the topics of home and shelter, and loneliness and companionship.
2. The terms "historically sensitive heritage" and "culturally sensitive heritage" are used here as they are defined in the German Museums Association's *Guidelines for German Museums—Care of Collections from Colonial Contexts* (2019, pp. 17–18).

REFERENCE

German Museums Association. (2019). *Guidelines for German museums: Care of collections from colonial contexts* (second edition). German Museums Association.

ACT

Audience (*x*) + Collaborative (*y*) +
Cultural Democracy (*z*) = **Act**

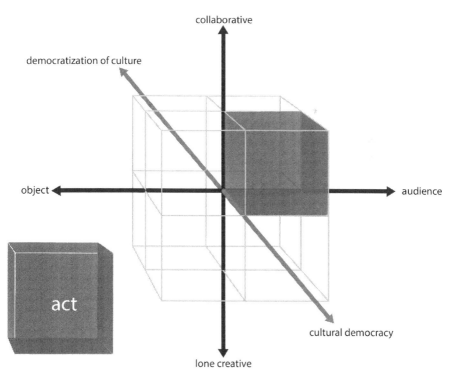

IMAGE COURTESY OF AUDREY JACOBS.

24

Collaborative Reach of a Site-Specific Exhibition That Addresses School Segregation

Katie Fuller and Patricia O'Rourke

This chapter looks at a collaboration between Katie Fuller, a curator and founder of the *Race and Revolution* art exhibition series, and Patricia O'Rourke, a PhD candidate at the University of Connecticut (UConn) whose research is focused on racial justice in education. The exhibition *Race and Revolution: Still Separate–Still Unequal*, co-curated with Larry Ossei-Mensah, traveled to Hartford, Connecticut, United States, in partnership with UConn's Dodd Center for Human Rights and the National Coalition on School Diversity. The show was on view at the Charter Oak Cultural Center from March through June 2018 and was free to the public. We discussed collaborating on an exhibition on school segregation with new partners, being both insiders and outsiders to the content, and addressing audience needs through outreach and public programs.

The exhibition addressed school segregation through the work of nine artist educators, each addressing the issue from their individual perspectives. The exhibiting artists were Dennis Redmoon Darkeem, Damien Davis, Uraline Septembre Hager, L. Kasimu Harris, jc lenochan, Carina Maye, Shervone Neckles, Nicole Soto-Rodriguez, and Marvin Touré. The exhibition fits the three-dimensional Dimensions of Curation Competing Values Model that Acts (x = Audience + y = Collaborative + z = Cultural Democracy). We will discuss each dimension of the model through how it applied to this community-focused social justice exhibition.

WHO WAS THIS EXHIBITION ON SCHOOL SEGREGATION FOR?

Katie: I wanted to show school segregation as a historical trauma. The concept was to post excerpts from historical documents alongside the artwork as historical evidence, and the contemporary artists spoke to how these issues are experienced now. The exhibitions were also influenced by where they were situated. As *Still*

Separate—Still Unequal traveled to different states, I worked with researchers in each state to understand how school segregation functioned. Mark Kohan and Glenn Mitoma, from UConn's Neag School of Education and The Dodd Center for Research, were generous sounding boards for me when *Still Separate—Still Unequal* launched in Brooklyn. We discussed having the show partner with UConn's Dodd Center for Human Rights and to include it in education conference programming. Glenn introduced me to Patricia, who led me through the *Sheff v. O'Neill* archives, a collection of documents from a landmark school desegregation case in Hartford, Connecticut. We pulled documents and quotations from the archive to obtain digital copies to print and post on the gallery walls alongside the artworks. Larry and I wanted to have teachers and students confront and wrestle with the racist logic of school segregation through the exhibition's artwork. Patricia was generating interest from schools, the library, and activist organizations.

Patricia: I was working alongside local activists in the *Sheff v. O'Neill* civil rights in education case and racial equity in education in the Hartford region. The purpose of the collaboration was to have the exhibition, as much as possible, firmly connected to the history of that case and the decades of struggle to realize its mandate since the State Supreme Court ruling in 1996. As we started the process, we had numerous conference calls from our different locations and shared our findings from the *Sheff* archives with partners at the National Coalition on School Diversity.

Community activists, artists, and organizers working on issues related to school segregation and social justice, as well as school administrators, were invited to participate in planning discussions regarding outreach, events at the exhibition, and other ways in which their work might connect. As we pored over the documents in the *Sheff* archives, I considered how fraught with emotion the issues involved were as a result of years of different experiences and frustration during and after the *Sheff* ruling. It felt important to select quotes that would encourage people to feel welcome, comfortable, and free to reflect on the pieces and the connection to the experiences in Hartford. We also needed to honor the history of those who had worked on the case and the movement before and after, and the tremendous amount of effort, energy, hope, love, and possibility that went into it.

There are many different ways to think about the audience for the exhibition: the whole greater Hartford region, those who had direct experiences related to the *Sheff* case, educators, community organizers and activists, and other visitors from the Northeast Regional Conference of the Social Studies event that was taking place at the same time. At the Dodd Center we made a great attempt to reach out to as many different groups and individuals as possible to explore opportunities for collaboration.

COLLABORATIVE PARTNERSHIPS

Patricia: We were lucky to find an English teacher engaged in teaching a class with a social justice theme at the Sport and Medical Science Academy, a Hartford Public School-run magnet school. Students participated in an in-depth project and created masks that were displayed at the exhibition. I provided lots of supporting documentation for the students to read and discuss. In addition to learning about the history of the *Sheff* case and segregation, I think that it was also valuable for them to experience being part of this collaborative effort.

Katie: Collaboration is a process of emergence. The Connecticut-based researchers and organizations explained to me what important themes might be communicated within the archives. Through meetings with Patricia, Glenn, and the National Coalition on School Diversity, we were making meaningful interactions between art, artist, and audience. In New York City, Larry and I met with each artist, prior to installation, and invited a handful of the artists to Hartford to present through performance or panel discussions. We had not intended to choose art educators for the exhibition. That we intuitively chose artists who were also teaching in schools was a powerful example of the emergence of collaboration.

CULTURAL DEMOCRACY: WHAT YOU THINK MATTERS, TOO

Katie: Cultural Democracy is rooted in discourse around topics such as race and racism. As a curator I wonder how artwork can be a conduit for these conversations—how it can be a vessel for people and absorb some of the pain and challenges that come with talking about issues like school segregation or racialized bodies in school discipline.

One of the art pieces speaks to this question. *Unfinished business: What you think matters too (Part III)* 2018, by artist jc lenochan, consists of wall space painted with chalkboard paint. On the ground in front of the chalkboard is a carpet of used and abandoned books he collected. The chalkboard displayed two questions: What was your race moment? What was your class moment? Fixed to the chalkboard was a small pouch containing chalk, inviting visitors to respond to the prompts. In order to respond, they had to walk on the books. As a curator I wondered how artwork can be a conduit for difficult conversations—how it can be a vessel for people and absorb some of the pain and challenges that come with talking about issues like school segregation or racism in school discipline. It's brave for young people to be answering such questions in a public space where their teachers and peers can read the comments. Cultural Democracy was written into the fabric of the exhibition themes. It has the potential to be written into pedagogy, as well.

Patricia: One aspect of Cultural Democracy is about fair and equitable access to cultural resources and participation in community and cultural life. We considered factors such as accessibility in location and ensuring there was no entrance fee. The gallery was open during the hours of the center, and people could move freely in and out of it. This made it feel more like the space belonged to the public than to an institution or other private entity. The center provides space for people experiencing homelessness, as well as for other community and youth programming. This led to many people visiting the gallery who might not have heard about it otherwise, just by being in the building and coming across it there.

ART MAKING WITH AN EXHIBITING ARTIST

Patricia: Student groups from two middle schools visited the exhibition and participated in activities. Teens from an afterschool program visited the exhibition as well and had the opportunity to work with a local artist who was also a community organizer. They were very interested in the pieces by Damien Davis. One of the adult mentors mentioned that they actually had the equipment to create the laser-cut acrylic kinds of pieces in Davis's work. Davis returned to Hartford and held a workshop to teach the students and mentors how to use the equipment, and he was also able to donate some supplies. One of the most important things that happened was that the students had an opportunity to hear about Davis's path in the arts and how his relationship with his mother and his mother's life experiences have contributed to the art that he was creating. It was an unexpected and special part of the collaboration.

CONCLUSION

Katie: The collaboration with UConn was exactly what I was hoping for when the exhibition first launched in 2017. Working with UConn showed me what was possible for an exhibition to be both activist and educational while also functioning as fine art. Larry was not able to participate in this conversation. During the two-year exhibition run, we worked together to source locations, as the show traveled the northeast.

Patricia: I appreciated the opportunity to participate in the type of model we selected for this exhibition. If it had been staged in Hartford without the intentional focus on the audience and collaboration, it would have been an entirely different exhibition. I think the location would have been hard to find and coordinate without local connections, and students from middle and high school likely would not have had the same level of participation. The model that was used encouraged active participation and evolving collaborations to develop over the course of the exhibition.

25

Boundless Hospitality

M FROM A DIFFERENT PERSPECTIVE

Sofie Vermeiren

In 2017, M Leuven reexamined the way it presents its collection. M chose to abandon its static, historical presentation in favor of more dynamic and narrative exhibitions. The general public was given a role, and participation became key. As part of this new approach and vision, a gallery has been dedicated to a co-creative project in which the public is actively involved.

The aim is to build an exhibition in which objects from the M collection are interpreted from the perspective of the participants. The overall theme of the exhibition and/or the choice of works of art are decided by the participants themselves. Throughout the process, they are challenged to look at and experiment from personal visions, interests, and experiences. This way, M wants to provide an enriching path for the participants and create an innovative exhibition for the public. When visitors with different backgrounds *read* the same object, multiple meanings are created. This is how M wants to make its visitors *aware* and introduce them to different views of our heritage. Eye-openers, you might say.

PROJECT *BOUNDLESS HOSPITALITY*: AN EXAMPLE OF ACT IN THE CURATORIAL MODEL

CONCEPT AND SETUP (MAY-SEPTEMBER 2016)

The first exhibition in this series of co-creative projects was *Boundless Hospitality*. Within the three-dimensional Dimensions of Curation Competing Values Model, this exhibition with its accompanying path fits on the axes Audience (*x*) + Collaborative (*y*) + Cultural Democracy (*z*) = Act. M explicitly chose to give ownership to the participants, to let them think and work together in the making of the exhibition, both curatorially and in terms of scenography, education, and communication. The participants were at various levels given great responsibility, with the support of museum experts. In several workshops the participants got to know each other and the museum staff, who gave the participants a better understanding of how the museum and the collection works, without being too directive or result-oriented. The museum experts acted mainly as a feedback platform; the participants' own choices and stories stood central.

In the end, their story was shared with the spectators, and they themselves gave tours and workshops, which also promoted interactions with other museum visitors. Because the exhibition is literally part of the series of collection presentations at M, the intention was to reach a broad audience.

For this project, M invited people with a migration background to take an intercultural look at its collection. The concept and choice for this target group was determined by a working group at M that included different profiles such as curators, but also staff from the departments of ancient art, modern art, and public relations. The concept was then tested by a number of experts. They offered their advice and thoughts about the exhibition concept linked to the target group and M's collection. This led us to choose the theme *hospitality*. The city of Leuven's diversity service helped to spread the call to participate across the different Leuven communities. Those interested in the project were invited to a meeting at the museum, where the project was explained. Eight participants committed to participate in the project.

PROCESS (SEPTEMBER 2016-JUNE 2017)

The eight participants, Liza Feyaerts (Russia), Akkacha Benazzouz (Morocco), Jing Kong (China), Julie Xinwei (China), Iwona Pom (Poland), Blanca Candia (Mexico), Gloria Margarita Vasquez (El Salvador), and Karen Vangansewinkel (Aruba), met regularly for just over a year with support of the M staff.

Over several sessions, they each selected two works from the M Collection in which they saw their personal stories reflected in some way. The first sessions focused on group dynamics, getting to know each other and the museum. Within the theme of *hospitality*, we started with two questions: Does your culture determine your identity, or do you have individual freedom of choice? Does your culture determine your view of art, or is it determined by your own personal associations?

Through active viewing exercises, based on the model of image literacy (association and observation), the participants learned what is involved in putting together an exhibition for an audience: how visitors see, what information works of art carry, how an arrangement gives extra information to the visitor and how works of art are viewed and analyzed from different perspectives (figure 25.1). To focus on the exhibition theme, we also used the place mat method (a word-and-image web around the exhibition concept of *hospitality*) using objects, newspapers, magazines, and works of art we associated with the scope of the theme.

The next step was the introduction to presentation and selection strategies in cooperation with M's curators. The M curators made a comprehensive and diverse long list of a hundred artworks from the collection. This list of images, without any art historical information, was given to the participants. In a subsequent session,

Figure 25.1. *Boundless Hospitality*, workshop.
PHOTO COURTESY OF ANDY MERREGAERT FOR M LEUVEN.

the participants and the curators shared their thoughts, feelings, ideas, and information about the various artworks. An M educator moderated these sessions, ensuring that everyone was given enough exposure and each idea was discussed equally. From there, everyone individually selected two works of art from the theme that evoked a strong story for them.

Finally, the presentation of the collection pieces was drawn up by an exhibition designer. This was done after he talked to the participants and took their wishes into account. For example, it was important to them that they could address the visitor directly at the start of the exhibition, that there was a carpet, that there was a space where people could take off their shoes, and that there was room for a guest book. The exhibition design itself should show hospitality. The participants also took mediating one step further. The personal stories linked to the art remained central.

EXHIBITION ON VIEW (JUNE 2017–APRIL 2018)

The eight participants welcomed the public to the gallery with a personal text in multiple languages. Visitors were then invited to take off their shoes and exchange them for Moroccan slippers. They could write their own stories or reactions in a guest book. The whole place exuded an air of hospitality. In the middle of the room, visitors could sit down on one of the many stools. Two large projection screens on either side of the room showed the participants' stories. On the first screen, the participants told the stories behind their choices. The

Figure 25.2. *Boundless Hospitality*, gallery view.
PHOTO COURTESY OF MILES FISCHLER FOR M LEUVEN.

video on the opposite wall showed the objects they were talking about. The camera zoomed in on object details. It was up close and very personal. For example, visitors saw a stained-glass window depicting Mary Magdalene washing Christ's feet. It inspired Blanca from Mexico to tell a story about sexual equality: "Mary Magdalene has such a humiliating task!"

Only then, at the back of the hall behind a sheer curtain, were the works of art presented. Because the participants' stories were so powerful and inspiring, and out of respect for the participants themselves, M chose to put the personal stories in the foreground, as opposed to the works of art that unravel all these stories. Visitors who wanted additional stories, music, or information about the works of art could get that from the audio guide.

REFLECTION

The cooperation with the participants did not stop at the start of the exhibition. After the opening, the public was invited to activities and were guided by the participants themselves. The participants were trained individually by an educator from M. They received a short basic training in guiding audiences, questioning techniques, and group dynamics.

The exhibition, which ran for about a year, reached a wide audience. A survey showed that our visitors appreciated this hall. The comments in the guest book were mainly positive. Many visitors directly addressed the co-curators of the exhibition: "Wow, beautifully done. Always very nice to know why someone chooses a particular piece of art. Also, the theme of hospitality comes across nicely with slippers, music, sofas, and food. Thank you!" The guides also noted that the audience lingered a long time in this room and watched an average of two to three short films (six minutes each). The participants themselves were also positive about the process and the exhibition. Karen from Aruba told us in an interview: "I really enjoyed it! Through this collaboration, I got to know a lot of people with all different backgrounds and stories. As a result, I noticed that people also all interpret *hospitality* differently. What is considered hospitable by one person may not be considered hospitable by another. You can also see these differences in the presentation." They presented themselves as ambassadors of the exhibition and, more broadly, of M. The various stories of the participants also showed their broader view of M's collection and of art in general.

Projects like this one require close cooperation between different colleagues of the museum (curator, scenographer, and audience mediator) and the participants to succeed. The museum's various departments learned a great deal from the participants. The latter's views of the art, the set, the stories, texts, and cultural mediation taught us not to be afraid to come out of our comfort zone and take a different approach to presenting a collection. The preparatory process and discussions with the participants were crucial.

Sofie Vermeiren

Part IV

Curatorial Change and Tools

26

One Museum, Three Dimensions of Curation

A SCRIPT

Jay Boda, Charlie Farrell, Madison Grigsby, and Anneliese Hardman

This chapter discusses the experiences of three graduate students reckoning with the Dimensions of Curation Competing Values Exhibition Model. As part of the Museums and Cultural Heritage Studies program at Florida State University, co-authors Charlie Farrell, Madison Grigsby, and Anneliese Hardman interned with The John and Mable Ringling Museum of Art (The Ringling) in Sarasota, Florida. Their work culminated with individual curatorial capstone projects. Within this context, the co-authors discuss their respective curatorial perspectives.

Co-author and edu-curator Jay Boda presents Charlie, Madison, and Anneliese's curatorial perspectives via *readers theatre*—an engaging teaching approach using oral storytelling and guided discussion to impart information and share idiosyncratic experiences (Saldaña, 2011; Tanner, 1993). Additionally, readers theatre fosters social learning through sharing varying perspectives, co-creating knowledge, and generating respectful discussion (Boal, 1979; Boda, 2020; Jeffries and Schramm-Pate, 2008; Savitt, 2002). For example, Love and Boda's (2017) script-based duoethnography described their co-curated visitor-centered exhibition experience. Similarly, Charlie, Madison, and Anneliese encourage museum studies classes, professional development workshops, and informal online meetups to perform the following readers theatre script to learn about their experience with the Dimensions of Curation Model.

THE SCRIPT

GET READY

Performing readers theatre in a classroom or lunch-and-learn is not complicated. It involves reading a script aloud as a group and discussing it afterward. A stage, memorizing lines, and acting ability are not needed. Readers should arrange themselves in a way that allows the audience to see and hear them. If there is no audience, readers should face one another.

THE CAST

The script's characters are the co-authors themselves, described in the following:

Jay Boda (JB): The associate director of academic affairs and collections at The Ringling. He leads a conversation with three Florida State University graduate students interning and completing curatorial capstone projects for their Museums and Cultural Heritage Studies program.

Charlie Farrell (CF): Charlie focused on performing arts curation and worked with Elizabeth Doud, The Ringling's Currie-Kohlman Curator of Performance Programs. Charlie's research focused on BIPOC artists and filmmakers in Sarasota.

Madison Grigsby (MG): Madison focused on The Ringling's circus collection and worked with Jennifer Lemmer Posey, Tibbals Curator of Circus. Madison researched historic circus posters and their exaggerated and otherwise fantastical claims.

Anneliese Hardman (AH): Anneliese focused on art exhibitions in nontraditional settings and worked with David Berry, vice president for visitor engagement and chief museum curator at Marie Selby Botanical Gardens (Selby) in Sarasota, Florida. Anneliese researched exhibition spaces beyond art museum galleries.

ONE MUSEUM, THREE DIMENSIONS OF CURATION

FIRST INTERVIEW, FIRST STEPS (RECORDED VIA ZOOM)

JB: Hi, everyone. Thanks for joining me to talk about your capstone projects. We'll do two interviews for our book chapter. This interview captures your preliminary ideas and plans for your curated exhibitions. Later, we'll do another interview to see if and how your ideas and plans changed and what you learned.

JB: Let's start with you, Charlie. Why did you choose to curate an exhibition for your capstone project?

CF: My goal is to be a curator, and I thought this would be a good opportunity to practice going through the steps from conceptual development, discovering artists, developing didactics, and imagining artwork in a space.

JB: Say more about working with artists.

CF: I love looking at art, but it's also about researching artists. You get to learn more about their process. You get to know about their history, about where they came from. It's a way to connect with art on a different level.

JB: Madison or Anneliese, do either of you want to jump in?

AH: Like Charlie, I'm interested in becoming a curator, but I'm also interested in curation as an academic concept. My capstone asks what curating means and what traditional curation looks like. It then asks what it looks like to curate nontraditionally.

JB: Explain what you mean about nontraditional curation.

AH: My project is hypothetical and challenges the boundaries of curation. It looks at curation within a botanical garden setting and explores how approach, object, and setting can be rethought in an outdoor space to involve smelling flowers or listening to music. It's important to me to incorporate multisensory and interpretive curating strategies for visitors who might not learn through only reading.

JB: Madison, why did you choose curation for your project?

MG: I'm actually not as interested in curation specifically. I really like exhibition design, which is what I hope to professionally do in the future. Like Anneliese and Charlie, I also like going through the academic process of weaving together the interesting parts of a story into one coherent narrative.

CF: To add to Anneliese's earlier point about nontraditional curation, it's important to ask: Does one person possess all the knowledge on a subject? Can a curatorial team be a mix of educators, curators, and community members? How can we also recognize community members as knowledge-keepers who have something valuable to contribute?

CURATORIAL CAPSTONE DESCRIPTIONS

JB: Let's talk about your specific projects. It's early, so you likely don't have everything figured out yet. But briefly describe your curatorial project ideas thus far.

CF: My project is a two-pronged event and exhibition proposal celebrating emerging BIPOC talent in Sarasota County. I'm planning to have an opening-night exhibition and reception in The Ringling's Community Gallery (an exhibition space inviting local organizations to share art and ideas). That will be followed by a film showcase featuring local filmmakers and film students.

AH: My project looks at the boundaries of exhibition and curation relating to nontraditional approaches, objects, and setting. I'll write an academic paper exploring my experience interning with Selby's exhibition department and create a hypothetical exhibition proposal, applying what I've learned about nontraditional curation.

MG: My project is an exhibition that will actually be installed in the Tibbals Learning Center of the Circus Museum at The Ringling. It's an exhibition of historic circus posters that explore the reality behind advertising. It interrogates the idea of what exactly "truth" means when it comes to exaggerated circus performances.

INITIAL LOCATION ON THE DIMENSIONS OF CURATION MODEL

JB: Sounds great. Now, let's try to locate where you think your curatorial projects will reside within the three-dimensional Dimensions of Curation Model. What type of exhibition do you think your projects will be?

MG: I initially thought this process would exclude me because I trend toward the Lone Creative. Instead, I'm working with the Curator of Circus to select posters and design an exhibition. I'd say I'm in the middle between an object and audience interpretive focus. I'm presenting information about the posters, but I'm also asking the audience to interpret the posters for themselves—to determine if they think what they see is fact, fiction, or exaggeration. There's freedom to investigate, but I'm guiding their response so, I'd say I'm within **MEDIATE: Audience + Lone Creative + Democratization of Culture.**

CF: My project has more of an object focus than an audience focus. I also see my project as more collaborative versus Lone Creative because I'm working with local contemporary artists in selecting objects and films. Within the z axis, I think I'm closer to democratization of culture because I'm not including wider audience input or response. So **AMPLIFY: Object + Collaborative + Cultural Democracy**?

JB: Well, looking at the model, I think what you described is closer to **EMPOWER: Audience + Collaborative + Democratization of culture.**

CF: Well, I feel like my intention would be **Amplifying** talents in the community. I don't think I want my audience to act in any way that's different than what they're already doing.

JB: Okay, let's go with **Amplify** for now and see how your project evolves through the semester. Anneliese, you have two potential ideas for your capstone but haven't decided which direction you're going in yet.

AH: Correct. I need to do more research about nontraditional curation and exhibitions first. From there, I will see which of my ideas applies better to Selby's exhibition program. One idea exhibits and sells the art of female Cambodian artists—encouraging visitors to **Act** by buying the art. The other idea creates a sensory experience for audience members, resulting in more free rein as they engage with materials. I think that would be an **Enriching** exhibition. **So, I think we're looking at an exhibition that ACTS or ENRICHES. ACT: Audience + Collaborative + Cultural Democracy; ENRICH: Object + Collaborative + Democratization of Culture.**

JB: Okay, we'll stop for now. We'll check in at the end of the semester after you've finished your curatorial projects. I'm looking forward to hearing about what you learn and create.

SECOND INTERVIEW, REFLECTION (RECORDED VIA ZOOM)

JB: Hello again, everyone. It's been a couple of months since we first discussed your capstones. You've finished and presented your projects. How'd they turn out?

CF: Mine turned out well! This project gave me the push I needed to start envisioning the cultural work I'd like to pursue.

MG: I'm happy with it, we just finished installation a few days ago.

AH: Overall, I am satisfied with my final project, although it took on a life of its own as I worked throughout the semester.

JB: Let's reflect on how your projects did and didn't change. Who wants to go first?

MG: Well, my exhibition didn't change too much from my initial plan (see figure 26.1). I made some minor tweaks. For example, I used a single QR code for all exhibition interpretation instead of a QR code for each poster.

Figure 26.1. Museumgoers experience Madison Grigsby's circus poster exhibition, *Fact, Fiction, or Fantastical Exaggeration?* PHOTO COURTESY OF JAY BODA.

JB: Nice work. I think your object labels entice visitors to use the QR code to learn more about each poster's true, false, or exaggerated claim.

MG: Thanks. That was definitely my intention.

FINAL LOCATION ON THE DIMENSIONS OF CURATION MODEL

JB: Speaking of curatorial intention, Madison, did you end up changing from **Mediate** within the Dimensions of Curation Model?

MG: No, I basically stayed with my original plan in terms of where the exhibition is on the model. There's probably a bit more audience interpretation than I had first expected, but it's still a **Mediated** experience.

JB: So, that's along the Lone Creative side of curatorial power. But I understand there was some collaboration between you and the exhibition preparation team, right?

MG: Yes, but discussions with prep were mostly related to the exhibit's technical layout and design details. Overall, the exhibition is mostly what I had in mind from the beginning.

JB: Okay. How about you, Charlie? Did your exhibition remain one that **Amplifies** artists and their works?

CF: Yes and no. It's still a collaborative project (see figure 26.2), but I transitioned from an object focus

Figure 26.2. Mock-up marketing material for Charlie Farrell's Emerging Artist Showcase.
PHOTO COURTESY OF CHARLIE FARRELL.

to an audience focus. And instead of having open-ended responses on the part of the audience, I decided to encourage people who attend the event to support Sarasota artists by asking them to learn about the artists and seek them out in the community. I'd say my project now falls within **Empower**. It's audience-centric, collaborative, and encourages the audience to take specific actions.

JB: Looking back, Charlie, why did you change your curatorial intention?

CF: While working on my project, I thought more about my whys and desired outcomes. I wanted to find ways to encourage the audience to go a step further. Asking them questions like: Which galleries are you going to? Which artists are you supporting?

AH: My project evolved from Cultural Democracy toward Democratization of Culture. Originally, I hoped that my exhibition ideas would either enrich an audience or help them act on what they experienced. Instead, my research paper ended up being more of an interrogation into three exhibitions hosted at Selby's Downtown and Historic Spanish Point campuses. These exhibition reviews ultimately informed my final exhibition proposal, *Flowering Fabrics: Batik Textiles of Indonesia*.

JB: Please say more about your new exhibition idea.

AH: My exhibition focused on Indonesian batik textiles and takes inspiration from past exhibitions at Selby (see figure 26.3). This idea features fourteen original

Figure 26.3. From The Selby's *Rainforest Masks of Costa Rica* exhibition. This exhibition's display and sale of indigenous masks specifically informed ideas of approach in Anneliese's capstone exhibition project, *Flowering Fabrics: Batik Textiles of Indonesia*.
PHOTO COURTESY OF ANNELIESE HARDMAN.

textiles from George Washington University's Textile Museum in the Museum of Botany and the Arts. It then incorporates outdoor components using textiles—like those you can buy from Etsy—to interpret the textile collection inside.

JB: In terms of the Dimension of Curation model, did you go with the **Enrich** or **Act** areas or end up somewhere new?

AH: Even though I workshopped my project with David Berry, I think I ended up within one of the Lone Creative options because I worked independently to choose the exhibition objects and design. However, my interpretive focus does heavily favor the audience, so I think my project ultimately fits into the **Mediate** category.

WORKING BACKWARD

JB: To recap: Madison, you started with **Mediate** and didn't change. Charlie, you started with **Amplify** and ended with **Empower**. Anneliese, you thought you'd either use **Enrich** or **Act** and ended up with **Mediate**. That demonstrates growth as you each started with a curatorial vision and carried it out based on what you learned along the way. Did you use the model to inform your projects, or would you recommend doing so?

AH: I didn't really use the model during my capstone, but I can see how the model could inform a curatorial team about bigger-picture goals. After determining the "what" and "why" of the project, curators can easily work backward to see the parts of the model that can help them work toward that intention.

MG: I like that idea of working backward. It's important to think about what you want visitors to take away from your exhibition first. Then look at the model to see how to get there. So, I think having the model inform you for that purpose would be helpful.

GOING FORWARD

JB: Given all the resources, time, and staff support at your ideal museum, would you continue to stay within the dimension you used in your capstone projects or try something different?

MG: I would like a more collaborative approach with more power in the hands of the museum team and their audience.

So, I'm leaning more toward exhibitions that **Act** and **Empower**—offering audiences the power of choice to interpret art for themselves. Maybe creating deeper personal interpretations can inspire them to meaningfully act.

AH: I think every exhibition fulfills a different purpose. I'll probably end up using each Dimension throughout my career based on the content of the exhibition and the expectations of the museum. I would also ideally like to incorporate collaboration into everything I do—through evaluation and feedback, or by working as a cross-departmental curatorial team. I believe that any amount of collaboration is likely better than none.

CF: I'll likely stay within more collaborative modes. When talking about diversity, equity, inclusivity, and accessibility, a curator is not an expert in all those areas. If you're truly an advocate for diversity, equity, inclusivity, and accessibility, you're going to naturally share power and authority by inviting different people in because there's always somebody who has a different experience than you who could bring something valuable to the table.

SUGGESTIONS FOR THOSE NEW TO THE MODEL

JB: Let's switch gears a bit. What would you suggest to someone who is new to curation or the Dimensions of Curation Model? How would you suggest they use it?

CF: I would recommend using the model as a visualization of your thinking. I don't think this model is meant to point fingers. It's not saying it's negative to have an interpretive focus more toward objects than audience or if you're a Lone Creative. It's just illuminating the thinking behind exhibition planning.

MG: I would say one of the most important things for students or early-career curators would be to study the theory. As the saying goes, learn the rules so you can break them. Look at exhibits you admire and try to understand what they're trying to accomplish and how. From there, try to locate them on the Dimensions of Curation Model.

LESSONS LEARNED

JB: How about what you learned since completing your curatorial projects?

AH: I felt pressure to do something "new" as I curated my exhibition. But I think a better approach is to look at a lot of exhibitions first and then borrow the best from each of these to create a new exhibition experience.

CF: Give yourself more time than you think, and involve other people in the process. It's more work, but it'll be worth it.

MG: Same thing. It's better to get more people involved from a project's start to get multiple perspectives versus working alone and having other departments come in later to make it more accessible and engaging.

JB: Great. Thanks again for sharing your projects and perspectives about the Dimensions of Curation Model. And congratulations again for graduating with your master's degrees. I'm looking forward to seeing what you do as you step into your new careers. Good luck!

Everyone: The end.

POST-READING GUIDED DISCUSSION

Readers theatre is an inherently socially constructivist learning experience (Tanner, 1993). After reading the script, readers and audience members should take the opportunity to share their reactions to the story, compare ideas, and co-construct knowledge together. Post-reading discussions should prompt for personal reflection and critical inquiry (Groh, 2012; Sallis, 2014; Savitt, 2002; Wulandari and Narmaditya, 2017). It is important to encourage readers and audience members to explore meaning making and compare differing perspectives demonstrated in the story. Educational outcomes typically include active/close reading and listening, critical analysis of ideas, unpacking varied understandings, and respecting differing points of view.

Boda (2020) employed readers theatre in a museum setting and found that staff and volunteer participants thought it was a positive learning experience because it shared perspectives from multiple museum roles. Participants also reported readers theatre fostered respectful conversation about potentially contentious topics. One participant said, "this kind of communication was valuable—and rare. I have never had such an open, honest discussion with a group [before]" (p. 92).

Charlie, Madison, and Anneliese had differing curatorial goals and experiences. Each found the Dimensions of Curation Model valuable to their curatorial learning process. As suggested in their conversation, the model does not value one perspective over another. They viewed the Dimensions of Curation Model as a guiding path for the intentions any curator or exhibition team might have.

REFERENCES

Boal, A. (1979). *Theatre of the oppressed.* Theatre Communications Group.

Boda, J. (2020). "Readers Theatre and Reflective Judgment in Museums" (27669035). Doctoral dissertation, Florida State University. Proquest.

Groh, A. (2012). "Using readers theatre to engage all learners." Master's thesis, Vanderbilt University. Vanderbilt University Institutional Repository.

Jeffries, R. B., and Schramm-Pate, S. (2008). *Grappling with diversity: Readings on civil rights pedagogy and critical multiculturalism.* Albany: SUNY Press.

Love, A. R., and Boda, J. (2017). Teaching visitor-centered exhibitions: A duoethnography of two team members. In P. Villeneuve and A. R. Love (Eds.), *Visitor-centered exhibitions and edu-curation in art museums.* Lanham, MD: Rowman & Littlefield.

Saldaña, J. (2011). *Ethnotheatre: Research from page to stage.* Walnut Creek, CA: Left Coast Press.

Sallis, R. J. T. (2014). Ethnographic performance and drama education: A meaningful communication between researcher, teacher, and student. *Youth Theatre Journal* 28(1), 3–17.

Savitt, T. L. (2002). *Medical readers' theater: A guide and scripts.* Iowa City: University of Iowa Press.

Tanner, F. A. (1993). *Readers theatre fundamentals: A cumulative approach to theory and activities* (second edition). Norman, OK: Clark Publishing Company.

Wulandari, D., and Narmaditya, B. S. (2017). Readers theater as a tool to understand difficult concept [sic] in economics. *International Education Studies* 10(5), 144.

27

You Say You Want a Revolution

EMPOWERING THE EDU-CURATOR

Emily Dellheim

For decades, museum scholars have been espousing the evolving relationship between museums and visitors, highlighting shifts that privilege educational practices and community engagement initiatives inclusive of diverse communities (Hirzy, 1992; Hooper-Greenhill, 2000; Villeneuve and Love, 2017; O'Neill and Wilson, 2010; Sandell, 2003; Simon, 2010; Villeneuve, 2007; Weil, 1999). The difficulties that museums faced in the wake of the COVID-19 pandemic underscore the continued need for museums to concretize their capacity to be visitor-centered; now, more than ever, museums need to reconsider the practices and capacities of their organizational change-makers (Krantz and Downey, 2021). Investing in the figure of the *edu-curator* (Villeneuve and Love, 2017) is a pertinent solution.

This chapter discusses affecting change in curatorial practice through the lens of professionalizing the edu-curator. I consider training needs regarding preservice and in-service practitioners, professional methods and competencies to carry out collaborative work, and suggestions for moving forward with the profession. In order to achieve this professionalization, I contend that the field needs to center the edu-curator role and implement the following professional objectives: (a) increase university-level and professional certificate training programs that provide theoretical underpinnings and conceptual frameworks, (b) reinvigorate job duties that reflect a commitment to research and practice, and (c) develop and implement new paradigms regarding education and leadership dispositions.

EDU-CURATION

I locate the sociocultural relevance of edu-curation in artist Theaster Gates's call to action to the art and museum world to "find new ways to imagine so that people can imagine new ways" (Guggenheim Museum, 2014). In fact, this sparked my own shift from a traditional curatorial trajectory toward visitor-centered exhibition practices. After experimenting with inclusive, community-centered museum programs with international and immigrant communities in Italy, I realized that as a scholar, educator, and museum practitioner, I needed further formal training in conducting research, creating programs that align with conceptual frameworks, and connecting art to learning theories and the educative needs of diverse audiences. By pursuing my PhD in Museum Education and Visitor-Centered Curation at Florida State University, I have been able to refine and expand my language of practice and connect with an important, collaborative network of like-minded professionals.

Edu-curation lies at the nexus of education and curation. It indicates a shift in curatorial practice from "Lone Creative" curators to collaborative and visitor-centered practice (Villeneuve and Love, 2017; Pegno and Brindza, 2021). Emerging from feminist systems theory, edu-curation relies on the following precepts: inclusivity and facilitating trust, incorporating voices from the margins, enhancing organizational culture, selecting appropriate methodologies, and contributing to social change (Love and Villeneuve, 2017). Edu-curation distributes authority among educators and curators and allows for hybrid roles and curatorial processes that embrace the varied—but mutually supportive—skill sets of its practitioners (Blake, Smith, and Adame, 2017; Hogarth, 2017). Both museum educators and traditional museum curators can become edu-curators and practice edu-curation. To do this type of work, there needs to be an institutional commitment to bring curators, educators, and community knowledge bearers into contact with each other to share and exchange viewpoints and skill sets (Willumson, 2007) in order to provide the visitor with "an experience" (Dewey, 1934, p. 37).

DIMENSIONS OF CURATION COMPETING VALUES MODEL

I draw upon the Dimensions of Curation Competing Values Exhibition Model as a fundamental edu-curatorial tool to adopt and disseminate. The trifecta of interpretive focus, curatorial power, and curatorial intent within the Competing Values Model provides a road map to enact multivocal curatorial practices that can best address the needs of museums and their communities in the twenty-first century. While acknowledging traditional practices, it also provides alternative options to the dominant paradigm—the Lone Creative curator—thus providing tangible means to respond to long-standing calls for museums to be visitor-centered. Recognizing that there is no one-size-fits-all curatorial approach, educational method, or exhibition, this model offers a variety of ways to intentionally curate exhibitions and collections to create the most situationally appropriate museum experience.

THE MAKING OF THE EDU-CURATOR—SOME HISTORICAL BACKGROUND

The twentieth century saw the rise of museum education, leading to the long-standing existence of education departments in art museums. During the late 1960s and 1970s, a museological shift increased focus on museum education and the professional needs of the museum educator through the creation of advocacy groups (International Council of Museums, n.d.-a; Kai-Kee, 2012). In the 1980s, researchers investigated the role and responsibilities of the museum educator (Eisner and Dobbs, 1986; Zeller, 1985) along with parallel studies regarding cognitive responses to viewing art and its relationship to learning in an art museum context (Housen, 1980; Parsons, 1987). During the 1990s, scholars urged for the central educational function of museums, as championed in the momentous American Alliance of Museums report, *Excellence and Equity: Education and the Public Dimension of Museums* (Hirzy, 1992) and echoed in Weil's (1999) proclamation that museums must shift from being about the object to being about the visitor.

Building upon the constructivist museum (Hein, 1998; Hooper-Greenhill, 1999), the 2000s continued to promote a visitor-centered focus, using museum education programming as a means to engage multiple voices (Hooper-Greenhill, 2000; Villeneuve, 2007). At the same time, curatorial work took on greater educational approaches, resulting in the "educational turn" to curation (O'Neill and Wilson, 2010). There has been much work in the past decade dedicated to how museums interact with their communities and engage with the social issues affecting them, vis-à-vis museum education (Boyd Acuff and Evans, 2014; Montgomery and Heller, 2017), yet the professionalization of the field itself continues to stall. Hierarchies between museum departments endure, and museum educators continue to work as reactionaries to curatorial decisions. Through decades of shifting museological focus to better incorporate the visitor and prioritize the educational function of museums, contemporary museum practices indicate that isolated disciplines and siloed roles are outmoded and that the future lies in the interdisciplinary, collaborative, and multifaceted figure of the edu-curator.

TRAINING PRACTITIONERS TO PROFESSIONALIZE THE FIELD

Putting the visitor-centered, collaborative approach of edu-curation into practice means that museums will have to shift their operations, while museum practitioners and the entities that train them will have to pursue new avenues of training and professional preparation. Traditionally speaking, the advancement of museum professions relied on the field having professional associations, university training programs, and specialized publications in which practitioners contribute their research (Latham and Simmons, 2019). In relation to the future professionalization of the edu-curator, acquiring the theoretical foundations and critical competencies developed through university training programs, professional certifications, or continuing education workshops, as well as engaging with the field through associations, conferences, and publications, will allow these practitioners to best catalyze and propagate innovations in the field. Edu-curators publishing their work would also enhance the outreach of the institutions that employ them by discussing art and exhibitions from a publicly minded point of view, with a voice that offers something different, independent, and complementary to that of the traditional curatorial essay. Following Latham and Simmons (2019), I propose that training needs should revolve around the following three areas: (a) subject area specialization, (b) professional dispositions, and (c) uniting practice with theory, research, and dissemination.

Among the small sample of existing training programs, some progressive graduate and certificate programs stand out. In the United States, The Ohio State University's graduate specialization in Museum Education and Administration, and Florida State University's Edu-curation certificate or master of arts and doctorate in Museum Education and Visitor-centered Curation contain courses focusing on learning theories, visitor research, and program design and evaluation. Tufts University's Anti-Racist Curatorial Practice Certificate provides training in anti-discriminatory curatorial methodologies, seeking to dismantle the hegemonic and colonial practices that historically and traditionally permeate art institutions. These types of programs are ripe for preservice practitioners and could allow mid-career educators to upgrade their skills, fill in the gaps in their previous education, and more effectively face the demands of the current profession.

UNITING PRACTICE AND RESEARCH

A clear articulation of research that is grounded in theoretical and conceptual frameworks adds to the credibility of the field and profession (Luke and Adams, 2007). In 2020, the International Council of Museums Committee for Education and Cultural Action created a special interest group dedicated to the professional development of museum educators (International Council of Museums, n.d.-b). Speaking from my personal experience as a member of this group, there is a strong desire among members to increase their skills in applied research, evaluation, and digital programming. At the turn of the century, Weil (1999) urged museum training programs to include visitor research and program evaluation as standard curricular components; Villeneuve, Love, and Viera (2014) reiterated the need for these competencies. One of the purposes of higher education programs is to teach students how to identify and apply appropriate research methods depending on the context. Importantly, training programs need to expand their focus from the *what* of subject area specializations, such as art history, art education, or museum studies, to emphasize the *how* and *why* offered through research and practice methodologies; this in turn creates practitioners who have the capacity to critique and improve their institutions, rather than just perpetuating existing practices (Latham and Simmons, 2019). Conducting research and evaluation also allows practitioners to make improvements to practice, whereas practice tests the merits of research and theories. As explained by Ambrose, et al., "practice and feedback are essential for learning" (2010, p. 124). Uniting research, practice, and evaluation allows the practitioner and the museum to create a feedback loop for continuous improvement and innovation. Valuing inquiry and the production of new knowledge within the museum engages and empowers museum practitioners and leads to more progressive, open, and resilient institutions (Pringle, 2019).

SUBJECT AREA SPECIALIZATIONS AND CONCEPTUAL FRAMEWORKS

Generations of curators and museum educators come from an educational background in art history (Eisner and Dobbs, 1986; Ebitz, 2005; Love and Villeneuve, 2017). However, as Eisner and Dobbs (1986) discussed, art museum educators are in a unique position that is not synonymous with art education, art history, or curatorship; we could also apply this to edu-curators, recognizing that a successful, professionalized field would require knowledge of all three areas, plus competency in the sociocultural realm.

As educational and training programs dedicated to this field evolve, it is fundamental that they clearly espouse their conceptual frameworks and philosophical viewpoints (Villeneuve, Love, and Viera, 2014). Not only does a conceptual framework apply to conducting research, but it also helps ground one's learning, providing the foundations from which one works. Embodying, sharing, and disseminating conceptual frameworks and philosophical lenses holds particular importance right now, as museums increasingly pledge to decolonize their practices and commit to diversity, equity, access, and inclusion. Callihan and Feldman (2018) examined how to weave an intersectional feminist agenda and social justice viewpoint into the operational fabric of the Minneapolis Institute of Art. Their Museum as Site for Social Action tool kit is an important example of how to use conceptual frameworks to ground and guide further work. Tying this back to the training of edu-curators, subject area specializations are not enough; we need conceptual frameworks that are going to address ways of thinking and bringing about social change through the public-facing work we conduct.

PROFESSIONAL DISPOSITIONS

Simon (2016) called upon museums to be relevant to their communities. Given the visitor-centered nature of edu-curators and museum educators, these staff members are often on the front lines of engaging marginalized groups and addressing issues of inclusion (Kletchka, 2021). Hence, demonstrating cultural competency and cultural humility are important skills (Brantmeier, 2020; Whitley, 2012); edu-curators need to be trained to adequately address social issues and facilitate this "wide-awakeness" (Greene, 1977). Effecting change to curatorial practice specifically requires acknowledgment and cultivation of professional dispositions (i.e., a practitioner's worldviews, attitudes, and beliefs). Research regarding education, museums, and organizational leadership indicates that practitioners should cultivate and be trained in empathy, communication, advocacy, active listening, facilitation, mediation, and other visitor-centered skills (Carr, 2007; Chung and Bemak, 2012; Gallegos, 2013; Greenberg, Antar, and Callihan, 2017; Harlow and Skinner, 2019). The Competing Values Model reflects this, placing emphasis on flexible, culturally sensitive, and situationally appropriate responses and uses of dispositions, and acknowledging that each museum exhibition or program may legitimately call for a variety of curatorial approaches reflected on the continua of the *x*, *y*, and *z* axes.

CONCLUSION: THE EDU-CURATOR AND THE COVID-19 TURN

From climate change and global migrations, to social, racial, and gender inequities sparking movements like Occupy Wall Street, Black Lives Matter, and the Women's March, the past decade has seen a flood of pressing social issues that involve communities inhabited by museums. Momentum for museums to engage with and advocate for their communities reached a tipping point in 2020 and 2021 with COVID-19. Art museum education departments were called upon as first responders to digitally engage the public and provide virtual exhibitions and programs in lieu of entry into the physical museum space (Harris, 2020). Reflecting on the state of the field, this is the moment to protect and sustain edu-curation in order to catalyze systemic change that will positively influence and shape generations of practitioners to come. As described in this chapter, implementing this solution requires reimagining the training, job description, and public position of edu-curators.

This is a breakthrough moment where museums need the competency and dynamism of edu-curators more than ever. Given their interaction with the public and understanding of community viewpoints, fears, and needs, museum educators and edu-curators are uniquely positioned to lead the museum in a crucial time in which museums need to connect with the public in new, long-term ways. The Competing Values Model provides a concrete path forward, where museum professionals, as well as visitors and community members, advocates, and leaders, may reenvision curatorial focus, power, and intent and facilitate a shift toward Cultural Democracy. This model activates intentional curatorial practices that can advance equity, empathy, and dignity for the exhibition team and museum visitors and should be part of the training of current and future practitioners.

REFERENCES

Acuff, J. Boyd, and Evans, L. (Eds.). (2014). *Multiculturalism in art museums today*. Lanham, MD: Rowman & Littlefield.

Ambrose, S. A., Bridges, M. W., DiPietro, M., Lovett, M. C., and Norman, M. K. (2010). *How learning works: Seven research-based principles for smart teaching*. Hoboken, NJ: John Wiley & Sons.

Blake, K. E., Smith, J. N., and Adame, C. (2017). Aligning authority with responsibility for interpretation. In P. Villeneuve and A. R. Love (Eds.), *Visitor-centered exhibitions and edu-curation in art museums* (pp. 87–97). Lanham, MD: Rowman & Littlefield.

Brantmeier, E. J. (2020). *Culturally competent engagement: A mindful approach*. Charlotte, NC: Information Age Publishing.

Callihan, E., and Feldman, K. (2018). Presence and power: Beyond feminism in museums. *Journal of Museum Education* 43(3), 179–92.

Carr, D. (2007). A vocabulary for practice. In P. Villeneuve (Ed.), *From periphery to center: Art museum education in the 21st century* (pp. 222–31). Alexandria, VA: National Art Education Association.

Chung, R. C., and Bemak, F. (2012). *Social justice counseling: The next steps beyond multiculturalism*. Los Angeles, CA: Sage.

Dewey, J. (1934). *Art as experience*. New York: Minton, Balch & Company.

Ebitz, D. (2005). Qualifications and the professional preparation and development of art museum educators. *Studies in Art Education* 46(2), 150–69.

Eisner, E. W., and Dobbs, S. M. (1986). Museum education in twenty American art museums. *Museum News* 65(2), 42–49.

Gallegos, P. V. (2013). The work of inclusive leadership: Fostering authentic relationships, modeling courage and humility. In Ferdman, B. M., Deane, B. R., Ferdman, B. M., and Deane, B. R. (Eds.), *Diversity at work: The practice of inclusion* (pp. 177–202). Hoboken, NJ: John Wiley & Sons.

Greenberg, A., Antar, A., and Callihan, E. (2017). Change-making through pedagogy. In Callihan, E. (Ed.), *The MASS action toolkit* (pp. 139–64). Minneapolis: Minneapolis Institute of Art.

Greene, M. (1977). Towards wide-awakeness: An argument for the arts and humanities in education. *Teachers College Record* 79(1), 119–25.

Harlow, D. B., and Skinner, R. K. (2019). Supporting visitor-centered learning through practice-based facilitation. *Journal of Museum Education* 44(3), 298–309.

Harris, G. (2020, April 23). Wave of museum educator redundancies worldwide sparks open letter. *The Art Newspaper*. https://www.theartnewspaper.com/news/open-letter-educator-redundancies-at-museums-worldwide

Hein, G. E. (1998). *Learning in the museum*. New York: Routledge.

Hirzy, E. C. (1992). *Excellence and equity: Education and the public dimension of museums*. Washington, DC: American Association of Museums.

Hogarth, B. (2017). Rethinking curator/educator training and interaction in the co-production of art museum exhibitions. In P. Villeneuve and A. R. Love (Eds.), *Visitor-centered exhibitions and edu-curation in art museums* (pp. 23–44). Lanham, MD: Rowman & Littlefield.

Hooper-Greenhill, E. (1999). Education, communication and interpretation. In E. Hooper-Greenhill (Ed.), *The educational role of the museum* (second edition, pp. 3–27). New York: Routledge.

Hooper-Greenhill, E. (2000). *Museums and the interpretation of visual culture*. New York: Routledge.

Housen, A. (1980). What is beyond, or before, the lecture tour? A study of aesthetic modes of understanding. *Art Education* 33(1), 16–18.

International Council of Museums. (n.d.-a). From the beginnings to now. http://ceca.mini.icom.museum/history-of-the-committee/from-the-beginnings-to-now/

International Council of Museums. (n.d.-b). What are special interest groups? http://ceca.mini.icom.museum/special-interests-groups/what-are-special-interests-group/

Kai-Kee, E. (2012). Professional organizations and the professionalizing of practice: The role of MER, EdCom, and the NAEA museum education division, 1969–2000. *The Journal of Museum Education* 37(2), 13–23.

Kletchka, D. C. (2021). Art museum educators: Who are they now? *Curator: The Museum Journal* 64(1), 79–97.

Krantz, A., and Downey, S. (2021). The significant loss of museum educators in 2020: A data story. *Journal of Museum Education* 46(4), 417–29.

Latham, K. F., and Simmons, J. E. (2019). Whither museum studies? *Journal of Education for Library and Information Science* 60(2), 102–17.

Love, A. R., and Villeneuve, P. (2017). Edu-curation and the edu-curator. In P. Villeneuve and A. R. Love (Eds.), *Visitor-centered exhibitions and edu-curation in art museums* (pp. 11–22). Lanham, MD: Rowman & Littlefield.

Luke, J. J., and Adams, M. (2007). What research says about learning in art museums. In P. Villeneuve (Ed.), *From periphery to center: Art museum education in the 21st century* (pp. 31–40). Alexandria, VA: National Art Education Association.

Montgomery, M. O., and Heller, H. (2017). Visitor as activist: A mobile social justice museum's call for critical visitor engagement. In P. Villeneuve and A. R. Love (Eds.), *Visitor-centered exhibitions and edu-curation in art museums* (pp. 153–65). Lanham, MD: Rowman & Littlefield.

O'Neill, P., and Wilson, M. (2010). *Curating and the educational turn*. San Francisco, CA: Open Editions.

Parsons, M. J. (1987). Talk about a painting: A cognitive development analysis. *The Journal of Aesthetic Education* 21(1), 37–55.

Pegno, P., and Brindza, C. (2021). Redefining curatorial leadership and activating community expertise to build equitable and inclusive art museums. *Curator* 64(2), 343–62.

Pringle, E. (2019). *Rethinking research in the art museum*. New York: Routledge.

Sandell, R. (2003). Social inclusion, the museum and the dynamics of sectoral change. *Museum and Society* 1(1), 45–62.

Simon, N. (2010). *The participatory museum*. Museum 2.0.

Simon, N. (2016). *The art of relevance*. Museum 2.0.

The Solomon R. Guggenheim Museum. (2014, April 26). Carrie Mae Weems live: Past tense/future perfect. Theaster Gates, Richard J. Powell and Carrie Mae Weems in conversation. https://www.youtube.com/watch?v=qbb6CLDCRYU

Villeneuve, P. (Ed.). (2007). *From periphery to center: Art museum education in the 21st century*. Alexandria, VA: National Art Education Association.

Villeneuve, P., Love, A. R., and Viera, A. (2014). Transitional approaches to art museum education: Models for practice, program evaluation, and research. In K. M. Miraglia and C. Smilan (Eds.), *Inquiry in action: Paradigms, methodologies, and perspectives in art education research* (pp. 169–85). Alexandria, VA: National Art Education Association.

Villeneuve, P., and Love, A. R. (Eds.). (2017). *Visitor-centered exhibitions and edu-curation in art museums*. Lanham, MD: Rowman & Littlefield.

Weil, S. E. (1999). From being about something to being for somebody: The ongoing transformation of the American museum. *Daedalus* 128(3), 229–58.

Whitley, R. (2012). Religious competence as cultural competence. *Transcultural Psychiatry* 49(2), 245–60.

Willumson, G. (2007). The emerging role of the educator in the art museum. In P. Villeneuve (Ed.), *From periphery to center: Art museum education in the 21st century* (pp. 89–94). Alexandria, VA: National Art Education Association.

Zeller, T. (1985). Art museum educators: Who are they? *Museum News* 63(5), 53–59.

28

M Leuven

A HOLISTIC APPROACH TO EXHIBITION MAKING

Peter Carpreau and Sofie Vermeiren

In the middle of Leuven's historic center stands M, a museum with a collection of more than 52,000 ancient and modern objects. This combination of objects makes the museum unique in Belgium. A few years ago, M adopted a new approach to its collection presentations and has since been developing a new museum language based on visual literacy and *transhistoricity*. The essence of visual literacy is the way in which the viewer finds or places a meaning in the viewed image. This has implications for how curators and museums can present images. Meaning is made by the viewer in the here and now. The historical context of the image is then less important. This opens up new possibilities for juxtaposing works from different times in meaningful ways or, in other words, for working transhistorically.

Up until 2017, M presented its collection in a permanent display, starting with the Middle Ages and ending with the twenty-first century. Research showed that visitors were spending less and less time in this classic arrangement and instead mostly visiting temporary exhibitions. M therefore decided to adopt a new approach. The idea of a permanent display was abandoned and replaced by more dynamic presentations that run over one or two years and showcase pieces of modern art alongside old masters.

With these various forms of presentation, M wants to show more than its own history and art history and appeal to different visitor profiles. The museum's temporary closing in 2017 provided space and inspiration to develop this story in concrete terms. The process of creating exhibitions was completely transformed. Whereas in the past the process was much more top-down (a curator makes an exhibition, and the team realizes it), we organized in cross-departmental groups to work together on new presentations. This gives everyone a fulfilling role based on their own expertise and strengthens cooperation.

Parallel to these collection presentations, the museum also runs an exhibition program with exhibitions of modern and ancient art. Depending on the content of a collection presentation or exhibition and the target group we have in mind, we use different methods in M during the cooperation process.

In this chapter we want to clarify these methodologies and our approach by looking at four exhibitions that fit into the Dimensions of Curation Model. This holistic approach allows us to appeal to different types of audience and to keep experimenting.

COLLECTION PRESENTATION: *THE POWER OF IMAGES* (JUNE 11, 2017–MAY 10, 2020)

This exhibition was the first in a series of new collection presentations in 2017. The exhibition was located in the first gallery, where our visitors are introduced to M and the collection. Because this sets the tone for the rest of the visit, the gallery had to convey the ideas of visual literacy and transhistoricity. The gallery provided an introduction that served as a guide for viewers who could then take the principles of visual literacy such as visual perception, visual creativity, visual language, or visual analysis with them during further visits. But it also had to help visitors understand that they were not entering a known art history story, but a museum where the classical historical approach has been abandoned in favor of other approaches.

Figure 28.1. *Power of Images*, gallery view.
PHOTO COURTESY OF ANDY MERREGAERT FOR M LEUVEN.

Peter Carpreau and Sofie Vermeiren

Several colleagues from different departments worked together on equal footing for this exhibition. It was the first time in M that we invested in the methodology of edu-curating. We found inspiration for this in the publication *Visitor-Centered Exhibitions and Edu-Curation in Art Museums* (Villeneuve and Love, 2017) and in discussions with Pat Villeneuve, whom we met at a conference in Manchester, United Kingdom. Colleagues from the departments of ancient art, modern art, scenography (exhibition design), production (installation), public mediation (education and interpretation), and communication worked together in the working group to create a new collection presentation. Everyone had a respected seat at the table, which was empowering. M was once a classically organized museum. To change the end product fundamentally, we had to reform the whole organizational structure.

Within the Dimensions of Curation model, this exhibition fits on the axes Audience Interpretive Focus (*x*) + Collaborative Curatorial Power (*y*) + Democratization of Culture Intent (*z*) = Exhibitions that Empower. That is why we explicitly chose to work together on this exhibition and to give the public a central role, where the visitor participated actively.

The research question "How does the viewer understand an image?" was central to the exhibition, but to avoid being too patronizing, we turned the question around to "How does an image tell a story?" The presentation was a mix of ancient and modern works of art. The spectator was challenged to look and to reflect on their own viewing patterns. Classic wall texts and art historical audio fragments were supplemented with question labels, interviews, personal stories on the audio tour, digital tools, drawing assignments, and touch labels (a label with a piece of fabric that the visitors can touch, for example) that provoked the visitor to look more closely and with more curiosity. Using these new museum strategies shifted the focus from the traditional art historical approach. In the current museum concept, the visitor actually learns to explore, to imagine, to value, and to understand images.

By moving away from a classical layout and focusing on visual literacy, M profiled itself as "a museum of the visual" rather than an art museum. This is sometimes regarded with suspicion, but many of our visitors say they appreciate this new approach and find it refreshing.

PUBLIC TRAJECTORY: *MADNESS. STUDENTS@M* (MARCH 15, 2019–JANUARY 24, 2021)

Students@M was part of a series of collection presentations in which the public was given the role of curator. The public is thus given the opportunity to work together with the team at M to create an exhibition in the museum halls. These pathways are located on the axes Audience (*x*) + Collaborative (*y*) + Cultural Democracy (*z*) = Exhibitions that Act of the three-dimensional model. Compared to the previous example, here we go one step further and give the participants co-ownership of the exhibition.

This process started in 2018. M chose to create an exhibition with Leuven students based on an interdisciplinary approach. Through a call for proposals,

Figure 28.2. *Madness. Students@M*, depot visit.
PHOTO COURTESY OF ANDY MERREGAERT FOR M LEUVEN.

we selected ten students with diverse backgrounds who would take on the role of public curator. They were given an empty gallery and access to the entire M collection. They helped determine the theme, the selection of works, the scenography (exhibition design), the mediation (interpretation and education), and communication. In other words, it was a unique opportunity for this young target group to take a look behind the scenes of a museum and make their own personal mark on the exhibition.

The participants were introduced to the museum, its collection, and its activities through guided tours, discussions with museum staff, and active viewing and association exercises. Together with the group and the M educators, they thought and philosophized about different perspectives, the process, and the intended target group. They viewed and analyzed works of art from different perspectives such as materials, stories (factual and personal), emotions, and art and society. The next step was to focus on an exhibition concept and choose a theme. This was partly simultaneous with the further investigation of the collection works. In brainstorming sessions, they sharpened ideas and sought a common denominator. Based on the various interests and ways of looking at the collection, "Madness" was chosen as a theme, and later became also part of the exhibition title.

The further selection of works for this was done along the way with the participants. As with the *Boundless Hospitality* project (see chapter 25), the next step was to engage them in a presentation where they could share their story with the audience. This was followed by a meeting with the exhibition designer

Peter Carpreau and Sofie Vermeiren

who then drew up a plan having talked to the participants. In this conversation, a number of specific questions were asked in order to translate the ideas into a presentation. The *labyrinth*, metaphor for a quest, eventually became the starting point. Just as in the previous project, the theme was also made visible in the scenography. The audience was invited literally to wander through the presentation and contemplate the various works. The participants also took mediating and communication one step further. They thought about making the process visible, about the stories they wanted to tell the audience, about the atmosphere and tone it should have. Finally, the diversity of backgrounds and education of the public curators was reflected in the exhibition.

With the collection presentation *Madness*, the participants went in search of the meaning of madness, but also the madness in each of us. In this exhibition, the students wanted to open up the concept of madness. All too often, it is given a negative interpretation, but madness can be looked at from a much broader perspective. Madness relates to notions and feelings such as despair, loss, confrontation, and disorder, but also to perception, distortion, ecstasy, and celebration—recognizable concepts. This was also made visible in the presentation. Various works of art, both ancient and modern, were juxtaposed with each other, and the students' views were shared with the audience in text, video, and audio tour. That deepened the viewing experience of the individual visitor by providing information that encouraged a different way of looking at and reflecting upon art and the theme itself. Finally, a guest book with specific questions and drawing cards provided additional communication with the visitors. The responses were generally positive and showed that the visitors really thought about the theme, not only from the perspective of the works of art but also from their own points of view.

RESEARCH EXHIBITION: *RODIN, MEUNIER, MINNE AND THE MIDDLE AGES* (MARCH 20, 2020–AUGUST 30, 2020)

M has a rich collection of sculpture that is subject to a great deal of research and recognized internationally. This sub-collection consists mainly of late medieval sculptures. It also includes a small but excellent series of sculptures by the Belgian social realist sculptor Constantin Meunier. The concept for the exhibition *Rodin, Meunier, Minne and the Middle Ages* started from the observation that Meunier took inspiration from medieval sculptures to make his own art timeless. Research showed that other nineteenth-century sculptors also worked in this tradition, and their inclusion in the story of the exhibition was important. This gave rise to the idea of investigating and confronting not only the influence of medieval art on Meunier's work but also on that of Auguste Rodin and George Minne.

Given the different backgrounds required to put this exhibition together, a decision was made to approach the curatorial process collectively. In terms of art history, there was a need for knowledge about Meunier, Rodin, Minne, and the world they inhabited. But it also required knowledge of medieval sculpture. To this end, experts from M worked together with specialists from the Rodin Museum (Paris) and the Meunier Museum (Brussels). The public aspect was also essential. The educational experts around the table soon noticed that the exhibition had themes

Figure 28.3. *Rodin, Meunier, Minne and the Middle Ages*, gallery view.
PHOTO COURTESY OF MILES FISCHLER FOR M LEUVEN.

of death, passion, and martyrdom. Sculptures such as *Mother Admires Her Dead Child* by George Minne, *The Martyr* by Rodin, and *The Old Mine Horse* by Meunier, especially in combination with the medieval funerary layouts and devotions, were in other words visualizations of emotions such as grief, sorrow, and loss. Based on this insight, we decided that the audio guide should not focus on the art. Instead, poets were asked to write poetry to accompany the works to bring the theme of farewell into the exhibition. The poems were recorded on the audio guide and could be listened to alongside the images. This piece of emo-curating proved to be a hit with the visitors.

Another aspect that the exhibition focused on was the visual elements of the artworks. One of M's curatorial specializations, as already shown in the example *The Power of Images*, is visual literacy and the human ability to create meanings through visual stimuli. The starting point that was the core focus of the exhibition was that the innovators of nineteenth-century sculpture in France and Belgium spent more time studying the art of the Middle Ages than had previously been assumed. To get the story across to the visitor, we opted for a presentation that invited the viewer to look and make visual connections without giving too much text or information. We achieved this by building each gallery around a specific visual theme, such as the *seated figure*, *the devotion (pieta)*, or *mother and child*. We selected images that visually fit within those themes and that showed clear visual parallels. This way, the audience was encouraged to look for themselves and to trust their own judgment more.

The exhibition clearly started from the object. It was the objects and the collection that were central, and the story was based around the works of art themselves. But the curatorial method was collective, with inputs from the different experts strengthening the common narrative. Through its visual approach, this exhibition positions itself on the axes Object (x) + Collaborative (y) + Democratization of Culture (z) = Exhibitions that Enrich.

CITYWIDE PROJECT: *BETWEEN HEAVEN AND EARTH* (MARCH 7, 2020–MARCH 31, 2024)

The city of Leuven is also home to Saint Peter's Church. This is the city's central and most important church and houses Leuven's most important works of art. The church displays masterpieces by Flemish masters, such as *The Last Supper* and *The Martyrdom of Saint Erasmus* by Dieric Bouts, and the *Eedelherent Triptych* or the *Triumphal Cross* by Jan Borman, in their authentic context. In addition, the church contains several other works of art and objects that are inextricably linked to the city's history and identity. The church is owned by the city and used by the church administration for its religious function. M manages the art treasures of the church.

The church building itself, a medieval Gothic construction, was the subject of a decades-long restoration. The inside of the building used to be divided into two parts. The large central part, the nave, was reserved for Catholic worship. The choir was furnished as a museum. These two parts were separated by a glass wall and there was an entrance fee for the museum.

The restoration was an opportunity to rethink the presentation in the church and to remove this separation between the church and the museum. The reasoning is simple. Almost all art objects in the church were made for context of the

Figure 28.4. *Between Heaven and Earth*, HoloLens experience.
PHOTO COURTESY OF DIRK LEEMANS FOR M LEUVEN.

church itself and have always functioned in a religious environment. Dividing that into religious and museum parts seemed rather artificial, even counterproductive. Furthermore, the city's greatest artistic asset was not used to its full potential. Saint Peter's Church and the works of Bouts have the potential to become a major international showcase for the city of Leuven. As the church occupies a central place in the city, both geographically and symbolically, a team including all stakeholders was put together. Representatives of the museum, the city, the building conservators, and the church were included. It was important to pay attention to all the different dimensions of such a project: the religious, the artistic, the tourist, the urban, the architectural, and the heritage.

For the concrete realization of the project, the team opted to highlight twelve different stories in the church. Some of the stories were about art and artists like Bouts; other stories were about folk beliefs, political history, or important crafts that are specific to the city. These stories were developed into an experience-oriented digital access. This mixed reality brings the masterpieces to life and lets visitors discover a bustling Leuven, past and present. With this new, innovative technology, M Leuven wanted to appeal to a new audience, without compromising on the information about the works of art. It is clear that this project focuses on the objects and the stories they tell, but also makes a connection to the city of today.

This project needed clear cooperation in order to unite all the different aspects that the church represents. Precisely because the church occupies a central place in the urban fabric, this was not a project where the museum curators knew all the answers. The religious community and the heritage community certainly contributed to the final result. In that sense, this project has been an example of cultural democracy. Our emphases on the axes Object (*x*) + Collaborative (*y*) + Cultural Democracy (*z*) resulted in exhibitions that Amplify. That was the ultimate aim of the project in the church. We wanted to make better use of the assets that Saint Peter's Church has and increase their impact both for international visitors and for the city's own residents.

DECISION

M Leuven is an agile museum. Its collection is versatile, and its mind open. It is a museum in a city characterized by an atmosphere of innovation. This also gives us the opportunity to experiment with the format of *exhibitions* and the medium of *museum*. The quality and success of an exhibition is the result of the way it was made and the way the curatorial choices were made. In the examples given here, it is clear that we do not choose one specific manner, but rather combine different methods. This ensures that Museum M's offerings are also much more varied and appeal to a more diverse and larger group of people. It also ensures that the projects we carry out are more in line with the worlds inhabited by our diverse audience.

REFERENCE

Villeneuve, P., and Love, A. R. (2017). *Visitor-centered exhibitions and edu-curation in art museums*. Lanham, MD: Rowman & Littlefield.

29

Inclusive Curatorial Practice

Lynette A. Zimmerman

Inclusive curation of art exhibitions is a complex topic. Inclusion, meaning to be part of something, has different nuances depending on the context in which it is being discussed. In the art gallery and museum world, curation is an act of selecting, organizing, and presenting art and artifacts in an exhibition for visitors to experience. It is the practice of storytelling. The curatorial process is an opportunity to be inclusive, accessible, and equitable. Inclusive curation appears to be trending, and researchers are examining potential models and frameworks that eliminate exclusionary practices. Creating experiences that address *why* an artist or body of work is important to exhibit now, in a particular location, speaking to a certain audience, is the key pillar in the creation of the Dimensions of Curation Competing Values Exhibition Model that I leverage at the Galleries at Kean University.

This chapter discusses the importance of understanding key concepts such as social justice, inclusion, audience engagement, leadership, awareness, structural design, and intersectionality. It will address inclusive curation based on my research and role as executive director of the Galleries at Kean, which has seven active art galleries producing purpose-driven experiences. The exhibitions and related programs target both internal audiences including students, faculty, and staff, and external audiences composed of community members living within a twenty-mile radius of Union, New Jersey, United States. Kean, the fourth-largest public four-year higher education institution in the state, is New Jersey's first urban research university and is a designated Hispanic-Serving Institution.

In this chapter, I draw from the theory of intersectionality and framework of Dimensions of Curation Model that embrace the internal versus external struggle of museums and galleries. The practice of creating connectivity through authenticity is captured through the implementation of blended curatorial practice of the Competing Values Model. Inclusive art curation, a practice naturally rooted in social justice, meaning fairness in society, is the synthesis of my approach.

CURATORIAL CHANGE ROOTED IN SOCIAL JUSTICE

What is social justice? Perhaps this is an unfamiliar way to open a conversation on curatorial change. However, by the end of this chapter it is my intent that you will be inspired to examine curation and the process of change through a social justice lens. Prior to this step, I encourage my colleagues to embrace a self-examination of their unique identities and take a moment to find out how their individuality influences their actions and experiences (Tatum, 2000). For me, social justice means equal economic, political, and social rights and opportunities for all.

I identify as a White, gay, female, able-bodied, and highly educated advocate for the arts, education, equity, inclusion, and women's and LGBTQ+ rights. Exposing my identity provides context and creates a platform for a deeper, more meaningful, and productive dialogue about the role of social justice in curatorial practice that can raise consciousness and lead to effective action (Tatum, 2020). My approach is insistent and direct in nature and deviates from the previous director's sole decree. It was essential during the early days of my tenure in 2020 to talk about racial injustice in the wake of George Floyd's murder.

Come Together, a group photography exhibition that visually addressed the struggles and injustices experienced by Black Americans and people of color in New Jersey, an exhibition my team and I curated, is an example of an exhibition that Acts (Audience Interpretive Focus + Collaborative Curatorial Power + Cultural Democracy). The artists, along with advocates and activists, participated in a virtual panel discussing racism, race, and the role artists play in societal change. By incorporating collaborative techniques, such as multiple curators racially representing Black, White, and Hispanic persons, and artists from varied racial groups, backgrounds, ages, sexual orientation, and gender, the exhibition was an example of creating an inclusive intersectional experience.

A recent exhibition, *Pulse Nightclub: 49 Elegies* by artist John Gutoskey, an out artist, addressed LGBTQ+ issues. Influenced by my identities, I used the Mediate curation model of Audience Interpretive Focus + Lone Creative + Democratization of Culture. This exhibition brought the LGBTQ+ community at Kean together, connected with the students in a meaningful way, and expanded the efforts of Kean's Office of Diversity, Equity, and Inclusion. It recognized and gave credence to a group of marginalized persons. Bayard Rustin, a lifelong civil rights activist and openly gay man instrumental in the organization efforts of protests and marches with Dr. Martin Luther King during the Civil Rights Movement, said, "it was an absolute necessity for me to declare homosexuality, because if I didn't, I was a part of the prejudice." He continued, "I was aiding and abetting the prejudice that was a part of the effort to destroy me" (Morgan, 2018, p. 8).

Museums and galleries have recently begun to address social justice issues (Katz and Reisman, 2020). Díaz (2020) highlighted the work of social justice curators in museums, particularly the work of Jasmine Wahi, the Holly Block Social Justice Curator at the Bronx Museum. As cited by Díaz (2020, p. 4), Wahi stated, "a social justice curator is a cultural worker who creates exhibitions that prompt dialogue and subsequent change toward a more socially equitable and just society." While the advent of this type of curator role is new, museums and galleries have always had an awareness of critical global issues; however, curation practice routinely did not reflect that understanding.

PRACTICE OF AWARENESS

Racism, sexism, ableism, and homophobia are critical topics that curators have the power to bring to the forefront of their work. On the contrary, if curatorial practices do not incorporate audience interpretation and collaborative approaches that bring different perspectives to the table, they may be participating in prejudicial practices. Critical consciousness in practice dissolves exclusionary systems (Robert, 2014), such as exhibiting only works with a Eurocentric view.

The Galleries at Kean have outlined future exhibitions that highlight a continued commitment to social justice and inclusive curatorial practice. For example, ableism will be addressed with the exhibition *Sight Unseen*. In *Aftermath*, social sustainability will be discussed within the context of disruption and disparities caused by war. Environmental sustainability will be examined in the exhibition of recycled materials by Sayaka Ganz in *Reclaimed Creations*. Cultural identity will be addressed in *East meet West: Hand-Tinted Vintage Photographs from Meiji Japan, 1880–1900* featuring a historical perspective on Japanese culture. Inclusive curation is happening at Kean, and it is not focused on a single identity (Robert, 2014). A single identity lens limits the view of the curator. It is essential that multiple identities be considered, and the intersectionality of humanity be examined to produce an inclusive exhibition.

Awareness of standard practices, such as the use of temporality in exhibition planning, telling a story that takes the viewer from the past to the present, is a potentially biased system. It may only highlight the experiences of one group while marginalizing those who have traditionally been excluded from the historical narrative. Although Robert (2014) implied that all exhibitions are based on biased temporal chronology, I disagree, as I have experienced exhibitions that purposely use inclusive practice to tell the stories of marginalized groups. However, unchecked practices can easily invoke discrimination and subjugation of the oppressed. Sandoval (2002) explained oppositional consciousness, also known as the methodology of the oppressed or the practice of deconstructive skills, to decode and rethink systems, in the context of feminism and the ways in which dominant White feminist theory sidelines other feminisms. Her exploration of feminism through lived experiences of women of color refreshes the construct of feminism. This can be applied to curation. Addressing sexism through art that encourages a call to action for social change could be a theme for the Galleries at Kean. Recognizing that not all persons share my perspective forces me to channel collaborative curatorial processes to achieve my goal, to be representative of many views and create an inclusive experience. Inclusivity is much more extensive than the opinions of a few; however, this brief example demonstrates that the creation of systems that guide inclusive engagement with culturally sensitive topics is possible. Acknowledging and understanding that unconscious bias and color-blind racial ideology, which according to Tatum (2017) is when White people deny or minimize the degree of racial inequality in existence, causes harm to people of color and perpetuates prejudice. The topics of race and racism must be discussed. When they are not, systems built to be exclusive continue and injure not only people of color but also White people. This is the moment when the theory of intersectionality plays a role.

INTERSECTIONALITY

Through the exploration of intersectionality, the curator, situated at the point of discrimination and oppression, is positioned to bring multiple perspectives into one exhibition. When racism, a known societal construct, is in place to purposefully marginalize groups of people, it is imperative that a curator's vantage include cross sections. For example, during the early phases of curation, will an exhibit discussing racism in the United States highlight sexism or homophobia within the Black community, or will it blindly assume a masculine, patriarchal, heteronormative society? Asking questions about intersectionality creates an inclusive platform of discussion, perspectives, and storytelling that results in a cohesive viewer experience. Exhibitions that leave a viewer feeling connected to something intangible, to the artist, or the work on display, is the goal of the experience. I have heard the term "authentic" used by viewers who attempt to describe how they are feeling. Intersectionality brings authenticity to the curatorial practice, resulting in an optimal experience.

STRUCTURAL DESIGN

The Galleries at Kean operates seven distinct art galleries, two that highlight student work and five that exhibit professional artists. Each employs its own purpose under the division's mission, "to be an impactful vehicle for social change and bring awareness to critical global issues." The art gallery spaces are spread across four buildings on Kean's main campus.

Profundo by Tamara Torres, an internationally recognized artist based in Trenton, New Jersey, who is known for her introspective abstract works, drew in a record number of students. Her work explores her story of struggle, poverty, and domestic instability as a woman of Puerto Rican descent. Survey results indicated that student viewers found the work impactful and the artist's story compelling. *Profundo* was an example of an exhibition that Inspires (x = Audience, y = Lone Creative, and z = Cultural Democracy). The artist, an Afro-Latina, called her viewers to act for the empowerment of women using a video installation as part of the exhibition, which demonstrates the effectiveness of the model.

Further examination into the success of this exhibition is done using intersectionality. The female undergraduate population in 2020 at Kean University was composed of 35 percent Hispanic undergraduate female students and 20 percent Black undergraduate female students (National Center for Education Statistics,

2022). This illustrates the intersection between the artist's identity and the female student population. It may be assumed that the intersectionality of race and gender may account for the positive reviews from the internal audience.

I advocate for the use of three-dimensional curation practice using a blended approach. *Come Together*, a collective exhibition, demonstrated the power of the Act three-dimensional model using Audience (x) + Collaborative (y) + Cultural Democracy (z). This model framed the topic of the Black Lives Matter movement in New Jersey by drawing on multiple artists' perspectives.

Viewers rarely walk away with a clear understanding of every curatorial detail, which is not the intent of inclusive curation. Instead, a person should leave with a feeling of authenticity that prompts an examination of their core values. *Come Together* captured connectivity between the artists and the viewers. The narrative resonated with both internal and external audience groups and generated positive impact through related panel discussions and conference presentations.

The Kean community and greater regional audiences represent a diverse spectrum of racial and socioeconomic groups. Understanding the composition of the Galleries' audience groups, relevant social topics, conflicts, and interests, I have employed the use of a blended three-dimensional model technique. This creates connection to a strong sense of purpose through art. While exhibiting living artists serves the Galleries at Kean well, deceased artists are also presented to offer another level of engagement to artistry. Ansel Adams's *Early Works*, art2art Circulating Exhibitions from the collection of Michael Mattis and Judith Hochberg, is an example of tethering history and art. This exhibition is an example of Disseminate a model of Object (x) + Lone Creative (y) + Democratization of Culture (z). *Early Works* struck a chord across racial lines and solicited similar positive reactions from multi-race viewers.

I recognize my own identities influence curatorial decisions and design of the exhibition program at Kean. Using a peer group of collegians to test the validity of the structure is essential to produce a diverse array of exhibitions that use the Dimensions of Curation Model. An example of the recently adopted blended model of curatorial is depicted in Table 29.1.

Over the past two years, following the blended model framework using the dimensional guide depicts the percentage of each model the Galleries at Kean implemented across twenty-four exhibitions (Figure 29.1).

Previously, the Galleries relied on one perspective and hierarchical organizational development archetype to select and curate the exhibitions. By eliminating the *why*, exhibitions were less connective, as evidenced by low attendance. Student participation waned over the years; however, community engagement remained relatively the same year after year. Use of the Sympathetic two-dimensional model of Audience (x) + Lone Creative (y) did occur for exhibitions held in the Human Rights Institute Gallery due to the involvement of the institute's director. Leadership plays a major role in institutional priorities and direction.

Table 29.1. Blended Model Spring and Summer 2022 Exhibitions at Kean University

Exhibition	Gallery	3-D Model	Theme	Gallery's Purpose	Mission Connection
Ansel Adams: Early Works	Liberty Hall Academic Center Gallery	Disseminate	Cultural Identity	Art in history	Social change, awareness, national parks, preservation of nature
Civil Rights Journey	Human Rights Institute Gallery	Empower	Cultural Identity	Social justice	Social change, awareness, global issues, racism, systemic corruption, civil rights, US history
In Knots	Nancy Dryfoos Gallery	Enrich	Cultural Identity	Emerging artists	Awareness, mental health
Profundo	The Karl and Helen Burger Gallery	Mediate	Cultural Identity	New Jersey artists	Social change, awareness, global issues, rape culture, domestic violence, women, Puerto Rico
Pulse Nightclub: 49 Elegies	Human Rights Institute Gallery	Empower	Cultural Identity	Social justice	Awareness, global issues, LGBTQ+ rights, gun violence, domestic terrorism, Latin LGBTQ+ community

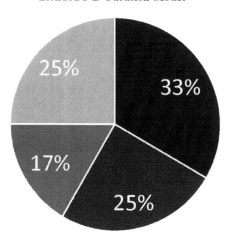

Blended 3-D Curation Model

- Object Interpretive Focus+Lone Curatorial Power+Democratization of Culture

- Audience Interpretive Focus+Collaborative Curatorial Power+Democratization of Culture

- Audience Interpretive Focus+Collaborative Curatorial Power+Cultural Democracy

- Audience Interpretive Focus+Lone Curatorial Power+Democratization of Culture

Figure 29.1. Two-Year Percentage Blended Model Outline

LEADERSHIP

Kean University welcomed its eighteenth leader in July 2020, Dr. Lamont Repollet. As Kean's first Black president, Repollet launched new efforts to engage secondary school students in a variety of programs serving as a pipeline to higher education. Diversity, equity, and inclusion efforts are a top priority under his leadership and are evident in research, curriculum development, hiring practices, and programming. The president's commitment to equity in action became the mantra for many nonacademic divisions, including the Galleries at Kean. The institution's direction is built into the framework of curatorial practice using the theory of intersectionality developed by Kimberlé Crenshaw. Alignment among Kean's priorities, the Galleries' mission, and the audience groups served is imperative to continuing to deliver authentic, meaningful art experiences.

AUDIENCE ENGAGEMENT

The principle of the twenty/sixty/twenty rule, derived from management theory, is a phenomenon applicable to many real-world situations (Jaworski and Pitera, 2015) and may prove useful with audience development. Chugh (2018) interpreted this principle to include three types of people, the *easy twenties*, *middle sixties*, and the *stuck twenties*. The easy twenties are intrinsically motivated to be unbiased and open. The middle sixties are silent, observant, and unmotivated to engage. The stuck twenties are entrenched in their ideas and unwilling to listen or change. When experimenting with inclusive curation, curators must be prepared to make points of view known in their process and realize that the stuck twenties are going to be the loudest and most unwilling to accept new narratives. By responding with clarity and cause, inclusive curatorial practice can be communicated to all types of people with the hope that the middle sixties are listening. This is the target audience. While researchers do not know how to debias the brain (Chugh, 2018), developing an engaged audience through targeted messaging and awareness building is an important step in expanding the impact of inclusive curation.

CONCLUSION

Using a blended three-dimensional model approach has broadened my perspective and given me new knowledge and critical understanding of the intersection of social justice, global issues, and awareness. It has prompted me to question old systems and standards of practice, look for bias and exclusionary points in current systems and practice, and address them with a growth mindset. This practice ultimately celebrates artists and the narratives they speak through their work. Purposefully implementing this model makes artists visible and the change they seek to create tangible. It further speaks to audiences seeking to connect, relate, and see themselves represented through art. Normalizing differences and connecting in authentic ways reduce suffering and pain, sending a message of awareness, acceptance, and an invitation for artists and viewers alike to have a seat at the table with an empowered voice.

There is more to learn, analyze, and investigate about how to connect with internal and external audiences in the name of art as a vehicle for social change. Ultimately, to act with purpose, drawing from a broad base of knowledge and understanding, curatorial practice can exist within a framework that supports experimentation and thoughtful engagement.

REFERENCES

Chugh, D. (2018). *The person you mean to be: How good people fight bias*. New York: Harper-Collins Publishers Inc.

Díaz, C. G. (2020, July 6). Why every art institution should have a social justice curator. *Grantmakers in the Arts*. https://www.giarts.org/blog/carmen-graciela-diaz/why-every-art-institution-should-have-a-social-justice-curator

Jaworski, P., and Pitera, M. (2015). The 20-60-20 rule. *Discrete and Continuous Dynamical Systems–Series B* 21(4), 1149–66.

Katz, S., and Reisman, L. (2020). Impact of the 2020 crises on the arts and culture in the United States: The effect of COVID-19 and the Black Lives Matter movement in historical context. *International Journal of Cultural Property* 27(4), 449–65.

Morgan, T. (2018, June 1). Why MLK's right-hand man was nearly written out of history. *History.com*. https://www.history.com/news/bayard-rustin-march-on-washington-openly-gay-mlk

National Center for Education Statistics. (2022). College enrollment rates. https://nces
.ed.gov/programs/coe/indicator/cpb/college-enrollment-rate

Robert, N. (2014). Getting intersectional in museums. *Museums & Social Issues* 9(1), 24–33.

Sandoval, C. (2002). Chicana feminism and postmodernist theory: Chela Sandoval's theory
of differential consciousness. In P. M. L. Moya (Eds.), *Learning from experience minority
identities, multicultural struggles* (pp. 79–80). Oakland, CA: University of California Press.

Tatum, B. (2017). *Why are all the Black kids sitting together in the cafeteria?* (Revised edition).
New YorK: Basic Books.

Tatum, B. D. (2000). The complexity of identity: "Who am I?" In M. Adams, W. J. Blumen-
feld, H. W. Hackman, X. Zuniga, and M. L. Peters (Eds.), *Readings for diversity and social
justice: An anthology on racism, sexism, anti-semitism, heterosexism, classism and ableism*
(pp. 9–14). New York: Routledge.

30

Toward an Interactive Model of Competing Values

FROM VISUALIZATION TO TOOL KIT

Morgan Joseph Hamilton

It can be tricky, if not challenging, to develop a visualization of an abstract idea that clearly illustrates its theoretical value and practical application. Visualizations can compromise conceptual nuance for labeled definition for the sake of simplicity and readability. In my time as a doctoral student, the phrase I heard again and again was "think of this model as a continuum, not a binary." Before I learned to appreciate the ambiguity of some theories, concepts, and models, I often mumbled to myself "but if it's a continuum, why do theorists draw a binary?" I learned that every line of even the simplest binary is made up of infinite points of variation between each pole. And in a quadrant model, you multiply each point by another dimension; the binary and quadrant models do not look so rigid anymore. They are representative of myriad nuanced positions, or directions, in which its user may go. The theoretical argument becomes a practical road map for museum professionals through the *Dimensions of Curation Competing Values Exhibition Model*.

Competing values in exhibition design builds upon Quinn and Rohrbaugh's (1981) two-dimensional model (*x* and *y* axes) of organizational effectiveness. Rather than axes describing organizational imperatives, the authors align the axes to interpretive focus (Object to Audience) and curatorial power (Lone Creative to Collaborative), resulting in four quadrants of curation. Using their experience in museums and visitor-centered exhibition planning, the authors were interested in curatorial intent through cultural policy orientations. From that perspective, they introduce a *third* axis that addresses *democratization of culture* and *cultural democracy*. Two-dimensional depictions of bi-axial (*x* and *y*) graphs and charts might be a familiar form of organizing information; however, they do not necessarily translate into three-dimensional depictions. Only so much information can be included on the page before it becomes obscured; a new approach to the visual model's design was developed to enhance user interaction and strength of the competing values.

In 2020, I developed a rudimentary three-dimensional animation of the model to accompany Love and colleagues' conference presentations. The animation shows the model as it develops from a curatorial idea, where it may fall on the x and y axis model, and how it interacts with the third z axis. The aim is for the user to more clearly see the eight areas of curatorial consideration. This chapter will explain how the visualization and tool kit was developed, why it is important to increase the use of the model, and how practitioners can use it right now.

PROTOTYPING AND PROFESSIONALIZATION

The first course I took in my doctoral studies was Visitor-Centered Exhibitions, taught by Dr. Ann Rowson Love. She introduced my class to the emergent Dimensions of Curation in a presentation about culturally responsive exhibition design. I remember the confusion my peers and I experienced when she presented the slide with the two-dimensional rendering of the three-dimensional model. Once she walked us through it, step-by-step, it clicked what the model meant and what it could do. The vulnerability of this model is that not everyone will have the opportunity to see it come together sequentially as we did. Because I come to this field from fine arts, I focused my studies and production on digital media including three-dimensional modeling and web design. I immediately saw the opportunity to bring the model to life through an animation that followed her step-by-step explanation.

I connected the Dimensions Model animation process to the larger goal of making it an accessible tool when I visited the Marie Selby Botanical Gardens in Sarasota, Florida. While interning for the Ringling Museum of Art, my peers and I were invited to a behind-the-scenes tour of the Selby Gardens exhibition of rare books on botanical illustration. The leather-bound volumes were open beneath vitrines, revealing brightly colored engravings of orchids and other epiphytes. While they were transfixing, it was a smaller volume tucked into a corner display shelf that caught my attention. It was a century-old book about botany for mothers to read to their children. Before that book, botany was an abstract profession undertaken in fields, forests, and universities. Nonexperts are introduced to a working knowledge of a scientific field through this translation of knowledge sharing in the form of child-friendly illustrations. That connection demonstrated to me how the model can turn expert knowledge into a collaborative, practical process of developing expertise in museum education.

Educators of all kinds are familiar with the process of developing lessons and programs that are engaging, impactful, and fun. An important step in this process is prototyping, an iterative procedure that brings together diverse knowledge and expertise to a common design. Prototyping opens a shared space of exploration and interpretation for small design groups, or interdepartmental initiatives; no one perspective is correct, no one approach is the best (Heidt, 2013; Mason, 2015).

In industrial design, finding the quickest and least expensive way to make a product is paramount. In edu-curation, a term that combines education and curation coined by Villeneuve and Love (2017), the most important aspect of this process is two-way knowledge exchange. Exhibition designers and educators find common ground, learn from each other, and produce an experience that increases their ability to facilitate visitor learning. When the design team receives feedback from the visitors, the prototyping process begins again in a loop of refinement.

Tools like this make specialized knowledge more accessible to practicing edu-curators and their collaborative teams. Professionalization of a field is a multifaceted endeavor that does not have a "you have arrived" sign for its professionals. Rather, it is a continuing effort on behalf of the people who are passionate about the work at every level, from volunteer in the gallery to researcher in the academy (Brady, 2018). Developing tools and tool kits is a worthwhile project that has proven to be beneficial to diverse professions such as program evaluation, exhibition design, and botany. A recognizable and territorial boundary around a profession, or professional closure, does not serve the field of museum education because edu-curators come from so many educational and professional backgrounds (Gorman and Sandefur, 2011; Kletchka, 2021; Krantz and Downey, 2021). What we should focus on is a collaborative expertise that is omnidirectional and open source, what this tool kit can help achieve. The curatorial team can design stronger exhibitions by bringing the Dimensions of Curation and its practical, interactive models into exhibition design in the museum. In time, these tools will change, multiply, and improve as the collective expertise of our field shapes them for versatile use.

VISUALIZING AND INTERACTING WITH THE MODEL

My first attempt to bring the competing values model off the page was a video animation that explores how a curator or educator might define their exhibition in a particular cubic sector. Though the animation clarifies the *shape* of the model in three dimensions, it lacks a certain engagement necessary for personal connections to it. I then designed an interactive, movable model using Three.js, a JavaScript library made for interactive visuals on websites. To fill out the tool kit, I developed an interactive version based on the Dimensions of Curation decision tree, allowing the user to make simplified choices to better locate, or guide, their exhibition design.

PHASE ONE: ANIMATED VISUALIZATION

A curatorial team should design an exhibition that suits the needs of the community it serves, so I will focus on multivocal, collaborative, and engaging exhibitions that Act as an example. Given enough information about an exhibition, the curatorial team can use the model to pinpoint their design in a sector and identify changes so they can consider moving toward an exhibition that Acts. Three frames of the animation (figures 30.1, 30.2, and 30.3) illustrate the curatorial idea at the center of the axes and how the idea is found at any point between the three axes (audience focused, collaboratively developed, and intending cultural democracy).

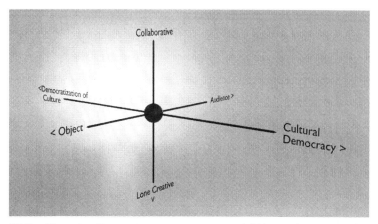

Figure 30.1. The animation prototype starts a curatorial idea at the crossroads of each axis. Every decision a curatorial team makes moves the idea toward object or audience, Lone Creative or Collaborative, or some in between. In three-dimensional space, each decision pushes the curatorial idea to a point between x, y, and z (Democratization of Culture or Cultural Democracy), describing a continuum of variation.

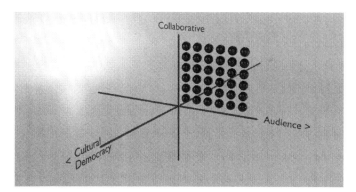

Figure 30.2. No two exhibitions are alike, and no single exhibition is exactly pinpointed by the axes and sectors.

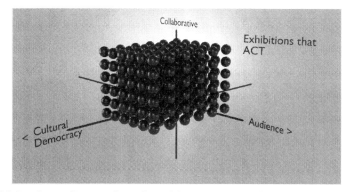

Figure 30.3. Depending on where the exhibition intentions lie on the continuum of each axis determines where one might find them on the model.

HOW YOU CAN USE THE ANIMATED VISUALIZATION

The animation prototype situates the three-dimensional model in a three-dimensional space, better representing how the curatorial decisions can move the project in a direction toward, or away from an exhibition that Acts. Remember, this example is just one of the eight cubic sectors (exhibitions that ___). The video may help to visualize how the curatorial idea builds from curatorial Focus, to Power, to Intent; it is represented by a point moving along the three axes.

PHASE TWO: AN INTERACTIVE, MOVABLE, CLICKABLE MODEL

Where the animation is a visual representation of the model in three dimensions, the interactive web model is interactive and self-guided. The prototype web model is made of three components, a list of the eight exhibitions that ___ on the right, an explanation of the selected exhibitions that ___ on the left, and a model of the three axes and eight cubic sectors in the center (figure 30.4). The model is an extension in operability from the animation, figuratively putting the model in the user's hands. When the user clicks on the list of exhibitions that ___, the model highlights and shows the resulting cubic sector, and the explanation updates.

HOW YOU CAN USE THE INTERACTIVE MODEL

One must remember that this is an abstracted, simplified depiction of the Dimensions of Curation Model, which is a continuum, not a set of solid boundaries. This tool is a means for the curators to see what sector their exhibition style falls

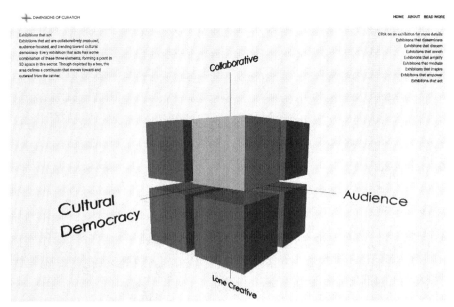

Figure 30.4. When the page loads, the model focuses on the exhibition that acts. From there, the user can click and drag the cursor to move and manipulate the model to see how the sectors and axes relate to one another. IMAGE COURTESY OF THE AUTHOR.

in. By clicking the other examples of exhibitions that ___, the user identifies how each axis interacts in three-dimensional space. With more information about the curator's exhibition design priorities, they can move farther away from, or closer to, exhibitions that act.

PHASE THREE: SELF-GUIDED DECISION TREE

The decision tree as depicted in Love, et al.'s article on Dimensions of Curation is a helpful visualization of the sequential order of defining exhibitions that ___. The interactive decision tree asks questions about how the curatorial team typically approaches their projects. Each choice moves the curators through the various aspects of exhibition design. This enables the curators to make better informed decisions about what, how, and why they are curating their exhibition.

HOW YOU CAN USE THE DECISION TREE

Think about whether your curatorial style is a solitary endeavor or a collaborative one. Do you typically focus on the object or the audience? Do your exhibitions *give* information to visitors, or are visitors implicated in the meaning-making process? The simplified, binary decisions are a way to meditate on how you tend to curate and educate (figure 30.5). There is not much room for nuance in the decision tree by design; finding where your choices lead you (to an exhibition that ___) can show trends in your curatorial process. Additionally, by choosing the *opposite* of your typical curatorial approach, you can see the types of exhibitions you avoid, or have yet to consider.

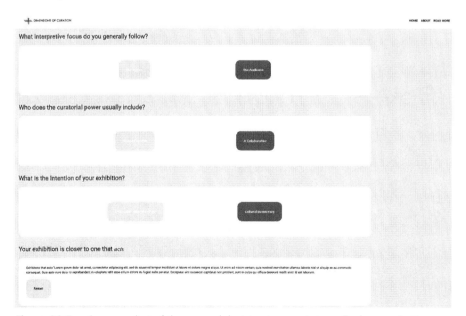

Figure 30.5. A screenshot of the opened decision tree prototype. Each green button indicates the option has been selected, resulting in an *exhibition that Acts*.
IMAGE COURTESY OF THE AUTHOR.

FUTURE DIRECTIONS

I do not claim that these tools are comprehensive; they are meant to assist with organizing abstract ideas and conceptual models by making connections to its parts. For example, the decision tree, as it exists at the time of this chapter, would be improved by working both directions. The user could make decisions in the order they are presented in the tool kit, or work from a finished or past exhibition and see how it aligns on the component axes. Currently, through simplified choices, the curator can generalize their exhibition style and see how certain choices lead to one of the eight exhibitions that ___. But providing an analytical approach starting from a current example would empower the curatorial team to make real-time, informed decisions about their exhibition design.

Regarding tool kits in the field, there are often checklists, templates, scripts, and opportunities to broaden your network. But according to culturally responsive best practices (Murawski, 2017; Kenney, 2021; MASS Action, n.d.; Seymour, 2022), they should be developed by a multivocal community of practitioners. I expect to find missed opportunities, areas that need more clarification, or areas that need simplification as edu-curators use the Dimensions of Curation and its tool kit. Through open-source collaboration, this tool kit has the potential to aid responsive and adaptable planning, design, and execution of visitor-centered exhibitions.

CONCLUSION

It is essential to remember that the Dimensions of Curation Model and its subsequent tool kit are not to prescribe rigid rules that dictate how one approaches curating for visitor engagement. They are a flexible continua that organize abstract ideas about the power and outcomes of curating in a visitor-centered culture. The curator may typically identify their style on the x axis delineating Audience from Object, and y axis spanning from Lone Creative to Collaboration continua. This model introduces the z axis which expands the model to include Democracy of Culture from Cultural Democracy to help the curator contemplate their intention. This third dimension turns the original model into an array of variations in curatorial intent, literally deepening the analysis of what, how, and why curators and educators design exhibitions.

Words can only do so much in describing the abstract qualities of axes and continua, which is where the animated visualization enters to depict them. It is beneficial to those of us who understand better through visualization while being open and transferable enough to leave room for future growth and development. The interactive three-dimensional model allows the user to build on their understanding of the animated visual by moving the model in space, deciding where to look and how to perceive the eight sectors. By turning, clicking, and seeing how the pieces fit, the curator or educator can build a more concrete understanding of the dimensions and how each sector relates to one another. The decision tree uses self-reflexive questioning so the curator or educator can think on their own work and approaches to see how they align, or misalign, with the model's dimensions. The user increases their awareness of success or missed opportunities while contemplating future improvements by following logical steps through the model's dimensions. These tools are distinct components of a whole story, one that is complex and nuanced. Each can be used in any order, on their own, or together to inform curatorial practices. They are also iterative as they can help describe or guide a project at any level or stage of design and production. Curators can use these tools at the beginning or final stages as a guide or a check on the work accomplished.

Tool kits are useful templates or strategies that democratize specialized knowledge, exemplified by the Regional Education Laboratory Program's *Program Evaluation Toolkit* and the *Getty Guide* (The Getty, 2011; REL, n.d.). Refocusing the process of professionalization on a process of collaborative expertise shares the responsibility of input and outcome, rather than defining who is or isn't a professional in the field. The visualization, interactive three-dimensional model, and self-guided decision tree serve as ways of sharing and developing expert knowledge. The Dimensions of Curation tool kit can put theoretical concepts and practical applications in the hands of curators, educators, and edu-curators to enhance the visitor and community experience. You can find the tools at the following links.

- Animated visualization: https://rowman.com/ISBN/9781538167359/Dimensions-of-Curation-Considering-Competing-Values-for-Intentional-Exhibition-Practices
- Interactive 3D model: http://morganjosephhamilton.com/docmodel/3dmodel
- Decision tree: http://morganjosephhamilton.com/docmodel/docmodel

REFERENCES

Brady, J. (2018). Toward a critical, feminist sociology of expertise. *Journal of Professions and Organizations* (5), 123–38.

The Getty. (2011). Complete guide to adult audience interpretive materials: Gallery texts and graphics. The J. Paul Getty Museum.

Gorman, E. H., and Sandefur, R. L. (2011). "Golden Age," quiescence, and revival: How the sociology of professions became the study of knowledge-based work. *Work and Occupations* 38(3), 275–302.

Heidt, M. (2013). Examining interdisciplinary prototyping in the context of cultural communication. In A. Marcus (Eds.), *Design, user experience, and usability. Health, learning, playing, cultural, and cross-cultural user experience. Lecture notes in computer science* (vol. 8013, pp. 54–61). New York: Springer.

Kenney, N. (2021, May 25). Exclusive survey: What progress have US museums made on diversity, after a year of racial reckoning? *The Art Newspaper.* https://www.theartnewspaper.com/2021/05/25/exclusive-survey-what-progress-have-us-museums-made-on-diversity-after-a-year-of-racial-reckoning

Kletchka, D. C. (2021). Art museum educators: Who are they now? *Curator: The Museum Journal* 64(1), 7997.

Krantz, A., and Downey, S. (2021). The significant loss of museum educators in 2020: A data story. *Journal of Museum Education* 46(4), 417–29.

Mason, M. (2015). Prototyping practices supporting interdisciplinary collaboration in digital media design for museums. *Museum Management and Curatorship* 30(5), 394–426.

MASS Action. (n.d.). *MASS Action toolkit.* https://www.museumaction.org.

Murawski, M. (2017, August 31). Museums are not neutral. *Art Museum Teaching*. https://artmuseumteaching.com/2017/08/31/museums-are-not-neutral/

Quinn, R. E., and Rohrbaugh, J. (1981). A competing values approach to organizational effectiveness. *Public Product Review* 5, 122–40.

REL. (n.d.). *Program Evaluation Toolkit*. https://ies.ed.gov/ncee/rel/Products/Resource/100644.

Seymour, T. (2022, August 24). What is a museum? Icom finally decides on a new definition. *The Art Newspaper*. https://www.theartnewspaper.com/2022/08/24/What-is-a-museum-icom-finally-decides-on-a-new-definition

Villeneuve, P., and Love, A. R. (2017). *Visitor-centered exhibition and edu-curation in art museums*. Lanham, MD: Rowman & Littlefield.

31

Dimensions of Education

ADAPTING THE CURATORIAL MODEL FOR MUSEUM EDUCATION

Audrey Jacobs and Ashley Williams

The *Dimensions of Curation Competing Values Model* offers museum professionals language to make strategic, dynamic decisions about exhibitions. As educators, we saw an opportunity for an adapted model that would extend the Dimensions of Curation Model's strengths and utility to programming considerations. An education-focused adaptation can support deliberate yet flexible decision-making for programming; it can also articulate curatorial values with an education lens. Educational programming—museum activities related to exhibitions, collections, or other museum aims—may in some cases form a foundational part of the curatorial process, but much museum education planning still takes place independent of curatorial activities. What programming will convey or complement exhibition goals and museum values? This tool does not sort program types into quadrants; on the contrary, some program types appear in each quadrant. We illustrate how each quadrant can influence one type of program, using the example of audio guides. We will conclude with a brief case study that highlights the tool in action in a co-curated exhibition.

COMPETING VALUES IN EDUCATION

We imagine the Dimensions of Curation Model and our adaptation expanding conversations into exhibition-related programming. While we interpreted the original model through learning theories, we kept the quadrant names (Exclusive, Traditional, Inclusive, and Sympathetic) so that the models may work as companions. Different educational approaches fit in the context of axes that describe educational focus and power. Hein's (1998) *Education Theories Model*, shifted counterclockwise ninety degrees, serves as a starting point for understanding

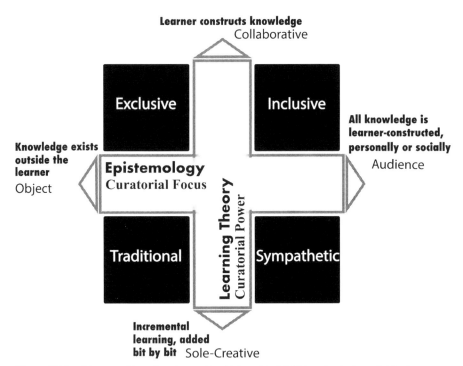

Figure 31.1. *Museum Education Competing Values Model.* This adapted model features language from both the *Dimensions of Curation* and *Educational Theories* (Hein, 1998).
IMAGE COURTESY OF THE AUTHORS.

these competing values (see figure 31.1). While we do not use Hein's quadrant names, we do adopt his *x* and *y* axes.

The *x* axis indicates where the educator centers their focus in designing programming, or the theory of knowledge. Curators navigate between a focus on the object (its art history, materiality, provenance, aesthetics, etc.) or the audience, and find a balance for their context between the two endpoints. Interpreting for an audience signals an educational, participatory, or otherwise community-driven position. Essentially, the curatorial question of being about something or for someone (Weil, 1999) is epistemological: where is knowledge located—in the object or its viewer? Stated like this, the question aligns with the continuum between visitors as receivers of knowledge and visitors as creators of knowledge. As learning moves farther right on this continuum, its nature changes to personal insights; these realizations and inspirations do not relate to the specific, physical history of the object but nevertheless give audiences insight into the object's social context (Surface and Ryan, 2018). At this right-hand endpoint, we understand that visitors create knowledge and museums frame exhibitions through a sociocultural context (Hein, 1998; Weil, 1999).

The *y* axis examines power and authority in pedagogical choices, echoing the Dimensions of Curation Model. In Hein's (1998) model, the learning theory continuum stretches between incremental, controlled learning to active learning that assumes the visitor constructs knowledge and collaborates in the learning process. In the Dimensions of Curation Model, the lone curator facilitates an exhibition's interpretation and communicates the meaning of an exhibition. On the opposite end, collaborative exhibition planning combines the efforts of a group for multifaceted exhibitions (McKenna-Cress and Kamien, 2013). In our Museum Education Competing Values Model, sharing authority can also vary from incorporating visitors' input to supporting visitors' autonomous decisions.

These competing values combine along the continua in the quadrants with varied implications for each learning context. Outcomes of different approaches change depending on the goals and circumstances of a given situation. For example, audio guides, a common and popular museum program (Smith and Tinio, 2008), range from traditional museum texts translated to an audio format (Pierroux and Qvale, 2019) to interactive and adaptive experiences (Kaghat, Azough, Fakhour, and Meknassi, 2020). Given their popularity and their ability to increase attention and memory (Schwan, Dutz, and Dreger, 2018), audio guides show us what variability a program may have based on the values and goals that make up its foundation.

KNOWLEDGE INDEPENDENT OF THE VISITOR + INCREMENTAL LEARNING = TRADITIONAL QUADRANT

The Traditional quadrant emphasizes the view that knowledge is independent of the visitor and that learning happens best in controlled, incremental stages (Hein, 1998). Like a classroom teacher preparing and delivering a lesson, the educator's authority determines learning paths. In this quadrant, visitors encounter knowledge presented to them. Educators may teach a lesson or lead a tour. But tours do not categorically fall within this quadrant: for several decades, museums have leaned on constructivist principles in programming strategies (Hein, 1998; Jeffery-Clay, 2015). We define the Traditional quadrant as learning that foregrounds objects, where the power to stimulate learning remains the educator's or educational material's domain.

Standard audio guides present information relating to the object and its historical or cultural context. Audio guides increase the amount of details and information visitors remember more than text alone (Barth, Candello, Cavalin, and Pinhanez, 2020; Schwan, 2018), especially with visual descriptions included (Hutchinson and Eardley, 2021). Relating information straightforwardly, as in the case of standard audio guides, allows visitors to engage with the exhibition content in a familiar, contemplative way.

KNOWLEDGE IS VISITOR CONSTRUCTED + INCREMENTAL LEARNING = SYMPATHETIC

In the Sympathetic quadrant, where the visitor constructs knowledge yet the educator controls the activities, programming emphasizes controlled, step-by-step processes of instruction. The curatorial model's interpretive focus on audience foregrounds the visitor's construction of meaning, and lone creative power underscores a conception of learning through expertly arranged information. Games can prompt closer looking through small, ordered steps that support the visitor's social and intellectual context; they give feedback on the visitor's progress on content learning through satisfying challenges (Ćosović and Brkić, 2019). This quadrant facilitates programming through stages, eliciting correct responses from visitors, incorporating visitor's personal and cultural contexts.

Audio programs that guide visitor interaction through progressive steps fall in the Sympathetic quadrant. The *Making Objects Speak* audio guide outlines a sequential process with incremental steps and socially relates the visitor to the content (Carbonelle, 2011). Visitors who use this guide, currently available on the website, take on the persona of a character in history as the guide ushers the visitor through its theme (Making Objects Speak, 2010). The program leans on incremental learning with content that falls within the purview of an expert or sole creative. The activity sequences stimulate the visitor to construct knowledge about the theme of the tour as it presents each new piece of information.

KNOWLEDGE IS VISITOR CONSTRUCTED + VISITOR CONSTRUCTS KNOWLEDGE = INCLUSIVE QUADRANT

The Inclusive quadrant aligns with collaboration and an audience focus. In this quadrant, the museum and community create educational experiences that encourage visitor-constructed meanings and personal interpretations of objects. Visitors actively construct knowledge through body and mind (Hein, 1998). Programming that includes collaborative art projects such as murals introduces kinesthetic components. Technology can also help when learning is collaborative or developed with the community. Virtual games are emerging that emphasize social learning through social media or aggregated responses and require visitors to interact with the game on their phones or physical components (Løvlie, et al., 2021; Vayanou, Ioannidis, Loumos, and Kargas, 2018).

Inclusive programs may use multiple perspectives or content options, guided by the visitor. Several interactive audio guides have used motion tracking to create a unique experience for each visitor (Kaghat, Azough, Fakhour, and Meknassi 2020; Yang and Chan, 2019; Zimmermann and Lorenz, 2008). Many augmented audio guides, like *SARIM*, allow visitors to explore a selection of sounds and audio comments (Kaghat, Azough, Fakhour, and Meknassi 2020). A forerunner in this technology, the *LISTEN* project provided information presented by a range of perspectives and personalities: reviewers, art historians, and restorers to name a few (Zimmermann and Lorenz, 2008). The content of these audio guides included pre-defined information from the museum and thus we imagine this program to be found on the continuum near the Exclusive quadrant. If some of the audio entries included perspectives from visitors, then it could shift more firmly into the Inclusive quadrant.

KNOWLEDGE INDEPENDENT OF THE VISITOR + VISITOR CONSTRUCTS KNOWLEDGE = EXCLUSIVE QUADRANT

The Exclusive quadrant places emphasis on subject matter related to the object and some collaboration between educator and visitor (Hein, 1998). These activities require understanding facts and discipline-based knowledge in a context connected to life. The learning in this quadrant likely includes hands-on projects that lead to conclusions corresponding to the world as described by scholarly fields. Programming like teaching artist activities, workshops, internships, and junior docent experiences underscore field-specific knowledge through directed, hands-on learning. Tours can cast the visitor in a professional role of a museum worker, with hands-on, dialogue-based projects (Murphy and Rose, 2019). These programs involve communication between visitor and educator and some shared decision-making. This sector lends itself to learning activities where professional knowledge is the goal. Educators consider carefully the evidence and organization that will support field-accepted conclusions since authority is shared, but the content is on the object.

New technology like artificial intelligence expands interactive possibilities for audio guides. Visitors to the Pinacoteca Museum in Brazil could ask the artificial intelligence–driven *Voice of Art* audio guide thousands of questions about artworks to access information they were curious about at their own pace (Barth, Candello, Cavalin, and Pinhanez 2020). The artwork's story—art history, materiality, and cultural context—takes center stage in this audio guide and the strategy of simulated conversation places this program north of the *x* axis on the far left end. Similar technology has been used to create Socratic interactions that spur reflection and transformation (Roussou, et al., 2019). This quadrant emphasizes active input from the visitor, while the content stems from museum-related fields (Hein, 1998). As visitors to the Pinacoteca Museum let their curiosity direct the information they receive, they collaborate in their learning.

PLOTTING OUR VALUES AND APPLYING THE MODEL

Programs can shift among the quadrants, and some projects can benefit from combining approaches. Educators can adjust where the program falls on the continuum, with consideration of the different values and needs of the program's context. Bringing in multiple quadrants balances the different needs of visitors and opens up more avenues for learning. To help think through the quadrants and review where programs might fit and shift on the model, we created a quick guide table (see table 31.1). Adapted from Gonzales's (2019) exhibition-type quick guide, table 31.1 asks questions educators can consider when developing programming to reflect the appropriate values for their learning goals. Educators can use this table to take inventory of current programs, to make adjustments to a program's baseline values, or as a guide to think through a new program. To illustrate how the Education Model and quick guide work, we used both to consider programming for an exhibition co-curated in Florida State University's Museum Education & Visitor-Centered Curation graduate program.

SOUNDSTITCHING THROUGH THE QUADRANTS

The 2022 Florida State University WJB Gallery exhibition, *Playing with Art: Cassia Kite and the Invention of Soundstitching*, highlighted how the artist translates

Table 31.1. Quick Guide: Thinking Through the Model

	Traditional	Sympathetic	Inclusive	Exclusive
How do learners and educators influence each other?	Educators provide knowledge to visitors; one-direction flow of influence	Educators prompt learners to make learning connections; educator influences learner heavily, learner influences educator a little	Two-way influence; lots of adjustments to learning based on interaction	Educators adjust learning moderately frequently based on learner input
How internal or external is knowledge?	Knowledge is external, located in the object, the field, the field expert	Knowledge is internally constructed but prompted by a subject-matter expert	Knowledge is internally constructed, especially with social and emotional influence	Knowledge is external; learner and educator work together to discover insights held in the object
How much personal interpretation is desirable for learning?	Minimal to no personal interpretation; the learner receives field-accepted information about the object	Learners interpret the informational inputs to make the desired connections	Insights about the object are almost exclusively filtered through personal interpretation and comparisons of interpretations made in groups	Learners interpret learning goals in a minimally personal way
How much does collaboration support learning?	Educators do not collaborate with learners; rather, they present to learners	Collaboration consists of educator prompting responses, learners responding, and educators offering corrections	Collaboration is foundational to learning	Learners collaborate in learning through directed activities; some collaboration on decisions
How much is the learner actively involved?	Learner receives information	Learner makes connections through responding to prompts	Learner is actively engaged in learning through mind and body, learner may be making significant decisions about direction of learning	Learning happens through active engagement, sometimes interacting with objects; learner may make some decisions about direction of learning
What is the educator's role?	Educators exclusively distribute the information; material may be delivered live, in person, recorded, or virtual	Based on information about learners, educators design material for learners to progress through and offer corrections	Educators support learners in exploration of self and subject matter, goal-setting, and progress	Educators design a project for learners and assist them through the learning goals, adjusting as needed

her stitched imagery into musical compositions. Kite's Soundstitching projects become multisensory experiences with musical compositions based on the rhythms of colors in the artist's embroidery (Kite, n.d.). *Playing with Art* used a visitor-centered curatorial process and, while we talked a great deal with the artist, decisions remained with the curatorial class. We think of the exhibition as falling in the Sympathetic quadrant on the Dimensions of Curation Model. We wanted to test the Education Model in conjunction with this Sympathetic quadrant exhibition and attend to different learners by incorporating programs from each quadrant. We first planned programs that would invite a range of engagement, from contemplative to playful. Using our quick guide table (see table 31.1), we asked ourselves the six questions in relation to each program to see where it fell on the continuum, and made adjustments. The co-curation team decided on four programs: an artist talk, a workshop, a zine activity, and a jam session. A weather event prevented the jam session, but the program was designed with Inclusive values in mind.

The first program invited Cassia Kite to convey her process directly through an artist talk. The values in this program rely on knowledge residing in the expert, as well as information being incrementally presented throughout the course of the talk. When we used the quick guide to think about the artist talk, our responses to each question fit within the Traditional column. The educator, in this case the artist, presents information to the visitor, and the visitor receives that information. Collaboration or personal interpretation is not necessary for this program. The program has strengths in allowing for the straightforward communication of an expert perspective on the art form and allowing visitors to receive information without expectations for participation or social interaction.

While the artist talk disseminated knowledge, we also wanted to encourage exploration of the artist's practice through social interaction. In a jam session, we intended to bring together community members and students from the school of music to the gallery to collaborate and create new musical meanings inspired by the art. Visitors could try composing and playing one of Kite's Soundstitchings. This programming fits within the Inclusive quadrant by underscoring participants' agency and collaboration with the artist while the co-curators facilitate the experience or step back entirely in a support role. In our planning, the jam session emphasized personal interpretations through visitors creating their own musical creations while still collaborating with the artist through using her work as inspiration.

After creating a zine, we found that this program could shift between the Sympathetic and Exclusive quadrants depending on what values we focused on when creating the content. We used this information to discuss how to edit the zine to more fully support learners through Sympathetic values. We wanted our zine to walk through Kite's process step-by-step and also include pages for visitors to practice stitching. We included questions that encouraged visitors' own creative reflections, prompting them to make connections. We situated our zine in the Sympathetic quadrant because the activities stimulate visitors to practice the artist's process and prompt self-reflection in small, controlled steps.

Our final program, an artist workshop, fits within the Exclusive quadrant. The artist workshop took place after the artist talk and invited visitors to learn with the artist. This program brought a hands-on dimension to learning Kite's media. Participants explored Kite's method of embroidering images through guided demonstrations, feedback, and conversation. Because the artist lecture and workshop were distinct parts of a larger activity, we used our table to understand the distinct pedagogical values inherent in the two parts. Programs might not always fit within one quadrant. In some situations, there may be too many participants to offer collaboration with the educator or even other participants; some subject matter may greatly benefit from incremental, controlled learning with feedback. Moving from one quadrant to another balances the different needs and constraints of disparate situations and opens up more avenues for learning.

CONCLUSION

Museum educators encounter competing values with each programming decision. Foundational decisions can make great changes in the shape of a program: how to structure content delivery and how to guide our learners, how our learners may interact with us and the content, and whether our program will concentrate on the knowledge held in objects or made through social and personal connections. Educators can create programming alongside or independent of an exhibition's curatorial alignment. When deeply considered and developed, educators can incite memorable, meaningful museum experiences in any quadrant. With this model, educators can navigate the tensions among competing values and make more considered decisions throughout their program design.

REFERENCES

Barth, F., Candello, H., Cavalin, P., and Pinhanez, C. (2020). Intentions, meanings, and whys: Designing content for voice-based conversational museum guides. In *Proceedings of the 2nd Conference on Conversational User Interfaces* (pp. 1–8). ACM Digital Library.

Carbonelle, B. M. (2011). Virtual field trips: Creating audio tours for teaching with visual culture. *Transformations: The Journal of Inclusive Scholarship and Pedagogy* 22(1), 139–42.

Ćosović, M., and Brkić, B. R. (2019). Game-based learning in museums: Cultural heritage applications. *Information* 11(22), 1–13.

Gonzales, E. (2019). *Exhibitions for social justice*. New York: Routledge.

Hein, G. E. (1998). *Learning in the museum*. New York: Taylor & Francis Group.

Hutchinson, R., and Eardley, A. F. (2021). Inclusive museum audio guides: "Guided looking" through audio description enhances memorability of artworks for sighted audiences. *Museum Management and Curatorship* 36(4), 427–46.

Jeffery-Clay, K. R. (2015). Constructivism in museums: How museums create meaningful learning environments. *Journal of Museum Education* 23(1), 3–7.

Kaghat, F. Z., Azough, A., Fakhour, M., and Meknassi, M. (2020). A new audio augmented reality interaction and adaptation model for museum visits. *Computers & Electrical Engineering* 84, 1–13.

Kite, C. (n.d.). *Soundstitching*. Retrieved August 1, 2022. http://www.cassiakite.com/Soundstitching.php

Løvlie, A. S., Ryding, K., Spence, J., Rajkowska, P., Waern, A., Wray, T., Benford, S., Preston, W., and Clare-Thorn, E. (2021). Playing games with Tito: Designing hybrid museum experiences for critical play. *Journal on Computing and Cultural Heritage* 14(2), 1–26.

Making Objects Speak. (2010). *Making objects speak: Portable audio guides for teaching with visual culture in the humanities.* http://jjcweb.jjay.cuny.edu/history/making_objects_speak/

McKenna-Cress, P., and Kamien, J. (2013). *Creating exhibitions: Collaboration in the planning, development, and design of innovative experiences.* New York: John Wiley & Sons.

Murphy, P. A., and Rose, D. (2019). Curator's curiosities: Active learning as interpretive pedagogy. *Journal of Museum Education* 44(1), 81–88.

Pierroux, P., and Qvale, A. (2019). Wall texts in collection exhibitions: Bastions of enlightenment and interfaces for experience. *Nordisk Museologi* 1, 39–50.

Roussou, M., Perry, S., Katifori, A., Vassos, S., Tzougantou, A., and McKinney, S. (2019) Transformation through provocation? Designing a "bot of conviction" to challenge conceptions and evoke critical reflection. In *CHI '19 proceedings: Conference on Human Factors in Computing Systems* (pp. 1–13). ACM Digital Library.

Schwan, S., Dutz, S., and Dreger, F. (2018). Multimedia in the wild: Testing the validity of multimedia learning principles in an art exhibition. *Learning and Instruction* 55, 158–57.

Smith, J. K., and Tinio, P. P. L. (2008). Audibly engaged: Talking the walk. In L. Tallon and K. Walker (Eds.), *Digital technologies and the museum experience: Handheld guides and other media* (pp. 63–78). Lanham, MD: AltaMira Press.

Surface, M. H., and Ryan, N. (2018). Developing close looking, creativity, and community through writing and art. *Journal of Museum Education* 43(4), 356–64.

Vayanou, M., Ioannidis, Y., Loumos, G., and Kargas, A. (2018). How to play storytelling games with masterpieces: From art galleries to hybrid board games. *Journal of Computers in Education* 6(1), 79–116.

Weil, S. (1999). From being about something to being for somebody: The ongoing transformation of the American museum. *Daedalus* 128(3), 229–58.

Yang, J., and Chan, C. Y. (2019). Audio-augmented museum experiences with gaze tracking. In *Proceedings of the 18th international conference on mobile and ubiquitous multimedia* (pp. 1–5). ACM Digital Library.

Zimmermann, A., and Lorenz, A. (2008). LISTEN: A user-adaptive audio-augmented museum guide. *User Modeling and User-Adapted Interaction* 18(5), 389–416.

Index

academic museum, 8, 43; teaching museum, 46; university museum, 45. *See also* FSU Museum of Fine Arts, Galleries at Kean University, LSU Museum of Art, Loeb Art Center, Ringling Museum of Art, Rollins Museum of Art, University of North Texas College of Visual Art and Design Galleries, University of Wyoming Art Museum

accessibility. *See* diversity, equity, accessibility, inclusion

act, 77, 154, 158, 169, 173-174, 187, 197, 204, 207

activism, 46-7, 82; activist, 50, 131, 135, 155, 157, 194

aesthetic preference, 141, 143

AI (artificial intelligence), 123

Alexander, Edward P., 6

ally, 12, 46-48, 50, 53

American Alliance of Museums, 4, 20, 179

amplify, 105, 107, 109, 113, 168-169, 173, 192

animation, 203-204, 206

Applebaum, Lauren, 5

artist residency, 85-87, 89

Artists' Association of China, 21

artmaking tutorials, 111,

arts colony, 118

art therapy, 112

audio guide, 161, 190, 211, 213-215; audio stories visitor guide, 148; audio tour, 187, 189

bilingual labels. *See* labels

BIPOC, 19, 266-7

Black History Month, 50

Black Lives Matter, 181, 197

board members, 58

board of trustees, 53

Boda, Jay, 165

Bonnefanten Museum, 96, 99-100

Bronx Museum, 194

Bucharest University, 106

Butler, Shelley Ruth, 36

Callihan, Elisabeth, 181

Cameron, Duncan F., 4

campus, 46, 73, 82-83, 172, 196

Carr, David, 112

censorship, 122-123

Charter Oak Cultural Center, 154

children, 19, 43, 55, 74, 96-97, 99-101, 112-113, 140-145, 147-149, 203; children's books, 41. *See also* young people

Civil Rights Institute, 43,

Civil Rights Movement, 194

climate action movement, 135

climate change, 4, 29, 79, 81-83, 135, 181

close looking, 73, 82, 124, 187; deep looking, 129

Clyfford Still Museum, 140-141, 144-145

co-creation, 4, 19, 28, 137-138

co-curation/co-curators, 4

collaboration, 5-7, 12, 18-19, 21, 28-29, 32, 34, 36, 41, 45; collaborative process, 47, 50, 53, 56, 58, 60-61, 64, 145, 147-148, 154-157, 194-195, 204, 208-209, 213-215, 217-218; collaboration with impacted/source communities, 112-113, 128; compensation for, 67, 70, 72, 74; institutional collaboration, 99, 133, 135, 140, 141-143, 170, 173-174, 178-179, 187; collaborative art, 103, 105; interdisciplinary collaboration, 86-87, 93, 96; pandemic's effects on, 75, 77, 82

college, 25-26, 28, 46-47, 50, 79, 83

colonialism, 45, 69, 180; postcolonialism, 5

community, 48, 154-156, 179, 197; community-based or co-curated approaches, 8, 58-60, 64; community members, 12, 17-19, 45, 52-57, 167-168,

217; community partners, 93, 214; community voices, 20, 43, 192, 208

community-driven approach, 106–107, 112, 212

community-driven perspective, 9, 120, 141

community participation, 4, 135, 159; community-specific collaboration 5; community collaboration 6, 145, 152; community expertise, 60, 63, 85–86, 128; community involvement, 103, 131, 181–182; source community, 105, 148; community identities, 113, 140, 177–178, 194

Competing Values Model. *See* Quinn and Rohrbaugh

Confucius Museum, 19

constructivism, 4, 74, 113, 129, 175, 179, 213

COVID-19. *See* pandemic

Creative Expression Lab. *See* gallery activities

Crenshaw, Kimberlé, 199

Crimp, Douglas, 37

cross-departmental partners, 43, 53–54, 174, 185

cross-discipline or integrated planning, 72, 79

cultural competency, 181

cultural democracy, 9, 45, 74, 82–83, 86–87, 105–106, 112–113, 117–118, 120, 125, 128, 131, 135, 156, 171, 182, 192, 208

cultural humility, 181

culturally specific art, 85–86

culture bearers, 85–87. *See also* knowledge bearers or knowledge-keepers

curricula, 122; curriculum development, 199; curricular goals, 43, 142

Czajkowski, Jennifer Wild, 12

curricular exhibition, 46–47, 50

Davies, Sue M., 7

diversity, equity, accessibility, inclusion (DEAI), 4–5, 18, 20, 40, 43, 48, 52–53, 56, 64, 94, 112–113, 119, 128–129, 131, 136, 142, 154–156, 159, 174, 177–178, 181, 188–189, 192, 194, 197, 199

decision tree, 9, 204, 207–209

decolonizing museums, 5, 181

democratization of culture, 9, 67, 70, 74, 94, 100, 117, 128, 143, 147, 168, 171, 197

Denver Art Museum, 143

Denver Museum of Nature and Science, 142

Department of Culture and Education of the German Consulate General Shanghai, 34

Des Moines Art Center, 17–20

dialogical approach, 61

Díaz, Carmen Graciela, 194

didactic labels. *See* labels

didactics, 50, 74, 82, 166

Dierking, Lynn D., 4

digitalization, 36

digital literacy, 122

digital tools, 187

discern, 82, 86,

disseminate, 9, 11, 67, 71–72, 75, 77, 94–95, 197

docent volunteers, 53, 215. *See also* volunteers

Dodd Center for Human Rights, 154–155

early learning, 140

educational turn, 179

edu-curation, 120, 122, 127, 177–182, 187, 204; edu-curator, 4, 18, 165, 208-9

emancipation, 69, 122

emotional expressions, 54

empower, 143, 147, 152, 171, 173–174, 187, 200

empowerment, 50, 75, 77, 145, 196

engagement, 3–6, 18–20, 36, 41, 43, 45, 46, 52, 56, 59, 64, 83, 95, 109, 111–113, 128, 132, 133, 166, 177, 193, 195, 197, 200, 204, 208

enrich, 77, 94–95, 97, 99–100, 169, 171, 173, 191

environmentalism, 54, 138, 195

environmental justice, 41, 43,

equity. *See* diversity, equity, accessibility, inclusion

evaluation, 61, 64, 145, 174, 180, 204

Everhart Museum, 109

exclusive, 8, 28, 34, 36, 82, 100, 113, 214, 217

extended labels. *See* labels

faculty, 8, 46, 48, 50, 82, 193

Falk, John H., 4–5

families, 17, 19, 43, 96, 100–101, 111–112, 140, 143, 148–149, 152; family

connection, 31, 61, 109–110; family exhibition, 147. *See also* children
Feldman, Kaywin, 181
feminism, 69, 181, 195,
feminist systems theory, 178
Florida State University, 40, 43, 165–166, 178, 180, 215,
Floyd, George, 194
Friedman, Milton, 37
FSU Museum of Fine Arts, 40–41, 43, 45

Galleries at Kean University, 193, 195–197, 199
gallery activities; activity bags, 43; activity stations, 152; Creative Expression Lab, 109–113; recording booth, 48, 50; Speed Stories, 74–75
gallery tours. *See* tours
generational knowledge, 109
George Washington University Museum and The Textile Museum, 173
globalization 4, 46
Goldsboro History Museum, 50
Gonzales, Elena, 215
Gray, Clive, 9
Greenslit, Jana Nicole, 5
guided discussion, 165, 175

Harris, Natalie, 5
Hein, George, 4, 129, 211–212
Heritage Center at Red Cloud, 85
hierarchy, 5, 18, 87, 92, 179; nonhierarchical exhibition, 55
hiring practices, 199
Hooper-Greenfield, Eilean, 4

immigrant, 8, 61, 178
inclusive, 9, 19–20, 28, 50, 56–57, 60–61, 70–71, 95, 120, 128, 132, 140, 143, 145, 177–178, 193–197, 200, 214, 217
Indigenous, 5, 60, 87, 110, 113
inspire, 77, 128, 131, 135, 138, 196
interdepartmental curation, 41, 59, 203. *See also* collaboration
interdisciplinary curation, 112, 187; interdisciplinary gallery, 79; interdisciplinary programming, 83; interdisciplinary roles, 179
International Association for Public Participation, 142

International Conference of Museums (ICOM), 22
intersectionality, 193, 195–197
interviews: for exhibition development, 48, 87, 106, 135, 137, 148–149, 151, 187; for evaluation 145, 162; for readers theatre, 166
iPads. *See* labels

Jiang, Xiaonan, 8, 207
junior executive board, 53

Kean University, 193–194, 196–197, 199
King, Dr. Martin Luther, 194
Kletchka, Dana, 5
knowledge bearers /knowledge-keepers, 8, 10, 105, 128, 178. *See also* culture bearers
Koke, Judy, 106
Korn, Randi, 3
Krogh-Jespersen, Sheila, 5

labels, 48, 61, 82, 92–93, 95; bilingual labels, 25, 143; didactic labels, 55; extended labels, 54; iPads as labels, 129; object labels 22, 74, 170; QR codes, 22–23, 25, 144, 169–170; question labels or touch labels, 187; translations, 70–71
Lakhóta, 85
Latham, Kiersten F., 5, 179
leadership, 4, 87, 177, 182, 193, 197, 199
Lehrer, Erica, 36
LGBTQ or LGBTQIA+, 17–20, 50, 194
Liu Haisu Art Museum, 34
lived experience, 18, 29, 41, 43, 45, 48, 112–113, 195
Loeb Art Center (Frances Lehman Loeb Art Center), 79, 82
lone creative or lone curator, 7–8, 10, 22–23, 48, 57, 67, 87, 89, 113, 117, 120, 135, 168, 170, 174–175, 178, 194, 197, 202, 208, 213
Lonetree, Amy, 5
Louisiana State University, 127
Love, Ann R., 8, 165, 180, 207
LSU Museum of Art, 127–128

marginalized voices, 4, 18–20, 47–48, 181, 194–196
Marie Selby Botanical Gardens,166, 203

Martin, Trayvon, 50
MAS (Museum aan de Stroom), 147–149
McCall, Vikki, 9
meaning making, 60–61, 113, 128–129, 175, 207
mediate, 117, 120, 122–125, 168, 170, 173, 194
Meunier Museum, 189
Mia (Minneapolis Institute of Art), 181
Missing and Murdered Indigenous Women (MMIW), 87–88
mission and vision statement, 56
M Leuven, 158, 185, 192
Montgomery Museum of Fine Arts, 52, 54, 56–57
mucem, 103, 105–107
Mulcahy, Kevin, 9
multiple voices or multivocality, 60–61, 71, 93, 95, 178–179, 204, 208
Musée de l'Homme, 105
Musée des Arts et Traditions Populaires, 105
Musée International du Carnaval et du Masque (International Museum of Carnival and Mask), 106
Museum Education Competing Values Model, 211
museum education or educator, 113, 178–180, 182, 203–204, 211
museum of mutuality, 56

nontraditional curation, 166–168
Northeast Regional Conference of the Social Studies, 155

object-based inquiry, 113
object-based learning, 5
object labels. See labels
Occupy Wall Street, 181
Ohio State University, 180
oral storytelling, 165
O'Sullivan, Terry J., 7

Padure, Cristian, 107
pandemic or COVID-19, 28–30, 32, 33–34, 37, 40, 74, 76, 83, 86, 109, 111, 113, 116, 118–119, 132, 145, 177; post-pandemic, 5, 33, 143
Paris, Scott, 112
participation, 4, 37, 43, 56, 8–87, 93–94, 120, 123–125, 128, 132. 135, 138, 141,

156–157, 158, 197, 217; participatory elements, 18, 74–75, 137, 147, 151; participatory practice, 36, 107, 132, 135, 212
Paton, Rob, 7
permanent collection, 52, 58, 60, 73, 79, 103, 109, 116, 185; semipermanent collection, 147
play, 97, 100, 143
post-critical museology, 4
prejudice, 106–107, 194–196
Price, C. Aaron, 5
professional certification, 179
professional development, 60, 64, 165, 180
professionalization, 177, 179, 181, 204, 209
programming, 3, 19, 32, 41, 43, 50, 52, 56, 83, 86, 112–113, 123, 128, 131–132, 140, 179–180, 211, 213– 215, 217–218
prototyping, 203–206
Provincetown Art Association and Museum, 116
public wellbeing, 36–37. See also well-being

QR codes. See labels
queer, 17–20
questioning: engagement strategy, 161; self-reflective, 208
question labels or touch labels. See labels
Quinn and Rohrbaugh, 6–8, 202
Quinn, Kimberly A., 5

racism, 4, 40, 46, 103, 107, 155–156, 180, 194–196
Radermacker, Anne-Sophie, 36
readers theatre, 165, 175
Recht-Op, 148
refugee, 50, 61
relational practice, 60, 64
responsive, 32, 36, 41, 60, 64, 203, 208
retrospective exhibition, 67, 69
Ringling Museum of Art, 165–168, 203
Robert, Nicole, 195
Rodin Museum, 189
Rollins College, 46–47, 50
Rollins Museum of Art, 46, 50
Roma, 103, 105–107
Ryan, Keri, 106

Saint Peter's Church, Leuven, 191–192
Salort-Pons, Salvador, 12

Sandell, Richard, 111
Sandoval, Chela, 195
scenography, scenographic design, scenographer, 8, 97, 124, 148, 158, 162, 187
school segregation, 154–156
screen culture, 120, 122–124
Segovia, Gloria, 5
sense of belonging, 20, 112, 143, 149
sexuality, 17–18, 50, 113, 194
Shandong Museum, 91, 93–95
shared ownership, 54, 143
Silk Road Arts Center, 21
Simmons, John E., 179
Simon, Nina, 4, 112, 128, 181
S.M.A.K. (Stedelijk Museum voor Actuele Kunst/The Municipal Museum of Contemporary Art), 70, 133, 135, 137
social change, 5, 22, 54, 120, 132, 178, 181, 194–196, 200
social distancing, 32, 33, 36
social justice, 47, 112, 154–155, 181, 193, 194–195, 200
social media, 25, 41, 43, 93, 214
social relevance, 4, 46, 181, 197
socioemotional learning, 109
Spectrum of Public Participation, 142, 145
Sport and Medical Science Academy, 155
Stadstriënnale Hasselt-Genk, 120
stereotypes, 106–107
storytelling, 29, 31, 43, 45, 74–75, 149, 165, 193, 196
students, 25–26, 28–29, 31, 43, 46–48, 50, 73, 82–83, 112–113, 123–124, 127–128, 131, 133, 135, 137–138, 143, 155, 157, 165–167, 180, 187, 189, 193–194, 196, 199, 217
Studio ORKA, 148–149
supported interpretation, 129
sympathetic, 8, 40, 45, 46–48, 129, 197, 213–214, 217

target group or audience, 95, 100, 107, 122, 147, 159, 186, 188, 193, 200
teaching museum. See academic museum
Thunberg, Greta, 135
tours, 19, 43, 94, 111–112, 133, 159, 188, 213–215; behind-the-scenes tour, 203; virtual tour, 50. See also audio guide

Tucson Museum of Art and Historic Block, 58–60, 63
Tufts University, 180
traditional, 4, 7–8, 17–20, 21, 23, 25, 33, 45, 52, 56, 61, 64, 67, 71, 82–83, 105–106, 113, 117, 120, 132, 178, 187, 213
training, 4, 9, 58, 60, 63, 122, 161, 177–182
transhistoricity, 185–186
translations. See labels
trust, 18, 29, 32, 53, 64, 142, 178, 190

university museum. See academic museum
University of Connecticut, 154–155, 157
University of North Texas, 28–29, 31–32
University of North Texas College of Visual Arts and Design, 28
University of Wyoming, 73
University of Wyoming Art Museum, 73–74, 77

Van Mensch, Peter, 4
Vassar College, 79, 81, 83
Viera, Alicia, 180
Villeneuve, Pat, 8, 56, 128, 180, 204
visitor-centered curation, 4–6, 12, 18, 41, 95, 101, 152, 165, 178–180, 202–203, 208, 215, 217
visitor engagement. See engagement
visual development (children's development), 141
visual literacy, 70, 185–187, 190
volunteer, 58, 175, 204
volunteer training, 60

wall texts, 25, 152, 187
water protectors, 41, 43, 45
web design, 203
Weil, Stephen, 4, 179–180
well-being, 5–6, 56, 101, 107, 113, 145. See also public well-being
Wessel, Brooke, 8, 207
Women's March, 181
workshops, 60, 111–112, 124, 133, 148, 159, 165, 179, 215

young people, 74, 86, 96, 98, 100, 113, 120, 122, 131, 133, 135–137, 142, 156, 188; youth, 124, 135, 156. See also children

Zoom, 29, 166, 169

About the Contributors

Peter Aerts is head of education and communication at S.M.A.K., Ghent, Belgium. After his MFA at St-Lucas Antwerp and The School of Communication Arts, London, Aerts had a career as an advertising art director and creative director. Aerts teaches creative problem-solving at Studio Communication Design, St-Lucas School of Arts. His S.M.A.K. team has a strong interest in audience engagement and outreach, with a particular focus on inclusion. He sees the development of new forms of museum experience inside and outside the museum walls as an ongoing, museum-wide process that should strive for strong local relevance with international resonance.

Nancy Ariza, a native of Brooklyn, New York, began her career as a museum professional at the Everhart Museum of Natural History, Science & Art in Scranton, Pennsylvania. After earning her bachelor's degree in education from Keystone College, La Plume, Pennsylvania, in 2019, she became the Everhart's assistant director of public programs, a role in which she served until transitioning into her current position of collections manager and registrar in 2022. Ariza's work includes overseeing all aspects of collections care and documentation; she is especially interested in the Everhart's expansive pinned butterfly, woodcut, and silkscreen collections.

Grant Benoit is an artist and educator who received his MFA in printmaking from Southern Illinois University in Carbondale in 2015. Benoit has taught in traditional and nontraditional educational institutions for the past ten years including Louisiana State University Museum of Art, Arrowmont School of Arts and Crafts, and the Bascom: A Center for the Visual Arts. Benoit is currently the director of education at Craft Alliance, an urban craft-centered school in St. Louis, Missouri.

Laura Ashley N. Bocquin is an artist and art educator with over eighteen years of experience in the field of nonprofit community engagement. From 2004 to 2022, she led a range of educational and enrichment programs for the Montgomery Museum of Fine Arts, with an emphasis on connecting local artists to the broader community. Currently, she teaches visual art and Advanced Placement art history for the Montgomery Academy and sponsors the school's Art Honor Society chapter, continuing her mission to help others connect with art. Bocquin earned her BA in English with a minor in art history from Auburn University at Montgomery, Alabama.

Jay Boda is the associate director of academic affairs and collections at the John and Mable Ringling Museum of Art in Sarasota, Florida—a division of Florida

State University. Along with leading The Ringling's Program Team, Boda teaches graduate courses for Florida State University's Museums and Cultural Heritage Studies program and collaborates with Museum Education and Visitor-centered Curation faculty and students. His research areas include visitor studies, performance-based pedagogies, and transmedia storytelling in museums. Boda is a combat veteran and honorably retired from the US Air Force in 2010.

Annie Booth is the curatorial assistant and visitor engagement coordinator at the Florida State University Museum of Fine Arts and a graduate of Florida State University with a MA in Museum and Cultural Heritage Studies and a certificate in Museum Education and Visitor-Centered Curation. She oversees Museum of Fine Arts' educational programming, internship program, and social media, specializing in visitor engagement. Conducting research and exhibition planning, she recently co-curated *A Shared Body* and *Boundless Terrain* at the Museum of Fina Arts. She has extensive experience working with a wide range of partners and stakeholders and presented her research at the Native American Art Studies Association conference.

Christine C. Brindza serves as senior curator and curator of art of the American West at the Tucson Museum of Art and Historic Block. She has spearheaded exhibitions that broaden representation of the American West, provide multiple access points, and consider relevance to local audiences. In her curatorial practice, she actively engages with various collaborators and integrates community expertise. Brindza has an MA in Archival, Museum, and Editing Studies and a BA in art history from Duquesne University in Pittsburgh, Pennsylvania, and is currently pursuing a PhD at the University of Arizona.

Peter Carpreau studied art science at the KU Leuven, Paris IV Sorbonne, and Cambridge. As scientific collaborator of the Ghent Museum of Fine Arts, he was one of the founders of the study center for Flemish art of the nineteenth and twentieth centuries. For fourteen years, he was head of the department of Old Masters and senior curator of M Leuven. He has several exhibitions in Belgium and abroad to his credit, including *Power and Beauty: The Arenbergs*, *Edgard Tytgat: Memory of a Much-Loved Window*, and *Michiel Coxcie, The Flemish Raphael*. Today he is the deputy director-general of the War Heritage Institute.

Nicole Cromartie is the director of learning and engagement at the Clyfford Still Museum. She is fifteen years into her journey as a museum educator, with experience in museum interpretation, public programming, evaluation, research, and curation. Early learning and collaboration in museums are her dual passions and fundamental to her thinking on making museum experiences meaningful, relevant, inclusive, and enjoyable for all. In 2021, Cromartie's first book was published, *Evaluating Early Learning: Planning for our Youngest Visitors*, which presents developmentally appropriate and culturally relevant practices for engaging young children in museums. Cromartie holds an MA in Curatorial Practice from California College of the Arts and a BA in art history from the University of Florida.

Xuejing Dai is the assistant researcher and deputy director of the exhibition and display department at Shandong Museum, China. She is also a doctoral candidate in the School of History and Culture at Shandong University, China. Her research interests include museum display and education.

Emily Dellheim is a museum educator, cultural practitioner, and artist who also works in higher education. She has ten years of experience working in curatorial and education departments within national and international museums, in addition to teaching university courses in art history and museum studies. Dellheim uses art to activate equitable encounters and community-driven inquiry, both inside and beyond the museum and classroom. Her work in Italy with immigrant communities has focused on creating inclusive, intercultural museum programs and forging accessible connections to art. She is currently pursuing her PhD in Museum Education and Visitor-Centered Curation at Florida State University.

Gerd Dierckx (born 1955, Belgium), founder and driving force of Rasa, curated a wide range of traveling exhibitions of contemporary art for children from 1992 onward. Each of her thirty exhibitions was a creative cross-pollination between artists and various professionals and shown at museums and cultural centers in Belgium and abroad. She began developing her holistic art approach allowing children to experience art with all their senses while working as an art educator at the KMSKA (Royal Museum of Fine Arts) in Antwerp (1978–1988) and later curated the first museum exhibitions for children, *Colour* and *Line*, in Belgium at the Stedelijk Museum in Sint-Niklaas (1989–1992).

Stefanie Dlugosz-Acton is the director of the College of Visual Arts and Design Galleries at the University of North Texas. She has worked at the Nelson-Atkins Museum of Art in Kansas City, Missouri; Cranbrook Center for Collections and Research, Bloomfield Hills, Michigan; The Sidney and Lois Eskenazi Museum of Art at Indiana University, Bloomington, Indiana; and the Dallas Museum of Art. Dlugosz-Acton received a BFA from the Kansas City Art Institute, Kansas City, Missouri, double majoring in fibers and art history and completed an MA in art history from Indiana University, Bloomington, Indiana, where she specialized in twentieth- and twenty-first-century art and design.

Charlie Farrell is a museum professional interested in contemporary art of the African diaspora. Farrell strives to build a practice that centers community and invites diverse audiences inside museums. Additionally, she is always excited to work with living artists and collaborate in bringing their vision to life. Past museums she has worked at include the John and Mable Ringling of Art in Sarasota, Florida; the Miami Museum of Contemporary Art of the African Diaspora in Miami, Florida; and the Saint Louis Art Museum in St. Louis, Missouri.

Kara Fedje, researcher/teacher/student/artist, is currently studying museum education and visitor-centered curation in the Department of Art Education at Florida State University. With more than twelve years of experience in the museum education field, she is interested in queering museum experiences and researching how visitors and non-visitors do and do not have a sense of belonging in museums. When not working, she enjoys adventuring with her partner, Dr. Monae Verbeke, and their daughter, Vivian Violet Verbeke.

Julia Ferloni is a French curator at Mucem (Museum of Civilisation of Europe and the Mediterranean), Marseille. She specializes in Oceanian art and societies. She taught this discipline at the Ecole du Louvre and was curator of the Oceania section at the Muséum d'Histoire Naturelle in Rouen, in collaboration with the Museum of New Zealand Te Papa Tongarewa (2011). She has specialized in participatory museum projects, including the exhibition *Carte Blanche à l'Hôpital d'Oissel* (Muséum Rouen, 2010), and the survey *Romani Professions and Know-How in Europe and the Mediterranean* (Mucem, 2019–2021), and *Barvalo* (Mucem, 2023), for which she is studying for a PhD at the Amsterdam School for Cultural Analysis (University of Amsterdam).

Roselyne Francken holds two master's degrees from KU Leuven, in Japanology and in art history. She was appointed curator of the Asia Collection at the MAS (Museum aan de Stroom) in Antwerp in October 2018. In addition, she is currently pursuing a PhD in art history with research set in the broader framework of the study of fin-de-siècle Japonisme in Belgium. Francken is a member of the independent working group Restitution Belgium that developed a series of ethical guidelines for the management and restitution of colonial collections in Belgium.

Katie Fuller is a doctoral candidate in art education with a certificate in Museum Education and Visitor-Centered Curation at Florida State University and lives in New York. She was an educator for eleven years before curating her first show in 2016. She has curated exhibitions nationally that challenge how racialized differences are projected. She works with local researchers, activists, and policymakers to write curriculum for the exhibitions and presents the content of the shows at education conferences, universities, and afterschool programs. Fuller's exhibitions have been reviewed by national art magazines. She is published in the *Journal for Social Theory in Art Education* and the *Journal for Cultural Theory in Art Education*.

Dr. Cecilia Garibay is principal of Garibay Group, a nationally recognized research and evaluation consulting firm. Her research focuses on the study and development of equity-focused research, evaluation, and organizational change in museums. She brings a bicultural/bilingual perspective to her work and specializes in culturally responsive approaches.

Madison Grigsby is a recent graduate of Florida State University's Museum and Cultural Heritage Program. During the second year of the MA program, she worked with the Circus Department at the John and Mable Ringling Museum of Art to create her own exhibition on historic circus posters. Grigsby is passionate about displaying stories that reveal our shared humanity, especially from those whose voices were not typically uplifted in the past. She looks forward to continuing this mission throughout her career as a museum professional.

Morgan Joseph Hamilton is a PhD candidate in Museum Education and Visitor-Centered Curation at Florida State University. His research interests include digital and virtual engagement, virtual and augmented reality, and network-based art experiences in the art museum. He is interested in locating areas of oversight and opportunity where art museum educators are developing their skills and networks in a rapidly professionalizing field. His current research focuses on art museum educators who developed digital programming during museum closures caused by the pandemic.

Originally from Sarasota, Florida, **Anneliese Hardman** has held positions at the Cambodia Peace Gallery in Cambodia; the Woodrow Wilson House in Washington, DC; Greyfriars Kirkyard in Edinburgh, Scotland; and other art-related sites. Hardman obtained her master's in Museum and Cultural Heritage Studies from Florida State University and her master's in Peace and Conflict Studies from the Paññāsāstra University of Cambodia. She is currently working toward her PhD in art history from the University of Illinois–Chicago with a focus on the revitalization of traditional Cambodian art following the Khmer Rouge genocide. Her other recent publications address innovative practices of museum curation.

Ashley Hartman, PhD, LCAT, ATR-BC, is an assistant professor of Art Therapy at Marywood University. Her research interests explore museum-based art therapy with diverse clientele as well as the exploration of intersectional aspects of one's identity using museum objects and therapeutic arts-based experiences.

Audrey Jacobs served as museum educator for the Heritage Center at Red Cloud, a museum on Očhéthi Šakówiŋ homelands in South Dakota. She built a wide range of school, youth, and adult programming: managing artist residencies, teaching continuing education, supporting middle school museum studies classes and elementary documentary filmmaking, and leading traditional tours. Now in the Museum Education and Visitor-Centered Curation program at Florida State University, her research builds on her previous work at the intersection of K–12 schools and art museums, investigating the use of museum studies in formal learning environments.

Jennifer Jankauskas has worked in the museum field for almost thirty years. Since 2011, she has held the role of curator of art at the Montgomery Museum of Fine Arts, curating contemporary art exhibitions and expanding the Montgomery Museum of Fine Arts' holdings of contemporary art. Jankauskas previously worked at the John Michael Kohler Arts Center, Artpace, American Federation of the Arts, and the Art Institute of Chicago. She has authored exhibition catalogs and contributed to scholarly publications. Jankauskas holds a PhD from the University of Leicester, United Kingdom, an MA from the Art Institute of Chicago, and a BFA from Ohio University.

Xiaonan Jiang is a doctoral candidate in the program of Museum Education and Visitor-Centered Curation at Florida State University. While pursuing her studies, she currently works as an associate professor at Shandong College of Arts in China. Her research interests include visitor-centered exhibitions, museum education, and museum family programs.

Patricia Lannes is a cultural agent whose work is centered on issues of equity and social justice. Her consulting work concentrates in creating frameworks and training programs to support a socially and culturally inclusive museum ecology. She is the founder of CALTA21, an initiative that uses art as a catalyst for strengthening immigrant voices. As the founder of CALTA21, she was nominated as a White House Champion of Change. She is the former director of education of the Leslie-Lohman Museum, New York, and of the Nassau County Museum of Art, New York. Lannes holds a degree in history from UDELAR, Uruguay, and is former chair of the Latino Network, American Alliance of Museums.

Alexia Lobaina is a museum educator, curator, and art historian specializing in the use of interpretive and accessible curatorial approaches. She currently serves as an interpretation specialist at Smithsonian American Art Museum and is a doctoral candidate in Museum Education and Visitor-Centered Curation at Florida State University. She has worked in the curatorial, education, and academic affairs departments of art museums, historic estates, and art foundations, implementing strategies that advocate for the visitor experience and promote collaborative exhibition development. Her research considers the ways museum spaces can continue transforming into alternative civic spaces of discussion, representation, and action.

Ann Rowson Love is associate professor and director of of the MA/PhD program Museum Education & Visitor-Centered Curation in the Department of Art Education at Florida State University. As the program director, she is also the faculty liaison with the program's partner museum, The Ringling, where she teaches and conducts visitor studies. She has more than thirty years of experience as a museum educator, curator, administrator, and scholar in art museums. She presents and publishes widely on collaborative curation, art museum interpretation, evaluation, and feminist systems thinking. Her co-edited books include *Visitor-Centered Exhibitions and Edu-Curation in Art Museums* (2017) and *Systems Thinking in Museums: Theory and Practice* (2017). She serves as Vice-Chair of the Curators Committee Professional Network of the American Alliance of Museums. She represented Curators Committee as part of the National Program Committee for American Alliance of Museums New Orleans in 2019 and as a member of the jury team for the Excellence in Exhibitions Competition in 2018 and 2019.

Meredith Lynn is an assistant professor of Art at Florida State University, where she is also curator of the Museum of Fine Arts. Specializing in contemporary art, her curatorial practice has recently been supported by the National Endowment for the Arts, the Florida Division of Cultural Affairs, the Minnesota State Arts

Board, the Indiana Arts Commission, and the Knight Foundation. She has previously served as the director of galleries at Indiana State University, the director of the Rourke Art Museum (Moorhead, Minnesota), and the director of the Nemeth Art Center (Park Rapids, Minnesota).

Lesley Marchessault is the chief development officer at Provincetown Art Association and Museum. A native of Burlington, Vermont, Marchessault grew up in Tallahassee, Florida, and received an MA in art history from Florida State University in 2009. She worked as a curator and arts educator before moving to Provincetown, Massachusetts, in 2011. At Provincetown Art Association and Museum, she has worn many hats, such as curator, membership manager, volunteer coordinator, and educator. She sits on the steering committee for Arts Foundation of Cape Cod's Creative Exchange, is chair of the Provincetown Cultural Council, and was a fellow in MassCreative's inaugural Create the Vote Fellowship in 2021.

Stefanie Metsemakers (born 1986) is head of education, audience engagement, and inclusion at the Bonnefanten Museum in Maastricht, Netherlands. Before joining the Bonnefanten, Stefanie worked at the Stedelijk Museum Amsterdam and the Van Abbemuseum in Eindhoven, Netherlands, where she initiated and coordinated educational programs and worked on several exhibitions. Stefanie holds a BA and MA in art history and a BA in arts in education. She completed internships at the Museum of Modern Art in New York and the Peggy Guggenheim in Venice, among others.

Elizabeth Nogrady is the Andrew W. Mellon Curator of Academic Programs at the Frances Lehman Loeb Art Center, Vassar College. She received her BA from Vassar and her PhD from the Institute of Fine Arts, New York University, where she specialized in Dutch and Flemish seventeenth-century art. She has held the positions of Moore Curatorial Fellow in the Department of Drawings and Prints at the Morgan Library & Museum and J. Clawson Mills Fellow in European Paintings at the Metropolitan Museum of Art; she also served as a specialist in Old Master Paintings at Christie's, New York.

Patricia O'Rourke is a research associate at the Institute for Municipal and Regional Policy at the University of Connecticut, working on projects to support just and equitable public policy. While completing doctoral studies in Education Curriculum and Instruction at the Neag School of Education at University of Connecticut, O'Rourke worked alongside educators, parents, and students in racial justice and social justice efforts in and beyond the Greater Hartford area as a Public Engagement Fellow at the University of Connecticut Dodd Center for Human Rights. O'Rourke also holds graduate certificates in Human Rights and Indigeneity, Race, Ethnicity, and Politics.

Marianna Pegno is director of engagement and inclusion at the Tucson Museum of Art. In this role, Pegno focuses on building a culturally relevant, community-based institution through programs, exhibitions, and partnerships. In practice and research, she is committed to exploring the implications of collaboration and multi-vocal narratives in art museums. Pegno holds a PhD in art and visual culture education and an MA in art history from the University of Arizona and a BA from New York University. In 2018, her dissertation was awarded the Elliot Eisner Doctoral Research Award in Art Education from the National Art Education Association.

Bailey Placzek is the Clyfford Still Museum's curator of collections and research and project manager for Clyfford Still's catalogue raisonné. She has been engaged in CSM's curatorial program and the research of the museum's collection since before its opening in 2011. Placzek's work is focused on advancing access to collections, promoting art's ability to foster connections among humanity across time, and deconstructing museum work to make it more transparent, collaborative, and fun. Recent curatorial projects include *Awful Bigness* (2023), *You Select: A Community-Curated Exhibition* (2022), and *Clyfford Still, Art, and the Young Mind* (2022). Placzek received an MA in art history from the University of Denver and dual BA degrees in art history and painting from the University of Kansas.

Ashley Pourier (Oglála Lakhóta) is curator of exhibits and collections at the Heritage Center at Red Cloud Indian School, Pine Ridge, South Dakota. Born and raised on the Pine Ridge Indian Reservation, she received her BFA degree from Carthage College in Kenosha, Wisconsin. Her time at the center has allowed her to support and advocate for Native artists. Ashley has served on local arts committees and boards, judged numerous art shows and competitions, and volunteers for arts and culture events. She continues education by attending numerous museum and arts conferences, leadership training, and Lakhóta Language classes.

Melanie Rosato has held positions at museums, libraries, and universities, garnering expertise in collections management, curation, and research since earning her BA in studio arts. She has written extensively for exhibitions while at the Everhart Museum of Natural History, Science, & Art, where she developed text for dozens of temporary and permanent installations. She has contributed reviews of literature and analyses of art historical subjects for blogs, as well as served as a community reviewer for the Feminist Library in London. She is from Scranton, Pennsylvania, where she continues to reside and work in the nonprofit industry.

Andy Shaw is associate professor at Louisiana State University, studio potter, coordinator of the Mid-Atlantic Keramik Exchange in Iceland, director of the Louisiana State University Ceramics Factory, and co-director of the first Queeramics Symposium. Shaw's residencies include SÍM Residency and Íshús Hafnarfjarðar both in Iceland, McKnight at Northern Clay Center, Arrowmont, Evelyn Shapiro Fellow at The Clay Studio, Archie Bray, and Nova Scotia College of Art and Design. His work is in the collections of the Garth Clark and Mark Delvecchio Collection at the Museum of Fine Arts Houston, the Crocker Art Museum, the Louisiana State University Museum of Art, the Philadelphia Museum of Art, and the Sanbao Ceramic Art Institute in China.

Prof. Dr. Emilie Sitzia holds a special chair at the University of Amsterdam and is an associate professor of Cultural Education at the University of Maastricht, Netherlands. She specializes in museum participatory practices, the impact of art on audiences, and word/image interdisciplinary studies. In 2019 she was a co-editor for the *Stedelijk Studies* issue *Towards a Museum of Mutuality*. Recent relevant publications include The Many Faces of Knowledge Production in Art Museums in *Muséologies* (2018), The Ignorant Art Museum: Beyond Meaning-Making in *International Journal of Lifelong Education* (2017), and the co-authored article with Julia Ferloni "When the Society Museum Gives Power: Challenges of Participatory Exhibition Co-creation at the Mucem" in *Culture & Musées* (2022).

Michelle Sunset (she/her) is a curator at the University of Wyoming Art Museum in Laramie, Wyoming. She holds two MAs from Florida State University, one in the History and Criticism of Art with specializations in Museum and Cultural Heritage Studies and the Visual Cultures of the Americas and the other in Museum Education and Visitor-Centered Curation. She has a BA in history from the University of North Florida. Her curatorial work is driven by curiosity and social justice. Since returning to the West, she is interested in subverting the myth of the cowboy through exhibitions like *Luke Gilford: Portraits of the Queer Frontier.*

Courtney Taylor is completing a Doctor of Design in Cultural Preservation at Louisiana State University, where she teaches museum studies and manages College of Art and Design Galleries. From 2016 to 2021, Taylor served as curator and director of public programs at Louisiana State University Museum of Art, where she directed collections, exhibitions, and public programs with a focus on building a robust exhibitions program, including developing numerous traveling exhibitions and catalogs, reinvigorating academic collaboration, and deepening community-based programming. Taylor holds an MA in Museum Science and Management from the University of Tulsa and a BA in history and art history from Hendrix College.

Pieter Jan Valgaeren is a curator, researcher, and lecturer. From his background in art history and law, he specialized in new media, hybrid art forms, technology, and intellectual property. He published on different topics such as intellectual property rights in the digital age, social media, media philosophy, and art in the public domain. In the past years he worked as a consultant for the European Union in art and technology and gave lectures at Universities in Berlin, Valetta, Tilburg, and Madrid. As a curator he worked on the intersection of art and law (TRADEMARKS festival) and on art and technology SCREEN IT festival (on the impact of our screen culture on digital art), and *Me, myself and I* (on the self-portrait in digital art). Currently, he is preparing *Ctrl-X* for Alt +1000 festival in Switzerland (on the representation of landscapes in digital art). In his presentation, he will deal with conceptualizing and representing digital arts in exhibitions and festivals, translating and mediation of post-internet art to wider audiences, and the position of digital arts in the current art world.

Aline Van Nereaux is an art historian with expertise in art mediation and education. She regularly uses this expertise to run art workshops and initiate projects in the museum world. Since 2019 she has been associated with S.M.A.K., the municipal museum of contemporary art in Ghent, Belgium, where she is responsible for public mediation, education, and various participation projects with a focus on children and youngsters.

Sofie Vermeiren studied art science at the KU Leuven and also followed her teacher training there. She has been working in the Flemish museum sector since 2000, where she set up several projects and training courses on public mediation and participation in a museum context. Today, she is head of the public mediation department at M Leuven. She is also a national correspondent for CECA/ICOM Belgium. In this role, she supports and helps publicize innovative mediation practices developed abroad and in Belgium to museum colleagues worldwide.

Pat Villeneuve is professor and director of arts administration in the Florida State University Department of Art Education and a 2021 Fulbright scholar to Belgium. She has had lengthy careers in museums and academe and has published and presented extensively on art museum education, edu-curation, visitor-centered exhibitions, paradigmatic change, and the Dimensions of Curation Model. Villeneuve developed the graduate program (MA and PhD) in edu-curation at Florida State University and published *Visitor-Centered Exhibitions and Edu-Curation in Art Museums* in 2017 with Ann Rowson Love. She keynoted the ICOM International Committee for Education and Cultural Action conference in Leuven, Belgium, in 2021.

Zida Wang is a doctoral candidate in the Museum Education and Visitor-Centered Curation program in the Department of Art Education at Florida State University. In addition to education, visitor services, and curatorial internships at leading US museums such as the Hirshhorn Museum and Sculpture Garden and Los Angeles County Museum of Art, he has curated contemporary art in China. He has assisted with curatorial programs and conducted visitor studies at The Ringling Museum during his doctoral program. His research interest focuses on collaborative curation, hybrid exhibitions, and socially engaged art. He is currently the museum education assistant at the Florida State University Museum of Fine Arts.

Tammy Wille holds a master's degree in art history and a teacher training degree. She has been responsible for public education at the MAS (Museum aan de Stroom) in Antwerp since 2011. Focusing on participation and engagement, Wille is constantly searching for innovative programs to inspire visitors and attract new audiences.

Ashley Williams is a doctoral student studying museum education and visitor-centered curation at Florida State University. She received her BA and MA in art history from the University of South Florida. Prior to her doctoral studies, Williams was a museum educator at the Glazer Children's Museum and Gallery221@HCC. She is presently a curator at the Gadsden Arts Center & Museum. Her current research focuses on the role of play in art museums for visitors of all ages and how museum educators can use play and digital programming for accessible experiences.

Ting Zhang has served as lecturer at the China Academy of Art since 2001. She holds a PhD in museology and her dissertation topic was "the development of art museums in Chinese universities." Her research interests lie primarily in art institution curatorial practice, and she is actively engaged in contemporary art curation, project management, and art criticism. Over the past decade, she has curated or co-curated more than twenty domestic and international art exhibitions. As an independent curator, writer and also a member of Experimental and Scientific Art Committee of Shanghai Artists Association, Zhang has focused on cross-cultural ecology and contemporary art expression in the international museum context, as well as research driven creation based on geographical comparison.

Lynette A. Zimmerman is an innovative entrepreneur, author, and higher education and arts administrator. Known for her growth mindset, she creates institutional change, advocates for a diverse workforce, addresses inequality in the curatorial process through collaboration, and believes in strong stakeholder relationships coming together to create unique inclusive art experiences. Zimmerman leads with equity and access, determined to ensure all persons have their voices heard and understood.